Nonlinear Dynamics, Chaos, and Instability

Nonlinear Dynamics, Chaos, and Instability: Statistical Theory and Economic Evidence

William A. Brock

David A. Hsieh

Blake LeBaron

The MIT Press
Cambridge, Massachusetts
London, England

This book was set in Times by the authors and was printed and bound in the United States of America.

Library of Congress Cataloging-in-Publication Data

Brock, William A.
    Nonlinear dynamics, chaos, and instability : statistical theory and economic evidence / William A. Brock, David A. Hsieh, Blake LeBaron.
        p. cm.
    Includes bibliographical references and index.
    ISBN 0-262-02329-6
    1. Statics and dynamics (Social sciences) 2. Economics, Mathematical. 3. Differential equations, Nonlinear. 4. Chaotic behavior in systems. I. Hsieh, David A. (David Arthur). 1953— .
II. LeBaron, Blake Dean. 1961— . III. Title.
HB145.B74 1991
330'.01'515252——dc20
                                91-8487
                                 CIP

William A. Brock dedicates this book to his daughter, Caroline, who keeps him humble, makes him laugh, and makes living worthwhile and to his wife Joan, whose love and laughter is the center of his life.

David A. Hsieh dedicates this book to his wife Priscilla, son Terence, parents C.C. and ZaZa, brothers Paul and Mike, and sister-in-law Tonia.

Blake LeBaron dedicates this book to his parents, Dean and Emily.

Contents

List of Figures ix

List of Tables xi

Acknowledgments xv

Chapter 1   Introduction   1

Chapter 2   The BDS Statistic   41

Chapter 3   The Changing Structure of
Stock Returns   82

Chapter 4   Nonlinearity in Foreign Exchange   130

Chapter 5   Summary, Relation to Other Work,
and Future Horizons   169

Appendix A   Size and Distribution of the BDS Statistic   206

Appendix B   Power and Distribution of the BDS
Statistic   218

Appendix C   Quantiles of the BDS Statistic   232

Appendix D   The Nuisance Parameter Property of
the BDS Statistic   235

Appendix E   Size of the BDS Statistic on Residuals   268

Appendix F   Distribution and Quantiles of the BDS
Statistic on GARCH Residuals   276

References   280

Index   314

Figures

Figure 2.1	$C_2(\epsilon)-C(\epsilon)^2$: AR1	78
Figure 2.2	$C_2(\epsilon)-C(\epsilon)^2$: MA1	78
Figure 2.3	$C_2(\epsilon)-C(\epsilon)^2$: Tent Map	79
Figure 2.4	$C_2(\epsilon)-C(\epsilon)^2$: Threshold AR	79
Figure 2.5	$C_2(\epsilon)-C(\epsilon)^2$: Nonlinear MA	80
Figure 2.6	$C_2(\epsilon)-C(\epsilon)^2$: ARCH	80
Figure 2.7	$C_2(\epsilon)-C(\epsilon)^2$: GARCH	81
Figure 3.1	GP Plot: Scrambled Normal	116
Figure 3.2	GP Plot: Sign Scrambled Normal	116
Figure 3.3	GP Plot: Scrambled AR	117
Figure 3.4	GP Plot: Sign Scrambled AR	117
Figure 3.5	GP Plot: Scrambled GARCH	118
Figure 3.6	GP Plot: Sign Scrambled GARCH	118
Figure 3.7	GP Plot: Scrambled Two State Variance	119
Figure 3.8	GP Plot: Sign Scrambled Two State Variance	119
Figure 3.9	Tent Map	120
Figure 3.10	Time Series Plot: Tent Map	120
Figure 3.11	GP Plot: Scrambled Tent Map	121
Figure 3.12	GP Plot: Sign Scrambled Tent Map	121
Figure 3.13	GP Plot: Scrambled Mackey-Glass	122
Figure 3.14	GP Plot: Sign Scrambled Mackey-Glass	122
Figure 3.15	Weekly Value Weighted Returns	123
Figure 3.16	Weekly S&P 500 Returns	123
Figure 3.17	Recurrence Plot: VW (1962-1986)	124
Figure 3.18	GP Plot: Scrambled VW1	125
Figure 3.19	GP Plot: Sign Scrambled VW1	125
Figure 3.20	GP Plot: Scrambled VW2	126

Figure 3.21	GP Plot: Sign Scrambled VW2	126
Figure 3.22	Recurrence Plot: S&P (1928–1985)	127
Figure 3.23	GP Plot: Scrambled SP1	128
Figure 3.24	GP Plot: Sign Scrambled SP1	128
Figure 3.25	GP Plot: Scrambled SP2	129
Figure 3.26	GP Plot: Sign Scrambled SP2	129
Figure 4.1	Rate of Change of $/BP Exchange Rate	158
Figure 4.2	Rate of Change of $/CD Exchange Rate	158
Figure 4.3	Rate of Change of $/DM Exchange Rate	159
Figure 4.4	Rate of Change of $/JY Exchange Rate	159
Figure 4.5	Rate of Change of $/SF Exchange Rate	160
Figure 4.6	GP Plot: $/BP Exchange Rate	161
Figure 4.7	GP Plot: $/CD Exchange Rate	161
Figure 4.8	GP Plot: $/DM Exchange Rate	162
Figure 4.9	GP Plot: $/JY Exchange Rate	162
Figure 4.10	GP Plot: $/SF Exchange Rate	163
Figure 4.11	Recurrence Plot: $/BP Exchange Rate	164
Figure 4.12	Recurrence Plot: $/CD Exchange Rate	165
Figure 4.13	Recurrence Plot: $/DM Exchange Rate	166
Figure 4.14	Recurrence Plot: $/JY Exchange Rate	167
Figure 4.15	Recurrence Plot: $/SF Exchange Rate	168

Tables

Table 2.1	Power Comparisons	77
Table 3.1	Nonlinear Diagnostic Statistics: Simulated Data	109
Table 3.2	Linear Filtering and Summary Statistics	110
Table 3.3	Estimated GARCH(1,1) Parameters	111
Table 3.4	Nonlinear Diagnostic Statistics: Stock Return Data	112
Table 3.5	Estimated GARCH-M(1,1) Parameters: Stock Return Data	113
Table 3.6	GARCH-M(1,1) Residual BDS Statistics	114
Table 3.7	Performance of Nearest Neighbor Forecasts: Regression of Actual Outcomes on Forecasts	115
Table 4.1	Summary Statistics of Log Price Changes: 1974-1983	146
Table 4.2	Autocorrelation Coefficients of Log Price Changes: 1974-1983	147
Table 4.3	BDS Test: Raw Data	148
Table 4.4	Distribution of BDS Statistics at $\epsilon/\sigma=1$	149
Table 4.5	BDS Test: Filtered Data	150
Table 4.6	Standard Tests of Nonlinearity: Raw Data	151
Table 4.7	Root Mean Squared Forecast Errors	152
Table 4.8	Power of Third Moment Tests for Different Models	153
Table 4.9	Third Order Moments of Filtered Data	154
Table 4.10	Tests of Nonlinearity: GARCH(1,1) Normal	155
Table 4.11	Tests of Nonlinearity: GARCH(1,1) Student-t	156
Table 4.12	Tests of Nonlinearity: GARCH(1,1) GED	157

Table A.1   Size of BDS Statistic: Standard Normal   206

Table A.2   Size of BDS Statistic: Student-t
             with 3 Degrees of Freedom   207

Table A.3   Size of BDS Statistic: Double Exponential   208

Table A.4   Size of BDS Statistic: Chi-square
             with 4 Degrees of Freedom   209

Table A.5   Size of BDS Statistic: Uniform Distribution   210

Table A.6   Size of BDS Statistic: Bimodal Distribution   211

Table A.7   Distribution of BDS Statistic: Standard Normal   212

Table A.8   Distribution of BDS Statistic: Student-t
             with 3 Degrees of Freedom   213

Table A.9   Distribution of BDS Statistic:
             Double Exponential   214

Table A.10   Distribution of BDS Statistic: Chi-square
             with 4 Degrees of Freedom   215

Table A.11   Distribution of BDS Statistic:
             Uniform Distribution   216

Table A.12   Distribution of BDS Statistic:
             Bimodal Distribution   217

Table B.1   Power of BDS Statistic: Tent Map   218

Table B.2   Power of BDS Statistic: AR1 (ρ=.5)   219

Table B.3   Power of BDS Statistic: MA1 (θ=.5)   220

Table B.4   Power of BDS Statistic: Threshold AR   221

Table B.5   Power of BDS Statistic: Nonlinear MA (γ=.8)   222

Table B.6   Power of BDS Statistic: ARCH (ϕ=.5)   223

Table B.7   Power of BDS Statistic: GARCH (ϕ=.1,ψ=.8)   224

Table B.8   Distribution of BDS Statistic: Tent Map   225

Table B.9   Distribution of BDS Statistic: AR1 (ρ=.5)   226

Table B.10   Distribution of BDS Statistic: MA1 (θ=.5)   227

Table B.11   Distribution of BDS Statistic: Threshold AR   228

Table B.12   Distribution of BDS Statistic: Nonlinear MA
              (γ=.8)   229

Table B.13   Distribution of BDS Statistic: ARCH (ϕ=.5)   230

Table B.14   Distribution of BDS Statistic: GARCH
              (ϕ=.1,ψ=.8)   231

Table C.1   Quantiles of BDS Statistic: Normal Random
              Variables with 100 observations   232

Table C.2   Quantiles of BDS Statistic: Normal Random
              Variables with 250 observations   233

Table C.3   Quantiles of BDS Statistic: Normal Random
              Variables with 500 observations   234

Table E.1   Size of BDS Statistic: AR1 Residuals (ρ=.5)   268

Table E.2   Size of BDS Statistic: AR1 Residuals (ρ=.95)   269

Table E.3   Size of BDS Statistic: MA1 Residuals (θ=.5)   270

Table E.4   Size of BDS Statistic: MA1 Residuals (θ=.95)   271

Table E.5   Size of BDS Statistic: ARCH Residuals (ϕ=.5)   272

Table E.6   Size of BDS Statistic: ARCH Residuals (ϕ=.95)   273

Table E.7   Size of BDS Statistic: GARCH Residuals
              (ϕ=.1,ψ=.8)   274

Table E.8   Size of BDS Statistic: NMA Residuals (γ=.5)   275

Table F.1   Distribution and Quantiles of BDS Statistic:
              GARCH(1,1) Standardized Residuals
              with 100 observations   276

Table F.2   Distribution and Quantiles of BDS Statistic:
              GARCH(1,1) Standardized Residuals
              with 500 observations   277

Table F.3   Distribution and Quantiles of BDS Statistic:
              GARCH(1,1) Standardized Residuals
              with 1000 observations   278
Table F.4   Distribution and Quantiles of BDS Statistic:
              GARCH(1,1) Standardized Residuals
              with 2500 observations   279

Acknowledgments

William A. Brock thanks Ehung Gi Baek, Dee Dechert, Simon Potter, Chera Sayers, Robert Savit, and José Scheinkman as co-conspirators in chaos as well as good friends for years of conversations on chaos. He acknowledges financial support from the National Science Foundation (Grant #SEC-8420872), the Guggenheim Foundation, the University of Wisconsin Graduate School, the University of Wisconsin Alumni Research Fund, and the Vilas Trust.

David A. Hsieh thanks José Scheinkman for his encouragement in the pursuit of nonlinear science. He acknowledges financial support from the Fuqua School of Business, Duke University.

Blake LeBaron thanks Simon Potter and José Scheinkman. He acknowledges financial support from the University of Wisconsin Graduate School.

Nonlinear Dynamics, Chaos, and Instability

Chapter 1

Introduction

Public interest in highly nonlinear deterministic and stochastic generators of time series has been stimulated by recent theoretical and experimental work on turbulence (chaos) in natural science, particularly in the wake of James Gleick's best-selling 1987 book, *Chaos*. (Also Eckmann and Ruelle 1985 survey theory and discuss documented instances of chaos in natural science.) Since economic time series appear "random" and are difficult to predict, it is natural for economists to take a look at chaos theory to see if anything can be applied to economics and finance. The Santa Fe Institute volume edited by Anderson, Arrow, and Pines 1988 discusses pathways by which complex dynamics and chaotic dynamics might emerge in an economy. Economic models have been constructed to generate deterministic equilibrium trajectories that appear random to the naked eye and to some statistical tests. Some of these economic models even have rational expectations equilibria that are deterministically chaotic. A good sample of some of this work is in the October 1986 issue of the

---

Part of this chapter draws on Brock 1988, 1990a, 1990b.

Journal of Economic Theory and in the survey article by Baumol and
Benhabib 1989. The book by H. W. Lorenz 1989 contains a nice
survey of this area. The appearance of this theoretical work is one
motivation for designing empirical tests for the presence of
deterministic chaos in actual data. Let us give a sneak preview of
what deterministic chaos is before we become more technical.

A standard example of a deterministic data generator that
appears random (or chaotic) to conventional statistical tests is a
computer pseudo random number generator. We shall use pseudo
random number generators as metaphors to exposit the ideas of this
chapter. For specificity, think of a computer generator of pseudo
random numbers uniformly distributed over the closed interval [0,1].
A well-designed pseudo random number generator will fool any
statistician into thinking that the time series so generated is truly
random. One would think that such a generator would have to be
"complex." Measurement of "complexity" will be discussed below.
Intuitively, complexity is measured by "dimension," which in turn
measures the number of effective dynamical modes or number of
degrees of freedom that ultimately generate the motion under scrutiny.
The motion may look very random to many statistical tests, even
though the number of active modes generating the motion is very
small. This kind of surprising effect arises from nonlinearity. What
is striking is that deterministic dynamical systems of very low
"complexity" can generate "random numbers" that fool many
statistical tests. This raises the intriguing possibility that new
statistical tests can be designed to detect hidden patterns in exchange
rates, macroeconomic variables, and stock market returns that have

never been detected before. Furthermore such patterns, if discovered, may aid in forecasting, especially over short time intervals.

We quickly point out that it will be impossible to tell from a data set of lengths available in economics, with computing machines of finite resolution, whether the data are generated by high-dimensional chaos. The hope is that new techniques based on chaos theory will help in detecting low-dimensional chaos or other types of nonlinearity masquerading as randomness.

This book is an attempt to whet the reader's appetite for some of this new material as well as show the reader how it is useful in economics and finance.

Testing for the presence of deterministic generators in a time series such as stock returns leads naturally to the broad recent literature on testing for the presence of temporal predictable structure in stock returns. We touch on some of that literature in this book. Before we go on, we should tell the reader the bottom line of this book, which comes in five parts.

First, evidence for the presence of deterministic low-dimensional chaotic generators in economic and financial data is not very strong.

Second, however, testing for such generators has led to the development of powerful new tools of statistical inference, which will be exposited in Chapter 2. A new test (Brock, Dechert, and Scheinkman 1987, hereafter denoted BDS) of the existence of potentially forecastable structure, nonstationarity, or hidden patterns has been applied to financial and macroeconomic time series data. The BDS test can also be adapted to test for the adequacy of fit of one's forecasting model. One just applies the test to the forecast errors from the model and check for hidden structure.

For example, if one suspects the presence of forecastable volatility (i.e., variance) in one's forecast errors, one fits this forecastable volatility, divide the forecast errors by the estimate of this volatility, and apply the BDS test to the resulting standardized forecast errors. If there is no remaining forecastable structure, then this standardized series should pass the BDS test. Otherwise, if there is still forecastable structure, then the model is incorrect, and one needs to specify a new model.

The BDS test is especially useful when one has no idea what kind of hidden structure to expect in the standardized forecast errors from the forecasting model. Since one's priors on the form of the forecastable structure in the data are already encapsulated in the model that one fits, the standardized forecast errors should have no forecastable structure left in them if the model is correct. If it is wrong, one is likely to have no idea in which direction one is incorrect. Therefore the procedure of testing standardized forecast errors for the presence of unspecified omitted structure is of practical importance. The procedure will be exposited in Chapter 2 and applied to stock returns in Chapter 3 and exchange rates in Chapter 4.

The BDS test is easy to use. Computer software now exists for the IBM PC (Dechert 1987) that enables one to calculate the BDS statistics in a matter of seconds on a personal computer. Some software is available as part of this book.

Third, there are two new graphical devices, called the Grassberger and Procaccia plot and the recurrence plot, related to the BDS statistics. These plots can be used to build a graphical depiction of our test, which compares the original series being tested for the presence of forecastable structure with a totally unforecastable series that has the same mean, variance, skewness, etc., as the original series under scrutiny. This is all developed in Chapter 3.

Fourth, a natural notion of instability, which also turns out to be a natural notion of measurement error propagation (uncertainty amplification or randomness multiplication), emerges from the literature on chaos theory and nonlinear science. This quantity is called the largest Lyapunov exponent, and analogues of it can be used to measure the amount of instability in a time series. This quantity is related to divergent speculative bubbles in rational expectations models of asset pricing. It can also be used to measure the rate of decay of forecast accuracy. The problem of estimating and quantifying economic instability is touched upon in Chapter 5.

Fifth, a general strategy of testing for various types of nonlinearity is presented. A leading notion of nonlinearity is this: a stationary stochastic process is linear if the best predictor upon the past is the best *linear* predictor. We show how to statistically test whether the best predictor is indeed the best linear predictor by using the methods presented in this book.

The organization of this book is as follows. Chapter 1 lays out basic concepts of chaos theory, such as deterministic data generators and measurements of complexity of such generators. A measure that we use here is the dimension plot, which indicates the number of operative modes or nonlinear factors that generate the data. Chapter 2 shows how to use the difference between dimension plots of the original data and dimension plots of a purely random data set with the same stationary distribution to detect hidden dependence in data that

looks random. It turns the diagnostic into a formal statistical test, i.e.,
the BDS statistic, which can also be used to test the adequacy of fit of
popular time series models.

Chapter 3 applies the BDS test to stock returns. The analysis
finds that, for certain time periods, there is forecastable structure or
left out (possibly unforecastable) nonstationarity in stock returns,
which is not completely captured by Generalized Autoregressive
Conditional Heteroskedastic (GARCH) models. Since these models are
becoming popular in finance (e.g., French, Schwert, and Stambaugh
1987 for a recent application), a challenge exists to modify these
models to account for the extra structure.

Chapter 3 also uses the recurrence plot, which is a device that
graphically detects hidden patterns in data and can show similarities
in patterns across series covering the same period of time. It is
another useful way to look at data that should be in the analyst's tool
kit, particularly as a diagnostic for nonstationarity and temporal shifts
in the dynamical structure generating one's data. It can be used to
date major economic events. It does a good job of dating such events
as the May 1962 "Kennedy Crash" and the oil shocks in stock returns.
It also does a good job in dating major shifts in monetary policy. The
interesting thing about the recurrence plot is that it can date such
events without reading the history books. In other words the data are
allowed to speak through the recurrence plot about which events are
important.

Chapter 4 applies the BDS statistic to foreign exchange rates.
It discusses how to use the third order moments to discriminate
between different classes of nonlinearity. It finds that, similar to

stock returns, GARCH models can account for most but not all nonlinearity in exchange rates.

Chapter 5 closes with a summary, a relation of our work to other areas of nonlinear tests, and suggestions for future research. It also presents some rather bold speculations about future evolution of this subject and future relevance to economics and finance.

Before we begin, it is important to state at the outset what this book's emphasis is. The area of testing for nonlinearity in time series is vast. In order to keep this book tightly focused, we will only treat the problem of testing for nonlinearities that are either deterministically chaotic or fairly closely related to such nonlinearities. In this spirit much, if not most, of this book will be devoted to developing, and applying to asset returns data, the BDS test.

Fortunately, however, even though the BDS test was designed to have high power against deterministic chaos, it turned out to have high power against some other nonlinear alternatives as well. As such it will be necessary to explain other areas of nonlinearity in time series analysis. But we do this only to the point where we can convey understanding of why the BDS test for chaos turns out to be good at detecting these other types of nonlinearity. In order to give the reader some appreciation for the general area of nonlinear time series analysis and some notion of how the material treated in this book fits into this large general area, we will give a very brief treatment in Chapter 5 to some other main components of the nonlinear time series area. This treatment will necessarily be brief to keep the book at a proper size.

At the risk of repeating, we wish to stress that from the point of view of those interested in the broad area of nonlinearity testing, our test for temporal dependence can be used as a test on the residuals of estimated models for neglected nonlinearity or neglected nonstationarity. Hence, in the nonlinear (or nonstationary) context, we recommend using our test as a "portmanteau lack of fit test" much in the same spirit as Box and Jenkins 1976 (p. 291) recommend using the Q statistic in the linear context. Appendix D shows that, under fairly broad and useful sufficient conditions, the first order asymptotic distribution of our test statistic is the same on the estimated residuals as on the true residuals provided the underlying model can be estimated $T^{\frac{1}{2}}$-consistently and the model truly describes the data.

At the end of the book we provide information on how to obtain source code to compute the test statistic. Chapters 2 through 4 show how to use the test statistic as a portmanteau lack of fit test by using it to evaluate parametric models fit to asset returns.

1.1 Basic Definitions and Concepts of Chaos

Before turning to a precise discussion of concepts from chaos theory, we urge the reader to consult the excellent survey of Eckmann and Ruelle 1985. Surveys written with the economist in mind are Brock 1986, 1988, Baumol and Benhabib 1989, and Boldrin and Woodford 1989b. We shall draw on Brock 1986, 1988 in much of what follows.

We need a basic definition:

Deterministic Explanation. The time series $\{a_t\}$ has a C^2 deterministic chaotic explanation if there exists a system (h,F,x_0) such that $a_t=h(x_t)$, $x_{t+1}=F(x_t)$, $x(0)=x_0$, where $h:R^n{\rightarrow}R^1$, $F:R^n{\rightarrow}R^n$ are both twice continuously differentiable, i.e., C^2. Furthermore we require that F have an ergodic invariant measure μ that is absolutely continuous with respect to Lebesque measure. (This just means that μ is "nondegenerate" and that limiting time averages exist and are independent of initial conditions, i.e., we can do time series analysis.)

Eckmann and Ruelle 1985 show that under regularity conditions there is a unique "natural" invariant measure. The invariant measure is a very intuitive notion. One computes the measure of a set A by counting the long-run fraction of time a solution $x(t,x_0)$ of $x_{t+1}=F(x_t),x(0)=x_0$ spends in A. Ergodicity, the property that all parts of the state space are visited by a typical solution $x(t,x_0)$, ensures that the long-run fraction of time spent in A is independent of the initial condition x_0.

A popular definition of "chaos" asks that the largest Lyapunov exponent, L, of F be positive. This is the definition of chaos that we use in this book. Positivity of the largest Lyapunov exponent is one way to capture the notion of sensitive dependence upon initial conditions (SDIC). SDIC is the hallmark of chaos. We caution the reader that different definitions of chaos exist in the literature. All of them that we have seen attempt to capture the notion of SDIC in some way.

The quantity L is defined by:

$$L = \lim_{t\to\infty}(\log\,(\,\|\,DF^t(x)\cdot v\,\|\,)/t), \tag{1.1.1}$$

where $F^t(x)$ denotes the t-th iterate of F starting at initial condition x, D is derivative, "log" is the natural logarithm, $\|\ \|$ is a norm, and v is a direction vector. Here "$\cdot$" denotes scalar product. It is known from the mathematical literature on chaos that, under the hypotheses assumed in the definition of a deterministic explanation, L exists and is independent of (x,v) for "most" initial conditions x and direction vectors v. (Cf. Brock 1986 for discussion and guide to the relevant references.)

This definition is easy to explain in plain English. We have a time series of data $\{a_t\}$ that we are scrutinizing for temporal dependence or potentially forecastable structure. For example $\{a_t\}$ could be monthly returns on the Dow Jones Industrial Average from 1948 to the present or the output of a computer random number generator. The definition says that $\{a_t\}$ has a deterministic explanation if there is some state vector x_t evolving according to the deterministic equation of motion, $x_{t+1}=F(x_t)$, and there is some function h(x) such that $a_t=h(x_t)$ for all t. Think of h as the output of a measuring apparatus or as a measured index such as the Dow Jones Industrial Average.

If the investigator knew h and F, and could measure x_t perfectly, then she could forecast future x's and, hence, future a's perfectly. In reality the state vector x and its dynamics, F, are unknown. One can only observe x indirectly by looking at the output of some measurement a=h(x). The "observer" function h is an attempt to formalize the notion of observation and measurement. There are stochastic versions of the definition where h and F are random functions. The stochastic versions are related to Kalman filtering frameworks in control engineering. At the risk of repetition, we turn now to explaining what invariant measures and Lyapunov exponents are.

Invariant measures are most easily explained by using the concept of a computer generator of random numbers. The invariant measure of a pseudo random number generator, F, which generates uniformly distributed random numbers on the interval [0,1], is the uniform measure on [0,1] itself. An invariant measure can be thought of as a histogram such that if one takes a large sample from the histogram and apply F to each point of that sample, one will get the same histogram back again. "Ergodic" is just a technical condition that ensures that time averages exist. Since we will be doing time series analysis, we need existence of time averages to do anything at all. Let us turn now to Lyapunov exponents.

Look at the case $h(x)=x$, i.e., one can observe the state x perfectly. Look at two initial conditions x_t and x_s that are near to each other and follow the trajectories $\{F^k(x_t)\}$ and $\{F^k(x_s)\}$, starting from x_t and x_s. In order for a deterministic map, F, to generate random looking behavior, nearby trajectories must diverge. In order for F to map a bounded set back into itself, locally diverging trajectories must eventually fold back on themselves. The largest Lyapunov exponent measures the rate of local divergence and averages this rate over a typical long trajectory generated by the map F.

Suppose one makes a small error in measuring the initial state and wants to forecast the state one period from now. The largest Lyapunov exponent is a measure of how fast the initial measurement error "multiplies" into error in one's forecast. There are versions of Lyapunov-like quantities for the case where h and F are random functions. More will be said about this below.

The content of the definitions and concepts laid out above will be more concretely illustrated by an example where $h(x)=x$.

Consider the "tent map":

$x_{t+1} = 2x_t,$ if $x_t \leq .5$

$x_{t+1} = 2-2x_t,$ if $x_t \geq .5.$ (1.1.2)

A number of basic properties of deterministic chaos are well illustrated by this simple recursion.

First, the tent map generates, for almost all (in the sense of Lebesque measure) initial conditions $x_0 \epsilon(0,1)$, trajectories such that for all numbers a and b such that $0 \leq a < b \leq 1$:

$$\#\{x_t, \ 1 \leq t \leq T \mid x_t \epsilon[a,b]\}/T \rightarrow (b-a).$$ (1.1.3)

Equation (1.1.3) says the long-run fraction of x_t's in the interval [a,b] is the length, (b-a). The map (1.1.2) has a nondegenerate invariant measure $\mu([a,b])=b-a$. This is like stochastic growth models used in general equilibrium asset pricing models with production. Indeed, for typical chaotic maps, almost all trajectories "converge" to some invariant measure μ. In the case of the tent map, this invariant measure is the uniform measure on [0,1].

Second, suppose one makes a small error in measuring the initial state so that one only knows that it lies in the interval

$I = [a-\epsilon,a+\epsilon], \ \epsilon>0.$ (1.1.4)

Now imagine that at date 1, one must forecast x_t based on the knowledge (1.1.4). The loss of precision in one's forecast (the length of the interval where one knows that x_t lies) grows exponentially fast as t grows. In the long run (i.e., as t goes to infinity), one knows nothing about x_t, except that it lies in [0,1]. This property means that one can *potentially* forecast x_t perfectly (if one could measure x_0 with infinite accuracy), but one can *practically* never succeed in long-run forecasting.

A third property of deterministic chaos (redundant given the two properties listed above but repeated anyway for emphasis) is that the time series $\{x_t\}$ appears stochastic even though it is generated by a deterministic system (1.1.2). More precisely, in the case of the tent map, the empirical spectrum and empirical autocovariance function are the same as that of white noise, i.e., the same as that generated by independent and identically distributed (IID) random variables.

Recall that for a mean zero, covariance stationary time series $\{x_t\}$, the autocovariance function is denoted by $\mu_{xx}(r) \equiv E[x_t x_{t-r}]$, for all integers $r > 0$. The autocovariances are zero for all r in the case that the series $\{x_t\}$ is independently and identically distributed (IID), i.e., the series is purely random and is totally unforecastable from its past. As we have seen, however, zero autocovariances for all $r > 0$ does *not* imply that series $\{x_t\}$ is unforecastable from its past.

A fourth property is that the Lyapunov exponent, i.e., the quantity L defined in (1.1.1), is positive for deterministic chaos. In the case of the tent map, $L = \log(2) > 0$. This means that nearby trajectories locally spread apart at an exponential rate.

A fifth property of deterministic chaos is that seemingly small changes in a shift parameter can lead to dramatic long-run changes in the long-run behavior of the dynamics. This is best illustrated by the "logistic" map, given by the difference equation:

$$x_{t+1} = \alpha x_t (1 - x_t), \tag{1.1.5}$$

where $0 \leq \alpha \leq 4$. The long-run behavior of the logistic map goes through a period doubling sequence of "pitchfork" bifurcations as α increases from zero up to the "Feigenbaum" value $\alpha = 3.57...$, at which point the long-run behavior becomes "turbulent." This fifth property teaches us that changes in the "tuning" parameter α can lead to abrupt changes in long-run behavior which could lead a time series statistician to falsely conclude that exogenous unforecastable stochastic shocks were present.

A sixth, and celebrated, property of chaotic maps is the universality of certain routes to chaos. The period doubling route, for example, is independent of the details of the map within a surprisingly broad class of maps——even higher dimensional ones (Feigenbaum 1983 (p. 128)). This property teaches us that it is not patently ridiculous to imagine that such events as the stock market crash of October 19, 1987, might have been a display of a route to chaos. This is especially true if one imagines that "economic" time speeds up during such events whereas data are collected in chronological time.

All six of the above properties have their counterparts in stochastic cases where h and F are random functions, which are discussed in Section 1.2 below. A constant theme that will run through this book is how one might determine from observed data whether h and F are genuinely random. Turn now to the problem of how one might test for *low-dimensional* deterministic chaos in time series. We emphasize "low-dimensional" because, from the point of view of practice, there is no difference between high-dimensional deterministic chaos and randomness. Computers have only finite resolution and data sets have only finite length in the real world.

Example (1.1.2) illustrates the need for a test for stochasticity beyond spectral and autocovariance analysis. Simply plotting x_{t+1} against x_t will not do because examples like

$$x_{t+1} = F(x_t,...,x_{t-q}), \quad q \geq 1, \tag{1.1.6}$$

can be generated that are chaotic, even though they are deterministic. One tests for chaos by calculating the "dimension" of $\{x_t\}$. Let us give a sneak preview of Chapter 2 here.

An efficient way to test for chaos is to consider the following quantity, called the correlation integral, studied by Grassberger and Procaccia 1983a,b, which is a measure of spatial correlation of scattered points or particles in m-dimensional space,

$$C_{m,T}(\epsilon) = \Sigma_{t<s} I_\epsilon(x_t^m, x_s^m) \times [2/T_m(T_m-1)], \tag{1.1.7}$$

where, $T_m = T-(m-1)$, $x_t^m = (x_t,...,x_{t+m-1})$, and $I_\epsilon(x_t^m, x_s^m)$ is an indicator function which equals 1 if $\| x_t^m - x_s^m \| < \epsilon$, and equals 0 otherwise. Here $\{x_t\}$ is a scalar time series under scrutiny for randomness. In order to use (1.1.7) to measure intertemporal local correlations and other dependence, one imbeds $\{x_t\}$ in an m-dimensional space by forming m-vectors $x_t^m = (x_t,...,x_{t+m-1})$ starting at each date t.

Chapter 2 will show that, for stochastic and deterministically chaotic systems, as $T \to \infty$,

$$C_{m,T}(\epsilon) \to C_m(\epsilon) \equiv \text{Prob} \{ \| x_t^m - x_s^m \| < \epsilon \} \text{ w.p. } 1, \tag{1.1.8}$$

for almost all initial conditions.

The probability on the right-hand side of equation (1.1.8) is easy to calculate for many examples. If $\{x(t)\}$ is independently and identically distributed (IID), then $C_m(\epsilon)=[C_1(\epsilon)]^m$ and $C_1(\epsilon)=E\{G(x+\epsilon)-G(x-\epsilon)\}$, where $G(x)\equiv Prob\{x_t\leq x\}$ is the cumulative distribution function.

Dimension (specifically the "information" or "correlation" dimension) is "estimated" by physicists (cf. the survey of Eckmann and Ruelle 1985), who plot $\log(C_{m,T}(\epsilon))$ against $\log(\epsilon)$ for large T and look for constant slope zones of this plot that appear independent of m for large enough m. Dimension is a measure of "complexity," i.e., the number of operative modes or operative degrees of freedom. This notion of "dimension" assigns "m" to objects that we think of as m-dimensional but can assign dimensions to objects such as fractals where we have little intuition as to what the dimension should be.

The definition of correlation dimension in embedding dimension m is defined as:

$$d_m = \lim_{\epsilon \to 0} \lim_{T \to \infty} \log[C_{m,T}(\epsilon)]/\log(\epsilon). \qquad (1.1.9)$$

The correlation dimension itself is given by:

$$d = \lim_{m \to \infty} d_m. \qquad (1.1.10)$$

For example, the "tent map" in (1.1.2) has correlation dimension $d=1$. Since an independent and identically distributed stochastic process (with a nondegenerate distribution function) has correlation dimension $d=\infty$, the correlation dimension can be used to distinguish deterministic chaos from truly random systems. In principle we can detect any deterministic chaos, given enough data. In practice, however, there is never enough data to detect high-dimensional chaos, so the best we can do is to detect *low*-dimensional chaos. When we speak of "low-dimensional chaos," we usually think of their correlation dimensions to be substantially lower than 10, perhaps 5 or 6.

Brock and Sayers 1988 and Scheinkman and LeBaron 1989b estimated various measures of dimension that were stimulated by the theoretical quantities above. Related measures of dimension that they looked at are:

$$SC_{m,T}(\epsilon,\delta) = [\log(C_{m,T}(\epsilon))-\log(C_{m,T}(\delta))]/[\log(\epsilon)-\log(\delta)], \qquad (1.1.11)$$

$$\alpha_{m,T}(\epsilon) = \log(C_{m,T}(\epsilon))/\log(\epsilon). \qquad (1.1.12)$$

The quantity, $SC_{m,T}(\epsilon,\delta)$, is an estimate of the slope of the plot of $\log(C_m(\epsilon))$ against $\log(\epsilon)$, as $\delta \to \epsilon$, i.e.,

$$\text{slope at } \epsilon = C'_{m,T}(\epsilon)\epsilon/C_{m,T}(\epsilon), \qquad (1.1.13)$$

where $C'_{m,T}(\epsilon)$ denotes the derivative of $C_{m,T}(\epsilon)$ with respect to ϵ. Note that the slope at ϵ is just the elasticity of C_m at ϵ. It measures the percentage change in new neighbors that a typical m-history x_t^m gets when ϵ is increased to $\epsilon+d\epsilon$. Hence dimension is a crude measure of the level of parsimony (the minimal number of parameters) needed in a dynamic model to fit the data.

Chapter 2 will show how to create a family of statistics based upon the correlation integral C_m. Recall that this is calculated by first putting

$$C_{m,T}(\epsilon) = \Sigma_{t<s} \, I_\epsilon(x_t^m, x_s^m) \times [2/T_m(T_m-1)], \qquad (1.1.14)$$

where $T_m \equiv T-(m-1)$.

The limit of (1.1.14) exists almost surely under modest stationarity and ergodicity assumptions on the stochastic process under scrutiny. Call this limit $C_m(\epsilon)$. If the stochastic process $\{x_t\}$ is IID, it will be shown that $C_m(\epsilon)=[C_1(\epsilon)]^m$ for all m and ϵ. That is to say, the correlation integral behaves much like the characteristic function of a serial string in that the correlation integral of a serial string of independent random variables is the product of the correlation integrals of component substrings. This motivates a test for independence called the BDS statistic:

$$W_{m,T}(\epsilon) = T^{\frac{1}{2}} \, [C_{m,T}(\epsilon)-C_{1,T}(\epsilon)^m] \, / \, \sigma_{m,T}(\epsilon), \qquad (1.1.15)$$

where $\sigma_{m,T}(\epsilon)$ is an estimate of the standard deviation under the IID null hypothesis. A formula for it will be given in Chapter 2. Brock, Dechert, and Scheinkman 1987 showed that, under the null hypothesis of IID, $W_{m,T} \rightarrow N(0,1)$, in distribution, as $T \rightarrow \infty$. Our Monte Carlo work will show that the W statistic has higher power against certain alternatives than, for example, the tests of independence based upon the bispectrum. The reason for this is that the bispectrum is zero for the class of processes with zero third order cumulants. There are many dependent processes with zero third order cumulants.

Chapter 2 will also show that the statistic (1.1.14) has the same limiting distribution for estimated residuals $\{u_{t,T}\}$, for econometric models of the form

$$y_t = F(I_t,\alpha) + u_t, \tag{1.1.16}$$

where I_t denotes past information, that can include past y's but not past u's, F is a conditional mean function to be estimated, and α is a vector of parameters that can be estimated $T^{\frac{1}{2}}$-consistently. The true residuals $\{u_t\}$ are IID with mean zero and finite variance. Here $\{u_{t,T}\}$ denotes the estimated residuals of (1.1.15) off of a sample of $\{y_t\}$ of length T. Indeed, this invariance result can be demonstrated, for the estimated residuals, for a broad class of models,

$$y_t = H(I_t, u_t, \gamma), \tag{1.1.17}$$

where u_t are IID, I_t is a set of regressors which may include past y's but not current and future y's, I_t is independent of u_t for all t, γ is a vector of parameters, and H satisfies certain regularity conditions.

The bottom line of all this for the practical user is that the BDS test can be applied to estimated innovations of econometric models like (1.1.15) and (1.1.16) to test whether one's data is being generated by a model within this class of models. Since this class of models is rather broad, the BDS test has practical value as a specification test.

1.2 Nonlinear Stochastic Models

The ability to use the BDS test on residuals of econometric models is an important result, which allows the BDS test to be used to detect nonlinearity in econometric models. In the time series literature, a number of nonlinear models have been proposed to explain behavior of data that cannot be generated by linear models. Priestley 1980 gives a general framework. Some well-known examples are as follows. Robinson 1977 proposes the nonlinear moving average, such as:

$$x_t = u_t + \alpha\, u_{t-1}\, u_{t-2}. \tag{1.2.1}$$

Granger and Andersen 1978 introduce the bilinear model:

$$x_t = u_t + \alpha\, x_{t-1}\, u_{t-1}. \tag{1.2.2}$$

Tong and Lim 1980 suggest the threshold autoregressive model:

$$x_t = \alpha\, x_{t-1} + u_t, \qquad \text{if } x_{t-1} < 1,$$

$$x_t = \beta\, x_{t-1} + u_t, \qquad \text{if } x_{t-1} \geq 1. \tag{1.2.3}$$

Engle 1982 puts forth the autoregressive conditional heteroskedasticity (ARCH) model:

$$x_t = \sigma_t\, u_t,$$

$$\sigma_t = [\alpha + \phi x_{t-1}^2]^{\frac{1}{2}}. \tag{1.2.4}$$

In all these examples, u_t is IID, $N(0,1)$. These models can generate x_t, which exhibit no autocorrelation but clearly are not independent of x_{t-1}. To detect nonlinearity, the econometrician can fit a linear time series model, making sure that the residuals are serially uncorrelated, and then apply the BDS test. A rejection means the model is nonlinear, so she knows that a nonlinear model potentially can give a better fit.

Although little theoretical work in economics gives rise to the above models, we do not consider this a weakness of nonlinear time series models. Rather, it is indicative of the difficulty in solving and analyzing nonlinear stochastic general equilibrium models. The nonlinear moving average and the bilinear model can be justified as second order approximations of the Volterra representation, which stationary (linear and nonlinear) time series possess. Threshold autoregressive and ARCH models have enjoyed slightly more attention in the theoretical literature. A threshold autoregressive model can be found in Aiyagari, Eckstein, and Eichenbaum 1985. The idea of their paper is that the price of a storable good will switch between two linear stochastic processes, depending on whether inventory is positive or zero. Hsieh 1988b presents a nonlinear stochastic rational expectations model of exchange rates under central bank intervention. This is a nonlinear switching model, similar to a threshold autoregression.

The most popular nonlinear model in empirical econometric work has been ARCH (and its generalizations), which is very useful in describing heteroskedasticity in many economic time series. There are, of course, theoretical reasons to believe that conditional moments are important determinants of asset prices, since most intertemporal asset pricing models give rise to Euler equations that involve conditional expectations of marginal utilities across assets and across time periods. It is therefore not hard to visualize conditional variances and covariances showing up in asset demand functions. The problem in generating an ARCH specification is that the Euler equation must be solved completely to obtain a characterization of the asset prices, a difficult task when the model is nonlinear. Recently, Lai and Pauly 1988 offered a model in which speculators in the foreign exchange market with incomplete information about market fundamentals use a Kalman filter to extract information and form expectations. The equilibrium exchange rate then turns out to be an ARMA process with conditionally heteroskedastic errors.

1.3   Confronting the Data

In serious confrontation of the theory of complex dynamics with data, the issue of appropriate time scale comes up. Let us explain. Returns on asset i over time period [t,t+h] are defined by:

$$r_{i,t,t+h} = (p_{i,t+h}+y_{i,t+h})/p_{i,t}-1, \qquad\qquad\qquad (1.3.1)$$

where $p_{i,t+h}$ denotes the price of asset i at date t+h and $y_{i,t+h}$ the dividends paid out at date t+h. An approximation to (1.3.1) that is used in much empirical work is $r_{i,t,t+h} = \log[p_{i,t+h}+y_{i,t+h}]-\log[p_{i,t}]$.

At the minute-to-minute level, Wood et al. 1985 have documented that returns tend to be higher at the opening of the exchange, fall over the first 20—30 minutes, look unpredictable in the middle, and rise in the last 20—30 minutes to the close; and that trading volume and price volatility follow the same pattern near the opening and the close. Market microstructure matters a lot at this frequency. See Marsh and Rock 1986 for details. We note in passing that Marsh and Rock argue that "nonlinearity" is quite evident at this frequency, and that the detail of market microstructure matters to price movements and matters a lot. This observation sets the stage for a remark that we want to make.

It is commonly argued by others not trained in the special problems inherent in economic and financial data sets that there is no data limitation problem in economics and especially in finance. Natural science methodology in testing for the presence of instability, chaos, and nonlinearity requires large amounts of data that come from a stationary dynamics, deterministic or stochastic. On the surface it appears that there is a huge amount of data, especially in finance. After all, financial data can be had at the tick-by-tick frequency.

The truth of the matter is that there are serious data limitations for financial economists. There are two ways to increase the number of observations in financial data. One can sample more frequently, say, every transaction. Such high-frequency stock return dynamics are contaminated by the dynamics of the bid/ask spread, which may be of interest to the market microstructure theorist but not to an analyst testing the stock price itself for nonlinearity. Alternatively, one can increase the number of observations by using longer histories while fixing the sampling frequency at a sufficiently long interval (e.g., daily or weekly) to avoid the dynamics of market microstructure. But one runs into nonstationarity problems. Most analysts in finance such as Fama 1976 will posit stationarity for periods no longer than five years and will posit it nervously at that. Many financial analysts such as Black 1976 will not posit a stationary parametric dynamics for stock returns for any period of time! This nonstationarity problem stands in sharp contrast to natural science. Fluid dynamics do not depend upon who is the Chairman of the Federal Reserve. These problems have forced us to invent some of the methods of testing for nonlinearity that are exposited in this book. Let us turn now to explaining why we should expect stock returns to be unpredictable especially at high frequencies. The same argument applies to asset returns in general.

Sims 1984 is the latest formalization that we have found of the standard economic reasoning that price changes must be unpredictable over small time intervals in a frictionless market like stock markets in modern countries. This is formalized by:

Definition (Sims 1984). A process $\{P_t\}$ is instantaneously unpredictable if and only if, as $v \to 0$,

$$E_t[(P_{t+v} - E_t[P_{t+v}])^2] / E_t[(P_{t+v} - P_t)^2] \to 1, \text{ a.s.} \qquad (1.3.2)$$

Here E_t is taken with respect to the information set I_t. ($\{I_t\}$ is an increasing sequence of sub sigma fields of a master sigma field, I.) In other words, for an instantaneously unpredictable process, prediction error is the dominant component of changes over small intervals. Of course, if $\{P_t\}$ is a martingale, which is defined by:

$$E[P_{t+v}|I_u, u \le t] = P_t, \text{ for all } v > 0, \qquad (1.3.3)$$

and $\{P_t\}$ has finite second moments, the ratio in (1.3.2) is exactly 1. Sims points out that, under (1.3.2), regressions of $P_{t+v} - P_t$ on any variable in I_t have $R^2 \to 0$, as $v \to 0$. Under (1.3.3), $R^2=0$. He also points out that (1.3.2) doesn't rule out predictability over longer time periods. He then argues that this roughly squares with empirical evidence in finance. "Short periods" for Sims is daily to weekly.

It is important to realize that (1.3.2) does not exclude predictability of higher order moments such as conditional variance. As an example, fix the "step size" v and let $P_{t+v}=P_t+e_{t+v}$ where $\{e_t\}$ is an ARCH process, i.e., e_{t+v} is distributed normal with mean zero and variance $h_{t+v}=a+bh_t$, $a>0$, $b>0$, h_0 given and positive. Easy computation shows the ratio in (1.3.2) to be unity for each v. This shows that although (1.3.2) excludes predictability of the conditional mean, it does not exclude predictability of the conditional variance.

Notice that (1.3.3) is the same as the equilibrium condition of the Lucas 1978 general equilibrium asset pricing model with constant marginal utility, $U'(c_t)=1$, zero discount rate on future utility, and zero dividends. Thus, in practice, (1.3.3) is "adjusted" by a discount factor, for example, $G_{t+1} \equiv \beta U'(c_{t+1})/U'(c_t)$, and net cash flow, y_{t+1}, over the period. In Lucas-type models, $U(c_t)$ denotes the utility function of an aggregate consumer that is a function of aggregate consumption c_t, $U'(c_t)$ is the derivative of $U(c_t)$ with respect to c_t, and β denotes the aggregate discount rate on the future.

Now recall that chaos theory teaches us that trajectories generated by chaotic maps are potentially perfectly predictable provided that one can measure the state perfectly. But if one measures the state today with error, then forecasts of the future state become worthless at an exponential rate. Hence nonlinear dynamicists sometimes say that chaotic dynamics are unpredictable. The financial logic outlined above leads us to believe that low-dimensional chaotic deterministic generators for stock prices and returns over daily to weekly time periods should be extremely unlikely, unless measurement error in the state is large or the "economic" time on which the dynamics run is faster than chronological time. The theme will be that if there is forecastable structure in stock returns, it must be difficult for traders to discover it. Randomness multiplication (Diaconis's term) phenomena that arise in chaos theory are an example of potentially difficult-to-detect forecastable structure that the methods of chaos theory are specifically designed to detect.

A dramatic example is recent work on quantifying unpredictability in weather forecasting (Casti 1991, Monastersky 1990). Much work in weather forecasting goes into forecasting the degree of precision of the forecast, and methods inspired by chaos theory are recently playing a role in this task. We see a possibility of related methods playing a similar role in economics and finance.

Before we turn to a preview of some evidence, we need to say a few words about the implications for economic decisions if there is deterministic chaos. One of the main points of contention in modern macroeconomics is whether the fluctuations we see in economic activity are due to *external* forcing such as shocks to supply (e.g., oil), shocks to the monetary system (e.g., the change in U.S. Federal Reserve policy from 1979 to 1982), or changes in fiscal policy (e.g., the Reagan "revolution"). Or, are they mostly due to *internal* self-magnifying dynamics, where an increase in activity in one part of the economy magnifies upward activities in other parts of the economy? The Grandmont 1986 volume contains a discussion of this debate stressing internal sources of fluctuations, while King, Plosser, and Rebelo 1988 concentrate on external sources of fluctuations.

The implications toward prediction and control of economic fluctuations of the two opposing views are dramatically different. On the one hand, if one believes the internal view is true then it follows that at least short-term prediction can be improved (perhaps dramatically) using methods tailor-made to predict such dynamics. Also, government stabilization policy may be able to control the fluctuations should it be deemed desirable to do so.

On the other hand, if the exogenous shock view is true then prediction (even in the short term) may be hard to improve by using more sophisticated methods rather than simple (e.g., linear) methods. Furthermore stabilization policy may be worse than useless. It may even be harmful. It is hard to think of two more dramatically different views with more dramatically different recommendations for prediction and control. Therefore it is of utmost importance to sort out, empirically, which view is the most correct. In reality, both views are likely to be correct to some degree. What is at issue is the degree to which each is correct. From the nonlinear-versus-linear perspective taken in this book, the two recent Ph.D. theses of Hiemstra 1990 and Potter 1990 contain the best and most detailed discussions of actual evidence for and against the two views. Potter emphasizes macroeconomic issues more than Hiemstra, who dedicates more space to finance. A rather related parallel debate in weather prediction is discussed in Casti 1991.

Let us turn now to a preview of some evidence, which is presented in more detail in Chapter 3, on this matter. Scheinkman and LeBaron 1989b have estimated the correlation dimension for 1226 weekly observations on the Center for Research in Security Prices (CRSP) value weighted U.S. stock returns index for 1962—1985. They get roughly 6. They calculate another estimate of dimension due to Takens which was also close to 6. Similar results for closing prices over the mid-1970s to the mid-1980s for gold and silver on the London Metals Exchange were reported by Frank and Stengos 1989. They get correlation dimension estimates between 6 and 7 for daily, weekly, and biweekly series. As will be seen in Chapter 3, the structure of stock returns changes over periods of time, and so it is not clear how one should interpret dimension estimates.

Part of the action in the stock market is related to interest rate movements. Look at the behavior of Treasury Bills taken from Ibbotsen and Sinquefield 1977 (p. 90, Exhibit B8). These data are also used by Gennote and Marsh 1986 to measure the risk-free rate of return. Brock 1988 reduced this series to stationarity by taking first differences. He then identified linear models by Box and Jenkins 1976 methods to remove temporally stationary linear dependence in the data. Note that prewhitening does not change the dimension of the underlying dynamics if they are chaotic. The dimension of the residuals (after fitting an autoregressive process of order 8 to the first differences of T-bill returns) is around 2. Furthermore the dimension of the bootstrap counterpart is much larger. The "bootstrap" counterpart is an IID series that has the same unconditional moments as the original series. We create this by drawing at random with replacement as in Efron 1982.

At first blush, this seems to be strong evidence consistent with a chaotic explanation. One cannot conclude that, however, because the largest Lyapunov exponent has not been estimated and shown to be positive. Also unlike Swinney's 1985 (p. 285) case for the Belousov and Zhabotinski chemical reaction, the dynamics have not been "reconstructed."

There is one thing that the scientist must always keep in mind when interpreting this evidence. During the period under scrutiny the government intervened in determining interest rates. There were periods where T-bill rates didn't move at all because the government was controlling interest rates. In other periods, for example, October 1979 to October 1982, the government was more concerned with the growth of the monetary base and less concerned with fluctuations in interest rates. Hence the "dynamics" is subject to "regime shifts." The bottom line is that government activity in the financial markets makes it even harder to interpret the evidence.

Let us sum up the evidence so far. There appear to be nonlinearities in stock returns and Treasury bill rates. There may be a low-dimensional (deterministic) chaotic process. But the results are also consistent with many other (stochastic) dependent processes that are not chaotic. In particular, it may be consistent with fractionally differenced stochastic processes. It also may be consistent with long periods of relative quietude followed by random periods of volatility bursts. If the length of the noisy periods are short compared to the quiet periods, then the estimated dimension will be small even though the series may not be chaotic. There is an intriguing suggestion of rough self similarity being present in many time series. Many economic time series exhibit rather infrequent volatility bursts at all time scales. Their structure can also change over time. This is consistent with the general theme of nonstationarity or regime changes.

This book will develop the theme that, even though conditional means may be hard to predict, it may be possible to predict (either linearly or nonlinearly) other conditional moments such as conditional variances, conditional skewnesses, and possibly the conditional moment generating function.   This has obvious implications for management of risks through put and call options.   This theme is related to the work of Bates 1987, who has shown how the differential between out-of-the-money put prices and out-of-the-money call prices can be used to infer information about conditional moments such as skewness in returns on the underlying security.   The knowledge that predictability of conditional moments exists in stock returns data has implications for searching for potentially profitable positions like those discussed by Bates.

Now that we have established some perspective on chaos and nonlinearity, we turn now to a discussion of possible pathways through which chaotic and other highly nonlinear dynamics may infect the economy.

1.4 Pathways to Chaotic Equilibrium Dynamics

As the reader can see from the surveys of Baumol and Benhabib 1989, those of Boldrin and Woodford 1990, and the conference volume edited by Grandmont 1986, there exists a rich population of economic models that produce equilibrium chaotic dynamics. In this section, we want to summarize the many different ways by which chaos can arise in equilibrium models. The extension to nonlinear stochastic models can be accomplished by adding exogenous noise to these models (although nonlinear stochastic models may arise from nonchaotic models).

First, we give a brief description of the Benhabib, Day, and Grandmont-type of results that show how chaotic rational expectations equilibria can be produced in overlapping generations models.

Second, since there have been objections that two period overlapping generations models generate results driven by parameter values that conflict with existing empirical studies, we state the Boldrin and Montrucchio result showing that any dynamics, hence chaotic dynamics, can be generated by the optimal solution of an infinite horizon growth model. Hence, when the model is turned into a rational expectations model (Sargent 1987a,b), we have chaotic rational expectations equilibrium dynamics in an infinite horizon model.

Third, since many economists of a more applied bent complain that model building in pure theory is too loosely disciplined by data, we discuss the possibility of chaos in models where parameter choice is disciplined in the style of the Real Business Cycle School (RBC) (King, Plosser, and Rebelo 1988). Indeed, since the Boldrin and Montrucchio 1986 result may be viewed as the analogue for dynamic recursive economics of the Sonnenschein, Mantel, and Debreu result for general equilibrium theory, discipline on parameter choice must be imposed in order to generate persuasive examples of chaotic equilibria. While the RBC approach can be criticized for not doing econometrics within the context of the model under scrutiny, we believe that it is a useful intermediate step that avoids paying the price of model specific development of econometric theory.

Fourth, since competitive equilibria are Pareto Optimal when markets are complete, given a competitive equilibrium, loosely speaking, there are weights, one for each consumer, such that the "welfare function" given by the weighted sum of consumer utilities is maximized by that equilibrium. In intertemporal general equilibrium models with recursive preferences and technology, the turnpike theorem of optimal growth theory puts limits on the possibility of complex dynamics in complete market models. See Marimon 1989 and Epstein 1987, as well as their references, for the most recent work on turnpike theorems applied to general equilibrium theory in both deterministic and stochastic setups. The bottom line is that the combined discipline of parameter choice for preferences and technology constrained by empirical studies in the manner of the RBC approach, recursive preferences and recursive technology, and complete markets makes it hard to construct examples of chaotic competitive equilibrium dynamics. In these models there are too many markets present to hedge against risks; there are too many devices available to smooth intertemporal consumption and production; and the desire to do so on both the production and consumption side is too strong to be consistent with complex dynamics. Therefore, we suggest the following channels by which complex equilibrium dynamics might appear. Some of these are taken from Arthur 1988, Boldrin 1988, Brock 1988, and Woodford 1989a,b.

1.   Introduce households that heavily discount the future and make their mass large enough relative to the rest of the economy. A recent paper that shows how this kind of mechanism can generate sensitive dependence upon initial conditions is Woodford 1990a.

2.   Introduce increasing returns and externalities. For example, many economists feel the growth and decay of cities must be explained by self-catalyzing internal effects.

3. Abandon the assumption of complete markets. For example, we believe that Bewley 1983 was the first to show how liquidity constraints can generate instability in recursive intertemporal general equilibrium models. Bewley showed how the dynamics induced by shutting down borrowing and lending markets can look like overlapping generations dynamics.

4. Allow agents to be price setters, not price takers. This will break the connection between equilibrium and Pareto Optimality.

5. Impose complex or chaotic dynamics directly in preferences and technology.

6. Abandon the equilibrium assumption. This would allow learning dynamics as in Anderson, Arrow, and Pines 1988.

7. Allow direct effects of some agents' actions upon the tastes or technologies of others. To put it another way, allow externalities as defined in Arrow and Hahn 1971 (Chapter 6). This would allow complex dynamics of fashion or technological diffusion to be transmitted to prices and quantities through the equilibration process. See Durlauf 1990a for a model of local technological externalities on a lattice structure that generates aggregative time series displaying a type of sensitive dependence upon initial conditions as well as a type of long term dependence that mimics the behavior of aggregative time series data.

8. Introduce exogenous forcing functions.

9. Introduce lagged effects in consumption and technology.

10.   Introduce fads and various kinds of positive feedback traders and noise traders into financial market models.

Although it is well known that lags are connected with instability and chaos, the main problem with lags of the "time to build" type in macroeconomics is that microentities will have an incentive not to initiate projects when everyone else is initiating them. This causes a smoothing effect across project initiation dates, which leads to a smoothing effect on project completions, which in turn leads to a smoothing effect on the resulting aggregative macroeconomic measures of investment activity. However, this smoothing effect may be checked if, for example, there are complementarities of the type discussed by Durlauf 1990a. In this case, initiation of expansion by one sector of the economy lowers marginal costs of expansion to neighboring sectors. Hence it may be possible for a large mass of economic activity to be subject to self-magnifying fluctuations rather than self-damping fluctuations. Let us turn now to a brief exposition of how chaotic rational expectations equilibria can appear in overlapping generations models.

1.4.1. Chaos in Overlapping Generations Models

The simplified version of the standard overlapping generations model presented below will allow us to exposit quickly the highlights of the Benhabib, Day, and Grandmont results as treated by Grandmont 1985.

Consider the following overlapping generations model. The young at date t maximizes the intertemporal utility function:

$$U(c_y(t), c_o(t+1)), \qquad\qquad (1.4.1)$$

subject to the budget constraints:

$$c_y(t)+M_y(t) = p(t)w_y, \text{ and}$$

$$p(t+1,e)c_o(t+1) = M_y(t)+p(t+1,e)w_o. \tag{1.4.2}$$

The intertemporal budget constraint for the young at date t is therefore

$$p(t)c_y(t)+p(t+1,e)c_o(t+1) = p(t)w_y+p(t+1,e)w_o. \tag{1.4.3}$$

The old at date t, having no bequest motives, consume all their income and wealth. Their budget constraint is:

$$p(t)c_o(t) = p(t)w_o+M_y(t-1). \tag{1.4.4}$$

To close the model, we need some requirements on $p(t+1,e)$. We treat two polar possibilities.

$$p(t+1,e) = p(t+1) \text{ (Rational Expectations)}. \tag{1.4.5}$$

$$p(t+1,e) = p(t-1) \text{ (Backward Expectations)}. \tag{1.4.6}$$

Finally, there are two market clearing conditions:

$$M_y(t) = M,$$

$$c_y(t)+c_o(t) = w_y+w_o. \tag{1.4.7}$$

Here U, $c_y(t)$, $c_o(t+1)$, $p(t)$, $p(t+1,e)$, $M_y(t)$, M, w_y, w_o denote utility function, consumption of young at date t, consumption of old at date t+1, price level at date t, point expectation formed at date t of price level at date t+1, nominal money balances demanded by young at date t, constant money supply, endowment of young, and endowment of old, respectively. Budget restraint (1.4.3) is obtained by adding the constraints in (1.4.2). Equations (1.4.5) and (1.4.6) are two expectation formation rules that we shall consider. Equations in (1.4.7) give equilibrium relationships.

Dynamic equilibria are easy to depict in this model by either using the young's offer curve or writing the equilibrium dynamics in terms of real balances

$$x(t) = M/p(t). \tag{1.4.8}$$

Assume $U(c,c')=u(c)+v(c')$, $u',v'>0$, $u'',v''<0$, $u'(0),v'(0)=\infty$, then write down the first order necessary conditions for optimum of the young to obtain the rational expectations dynamics, in terms of $x(t)$, using $M_y(t) = M$,

$$A(x(t)) = u'(w_y-x(t))x(t)$$

$$= v'(w_o+x(t+1))x(t+1)$$

$$= B(x(t+1),a). \tag{1.4.9}$$

Here "a" represents a one-dimensional arc in the space of parameters defining the tastes and endowments of the old. This one-dimensional

arc will be chosen to play the role of the shift parameter in the Ruelle
and Takens scenario and will be used to generate a Feigenbaum period
doubling route to chaos as in Grandmont 1985 (Figure 4, p. 1030).

Now observe that concavity of u implies $A'>0$ and $w_y>0$
implies $A(0)=0$. Invert A to write (1.4.9) in the form

$$x(t) = F(x(t+1),a)), \quad F=A^{-1}(B). \tag{1.4.10}$$

The "forward perfect foresight dynamics" are generated from (1.4.10)
by putting

$$x(t+1) = p(t+1)/M. \tag{1.4.11}$$

Forward perfect foresight dynamics correspond to rational point
expectations equilibrium dynamics. The "backward perfect foresight
dynamics" are generated by putting $x(t+1)=x(t+1,e)=p(t+1,e)/M=$
$p(t-1)/M=x(t-1)$, which leads, from (1.4.10) to

$$x(t) = F(x(t-1),a). \tag{1.4.12}$$

Backward perfect foresight dynamics correspond to the equilibrium
dynamics of a sequence of "Hicksian" temporary equilibria where
expectations $p(t+1,e)=p(t-1)$. Note that (1.4.12) is in the form earlier
treated in this chapter where we discussed the period doubling route
to chaos. Recall that one must assume $F(x,a)$ has a unique maximum,
$x(a)$, that $M(a)=F(x(a),a)$ increases, and that F is C^2 with nontrivial
curvature at $x(a)$.

To obtain the above conditions on F(x,a), which we need to get a period doubling route to chaos, all one needs is to impose similar conditions on B(x)=v'(w_o+x)x, since A'>0. That is, one needs B to be hump-shaped with the size of the hump increasing along an arc in the space {w_o, v(y,b)}. Here v(y,b) will denote a family of concave, increasing functions v(.,b) parameterized by the vector b. For example, look at the class

$$f(z) = z^d/d, \ -\infty < d \leq 1, \ B(x,a)=[w_o(a)+x]^{d(a)-1}x. \qquad (1.4.13)$$

Now one constructs an arc (w_o(a),d(a)) so that the above conditions for a Feigenbaum cascade are satisfied. See Grandmont 1985 for the details.

We have shown above that one can easily generate chaotic backward dynamics. To generate an example of chaotic rational expectations dynamics, all one needs to do is to pick out the above backwards dynamic path out of the multiplicity of forward dynamic paths consistent with the rational expectations dynamics (1.4.10). There will be a multiplicity of forward dynamic paths because given an x(t), in many cases, there will be at least two x(t+1)) consistent with (1.4.10) due to the humped shape of F.

Objections have been made (e.g., Boldrin 1988) to using overlapping generations models to generate realistic examples of chaotic dynamics in economics. The criticism is that one would like to obtain dynamics whose fluctuations are commensurate with fluctuations observed at business cycle frequencies and overlapping generations models realistically parameterized cannot do the job (Sims 1983). Let us turn now to another class of models that may be used to generate chaotic dynamics. We shall consider a class of infinite horizon, recursive, growth models with concave one-period payoff functions.

1.4.2. The Boldrin and Montrucchio Theorem

We follow Boldrin 1988 in our presentation of the Boldrin and Montrucchio theorem.

Theorem 1.1 (Boldrin and Montrucchio 1986). Let $F:X \rightarrow X$ be a C^2-map describing a dynamical system on the compact convex set X contained in R^n. Then there exist a set D, a return function V, and a discount factor b in $(0,1)$ satisfying A1 and A2 below such that F is the policy function h that solves the problem:

$$W(x) = \max \{V(x,y)+bW(y) \text{ s.t. } (x,y) \text{ in } D\}. \tag{1.4.14}$$

A1: $V:D \rightarrow R$ is strictly concave and C^2. $V(x,y)$ is increasing in x and decreasing in y.

A2: The set D contained in $X \times X$ contained in R_+^{2n} is convex, compact, and has nonempty interior. The set X is convex, compact, and has nonempty interior.

Proof. See Boldrin 1988 and his references.

While the Boldrin and Montrucchio construction may be thought to have removed some of the objections to the use of overlapping generations models, there still remains the issue of whether the parameter values needed to calibrate the model are consistent with values established by empirical studies. Work by Benhabib and Rustichini 1989 and Woodford 1989a has tried to come up with models of the type treated in Sargent's books 1987a,b, where the parameter values for tastes, technology, and trading constraints are consistent with parameter values established by empirical studies, and the model generates competitive equilibrium paths that are deterministically chaotic. At this stage the jury is still out on whether this can be done in a convincing way. We stress that there is no controversy concerning whether nonlinearity and nonstationarity are important characteristics of economic and financial data. What is at issue is whether the special form of nonlinearity known as low-dimensional deterministic chaos is present. Let us turn now to Chapter 2 where we develop testing procedures that are capable of detecting deterministic chaos, nonstationarities, and nonlinearities of general form.

Chapter 2
The BDS Statistic

In this chapter, we present a new test for nonlinearity, called the BDS statistic, from the paper by Brock, Dechert, and Scheinkman 1987. The statistic is derived from the correlation integral from equation (1.1.5) in Chapter 1. It tests the null hypothesis that a time series x_t is independent and identically distributed (IID) against an unspecified alternative using a nonparametric technique. In Section 2.1, we derive the asymptotic distribution of this statistic under the null hypothesis of IID. In Section 2.2, we perform Monte Carlo simulations to show that the asymptotic distribution is a good approximation of the finite sample distribution for more than 500 observations, when the data are normally distributed, although skewness and leptokurtosis do not appear to create any additional problems. In Section 2.3, we examine the power of the BDS test against a number of alternative hypotheses, including chaotic processes and nonlinear stochastic processes. In Section 2.4, we show that the presence of "nuisance" parameters does not change the asymptotic distribution of the BDS statistic, provided

---

This chapter is mainly based on Hsieh and LeBaron 1988, except for Section 2.4, which is based on Brock and Dechert 1988b.

that the nuisance parameters are $T^{\frac{1}{2}}$-consistently estimated. In Section 2.5, we use Monte Carlo simulations to show this fact in a regression context; in addition, we also show that standardized residuals from an ARCH or GARCH model do not behave as well. In Section 2.6, we deal with some of the remaining aspects in the application of the BDS statistic.

2.1 The Asymptotic Distribution of the BDS Statistic

Let $\{x_t\}$ be a sequence of (scalar) observations of length T. The Brock, Dechert, and Scheinkman (BDS) statistic is calculated as follows. Form m-dimensional vectors, called m-histories, $x_t^m = (x_t, x_{t+1}, ..., x_{t+m-1})$. Calculate the correlation integral:

$$C_{m,T}(\epsilon) = \Sigma_{t<s}\, I_\epsilon(x_t^m, x_s^m) \times [2/T_m(T_m-1)], \qquad (2.1.1)$$

where $T_m = T-m+1$, and $I_\epsilon(x_t^m, x_s^m)$ is an indicator function that equals 1 if $\| x_t^m - x_s^m \| < \epsilon$, and that equals 0 otherwise. $\| \ \|$ is the sup norm. The correlation integral measures the fraction of pairs of points (x_t^m, x_s^m) that are within a distance ϵ of each other.

Brock, Dechert, and Scheinkman 1987 employed the correlation dimension to obtain a statistical test of nonlinearity. We can summarize their results as follows. Under the null hypothesis that $\{x_t\}$ is IID, with a nondegenerate cumulative distribution F, we can show that for fixed m and ϵ,

$$C_{m,T}(\epsilon) \rightarrow C(\epsilon)^m \text{ w. p. 1, as } T\rightarrow\infty, \qquad (2.1.2)$$

where $C(\epsilon) = \int[F(z+\epsilon)-F(z-\epsilon)]dF(z)$. Also $[C_{m,T}(\epsilon) - C(\epsilon)^m]$ has an asymptotic normal distribution, with mean zero and variance:

$$\sigma_m^2(\epsilon) = 4\, [\, K^m + 2\, \Sigma_{j=1}^{m-1}\, K^{m-j}\, C^{2j} + (m-1)^2\, C^{2m}$$
$$- m^2\, K\, C^{2m-2}\,], \tag{2.1.3}$$

where $C = C(\epsilon)$, and $K = K(\epsilon) = \int[F(z+\epsilon)-F(z-\epsilon)]^2 dF(z)$. We can consistently estimate $C(\epsilon)$ by $C_{1,T}(\epsilon)$, and $K(\epsilon)$ by:

$$K_T(\epsilon) = \Sigma_{t<s<r}\, h_\epsilon(x_t^m, x_s^m, x_r^m) \times [6/T_m(T_m-1)(T_m-2)], \tag{2.1.4}$$

where $h_\epsilon(i,j,k) = [I_\epsilon(i,j)I_\epsilon(j,k)+I_\epsilon(i,k)I_\epsilon(k,j)+I_\epsilon(j,i)I_\epsilon(i,k)]/3$.

Therefore, we can consistently estimate $\sigma_m^2(\epsilon)$ by $\sigma_{m,T}^2(\epsilon)$, which is obtained by replacing C and K in (2.1.3) with $C_{1,T}(\epsilon)$ and $K_T(\epsilon)$. Then the BDS statistic:

$$W_{m,T}(\epsilon) = T^{\frac{1}{2}}\, [C_{m,T}(\epsilon)-C_{1,T}(\epsilon)^m]\, /\, \sigma_{m,T}(\epsilon), \tag{2.1.5}$$

has a limiting standard normal distribution under the null hypothesis of IID.

Rather than giving the proof in the original Brock, Dechert, and Scheinkman 1987 paper, we can provide a more general result using the theory of U-statistics, and apply it to the IID case.

Theorem 2.1. Suppose $\{x_t\}$ is a weakly dependent time series, satisfying conditions (a), (b), or (c) in Theorem 1 in Denker and Keller 1983 (p. 507). Define:

$$w_{m,T}(\epsilon) = [C_{m,T}(\epsilon) - C_{1,T}(\epsilon)^m] / \sigma_{m,T}(\epsilon), \tag{2.1.6}$$

Then

$$w_{m,T}(\epsilon) - [C_m(\epsilon) - C(\epsilon)^m]/\sigma_m(\epsilon) \tag{2.1.7}$$

is asymptotically normally distributed with mean zero and variance $[\omega_m(\epsilon)/\sigma_m(\epsilon)]^2$.

Proof. Consider $C_{m,T}(\epsilon) = \Sigma_{t<s} I_\epsilon(x_t^m, x_s^m) \times [2/T_m(T_m-1)]$. This is a U-statistic, whose kernel is $I_\epsilon(x_t^m, x_s^m)$. Let $G(x_t^m)$ be the unconditional distribution of x_t^m. Define:

$$C_m(\epsilon) \;\; = \int \int I_\epsilon(x_t^m, x_s^m) \, dG(x_t^m) \, dG(x_s^m), \tag{2.1.8}$$

$$k_m(\epsilon, x_t^m) = \int I_\epsilon(x_t^m, x_s^m) \, dG(x_s^m) - C_m(\epsilon), \tag{2.1.9}$$

$$v_m^2(\epsilon) \;\; = E[\, \{\Sigma_{t<T} k_m(x_t^2)\}^2 \,]/T. \tag{2.1.10}$$

If $v_m^2(\epsilon)$ is finite and positive as $T \to \infty$, then Denker and Keller 1983 show that $[C_{m,T}(\epsilon) - C_m(\epsilon)]/2v_m(\epsilon)$ is asymptotically a standard normal distribution.

To compute the covariance between $[C_{m,T}(\epsilon) - C_m(\epsilon)]$ and $[C_{1,T}(\epsilon) - C_1(\epsilon)]$, we need to calculate:

$$v_{1m}(\epsilon) = E[\, \{\Sigma_t k_1(x_t)\}\{\Sigma_s k_s(x_s^m)\} \,]/T. \tag{2.1.11}$$

Thus, the 2×1 column vector $[C_{m,T}(\epsilon)-C_m(\epsilon) \quad C_{1,T}(\epsilon)-C_1(\epsilon)]'$ has a multinormal distribution, $N(0,\Omega)$, where Ω is the matrix whose elements are $\Omega_{11} = v_m(\epsilon)$, $\Omega_{12} = \Omega_{21} = v_{1m}(\epsilon)$, and $\Omega_{22} = v_1(\epsilon)$. Then we can apply a Taylor series expansion on $w_{m,T}(\epsilon)$ to show that

$$[C_{m,T}(\epsilon)-C_{1,T}(\epsilon)^m-C_m(\epsilon)+C(\epsilon)^m] \qquad (2.1.12)$$

is asymptotically normally distributed, with zero mean and variance:

$$\omega_m(\epsilon) = [1 \ \ -mC(\epsilon)^{m-1}] \ \Omega \ [1 \ \ -mC(\epsilon)^{m-1}]', \qquad (2.1.13)$$

which can be calculated as:

$$\omega_m^2(\epsilon) = 4 \ [\ 4C(\epsilon)^2 v_1^1(\epsilon) - 4C(\epsilon)v_{1m}(\epsilon) + v_m^2(\epsilon) \ ]. \qquad (2.1.14)$$

Thus, $[C_{m,T}(\epsilon)-C_{1,T}(\epsilon)^m-C_m(\epsilon)+C(\epsilon)^m]/\omega_m(\epsilon)$ is asymptotically a standard normal distribution.

Multiplying by $[\omega_m(\epsilon)/\sigma_m(\epsilon)]$, and noting that $\sigma_{m,T}(\epsilon)$ converges to $\sigma_m(\epsilon)$ in probability, we obtain the desired result, namely, that $w_{m,T}(\epsilon) - [C_m(\epsilon)-C(\epsilon)^m]/\sigma_m(\epsilon)$ is asymptotically normally distributed with mean zero and variance $[\omega_m(\epsilon)/\sigma_m(\epsilon)]^2$. In other words, $w_{m,T}(\epsilon)$ can be approximated by a normal distribution with mean $[C_m(\epsilon)-C(\epsilon)^m]/\sigma_m(\epsilon)$ and variance $[\omega_m(\epsilon)/\sigma_m(\epsilon)]^2$. Q.E.D.

Before we proceed further, we have six remarks. One, under the null hypothesis that $\{x_t\}$ is IID, direct calculation shows that $C_m(\epsilon)=C_1(\epsilon)^m$ and $\omega_m(\epsilon)=\sigma_m(\epsilon)$, so that $w_{m,T}(\epsilon)$ is asymptotically a standard normal

distribution.   This   verifies   the   result   in   Brock,   Dechert,   and
Scheinkman 1987. In actual applications, we calculate the test statistic:

$$W_{m,T}(\epsilon) = T^{\frac{1}{2}} [C_{m,T}(\epsilon) - C_{1,T}(\epsilon)^m] / \sigma_{m,T}(\epsilon) \qquad (2.1.15)$$

and obtain its critical values using the standard normal distribution.

Two, suppose under a specific alternative hypothesis, $\{x_t\}$ is
not IID, but it is weakly dependent, satisfying conditions (a), (b), or
(c) of Theorem 1 in Denker and Keller 1983. In that case, we know
that $w_{m,T}(\epsilon)$ is asymptotically normal, with mean $[C_m(\epsilon) - C(\epsilon)^m]/\sigma_m(\epsilon)$
and variance $[\omega_m(\epsilon)/\sigma_m(\epsilon)]^2$. To calculate these two quantities, we
need to compute $C(\epsilon)$, $C_m(\epsilon)$, $\sigma_m(\epsilon)$, and $\omega_m(\epsilon)$. In addition, we must
verify that $0 < \sigma_m(\epsilon), \omega_m(\epsilon) < \infty$ to ensure that the variance $[\omega_m(\epsilon)/\sigma_m(\epsilon)]^2$
is well defined. Note that if $C_m(\epsilon) \neq C_1(\epsilon)^m$, the test will reject the null
hypothesis of IID with probability one as $T \to \infty$.

In general, $C(\epsilon)$, $C_m(\epsilon)$, and $\sigma_m(\epsilon)$ are relatively simple to
compute using Monte Carlo integration. To estimate $C_m(\epsilon)$, draw x_i^m
and x_j^m independently from the unconditional (stationary) distribution
of $\{x_t^m\}$. $C_m(\epsilon)$ is the fraction of draws for which $\| x_i^m - x_j^m \| < \epsilon$. To
estimate $K(\epsilon)$, draw x_i^m, x_j^m and x_k^m independently from the
unconditional (stationary) distribution of $\{x_t\}$. $K(\epsilon)$ is the fraction of
draws for which $\| x_i^m - x_j^m \| < \epsilon$ and $\| x_j^m - x_k^m \| < \epsilon$. Then $\sigma_m(\epsilon)$ can be
estimated using the estimates for $C_1(\epsilon)$ and $K(\epsilon)$. For a sufficiently
large number of draws, say 250,000, this procedure yields fairly
accurate estimates of $C(\epsilon)$, $C_m(\epsilon)$, and $\sigma_m(\epsilon)$.

It turns out that $\omega_m(\epsilon)$ is much harder to compute, since it
involves calculating $v_1^2(\epsilon)$, $v_m^2(\epsilon)$, and $v_{1m}(\epsilon)$, which may contain many
terms when $\{x_t\}$ is dependent. We can truncate the infinite sums in

$v_m^2(\epsilon)$, and $v_{1m}(\epsilon)$. To avoid negative values of $\omega_m(\epsilon)$, we suggest making the following adjustments:

$$v_m^2(\epsilon) = E[k_m(x_1^m)2] + 2 \Sigma_{t>1} (1-t/T_m) E[k_m(x_1^m)k_m(x_t^m)].$$

$$v_{1m}(\epsilon) = E[k_m(x_1)k_m(x_1^m)] + \Sigma_{t>1} (1-t/T_m) E[k_m(x_1)k_m(x_t^m)]$$

$$+ \Sigma_{t>1} (1-t/T_m) E[k_m(xt)k_m(x_1^m)]. \qquad (2.1.16)$$

The truncated sums of $v_m^2(\epsilon)$ and $v_{1m}(\epsilon)$ can be used to calculate $\omega_m(\epsilon)$.

Three, although IID implies $C_m(\epsilon)=C(\epsilon)^m$, the converse is not true. Dechert 1988 gives some pathological examples when $\{x_t\}$ is not IID but $C_m(\epsilon)=C(\epsilon)^m$. This means that BDS should be able to detect most nonlinearities, except for certain pathological cases.

Four, the case when x_t is a vector rather than a scalar is treated in Back and Brock 1988a.

Five, the asymptotic distribution of other functions of $C_{m,T}(\epsilon)$ can be obtained using the Taylor series expansion in the same way.

The sixth and final remark is that the asymptotic distribution of the BDS test does not depend upon the existence of higher order unconditional moments. This is verified in the simulations in Section 2.2 for the IID case (using the Student-t with 3 degrees of freedom), and in Hsieh 1991 (using the Cauchy distribution). This is not true for most of the other nonlinearity tests, such as Tsay 1986, Engle 1982, and Hinich 1982, which typically require finite unconditional moments of the fourth or higher order.

We turn now to the finite sample behavior of the BDS statistic.

2.2 The Finite Sample Distribution of BDS under IID

In any application of a test that relies on its asymptotic distribution, one must make sure that the finite sample distribution is actually well approximated by the asymptotic distribution. For the BDS statistic, there are more complications, since the BDS test is computed for a given imbedding dimension, m, and a given distance, ϵ (in number of standard deviations of the data, σ). The choice of m and σ must therefore be determined. Although the asymptotic distribution is proven for any fixed choice of m and σ, we know intuitively what will happen in a finite sample. If m is too large relative to the sample size, the BDS statistic will be very ill-behaved, because there are too few independent (nonoverlapping) points. If σ is too small or too large, the BDS statistic will also be ill-behaved, because there are too few or too many points "close" to any given m-vector. Last, the shape of the data distribution also matters, since it affects how far the points are spread apart.

We access the finite distribution of the BDS statistic under the null hypothesis of IID by Monte Carlo simulations. We generate pseudo random numbers for three sample sizes (100, 500, 1000) and six distributions:

N: Standard normal
t(3):   Student-t with 3 degrees of freedom
D: Double exponential distribution
$\chi^2(4)$:   Chi-square with 4 degrees of freedom
U: Uniform distribution
BM: Bimodal mixture of normals:
                .5 N(3,1) + .5 N(-3,1)

All these distributions are scaled so that their standard deviations equal 1. The normal is typically regarded as the base model. The other distributions represent departures from normality. The Student-t and the double exponential represent heavy-tailed data, which are frequently observed in short-term changes in asset prices. The chi-square with 4 degrees of freedom, $\chi^2(4)$, represents skewed data. The uniform is a thin-tailed distribution that has no mode. The bimodal mixture of normals is intended to simulate departures from unimodality.

Since BDS potentially has power against chaotic behavior, a good pseudo random number generator is needed for the Monte Carlo study. We make use of the following congruential pseudo random uniform number generator. Start with a seed value, S_0. Successive seeds are obtained as follows:

$$S_t = 7^5 S_{t-1} \quad (\text{mod } 2^{31}-1). \tag{2.2.1}$$

A pseudo random uniform number can be obtained by:

$$x_t = S_t / 2^{31}. \tag{2.2.2}$$

We can write $x_t = B \, x_{t-1} \, (\text{mod } 1)$. Since B is a large number, it is easy to see why the BDS test will be unable to detect this generator. A small change in x_{t-1} may lead to a large change in x_t.

To further increase the "randomness" of the generator, we use a shuffling method due to Marsaglia and Bray 1968 and examined in Learmonth and Lewis 1973. Before any pseudo random numbers are generated, a table of 128 uniform random numbers is created. Then for each new pseudo random number, two seed values are calculated. The first one is used to pick one of the 128 positions in the table. The uniform random number in that position is used, and is replaced by the uniform random number generated by the second seed. The simulations are done using FORTRAN programs running on three different Digital Equipment machines (a VAX 8550, a VAX 8650, and a MicroVAX II), and an IBM personal computer (Model PS/2-70A21).

   In the Monte Carlo experiments, we try three sample sizes, T=100, 500, and 1000. For each sample, we compute BDS statistics for ϵ=.25, .5, 1.0, 1.5, and 2.0 times the standard deviation of the sample. For T=100, we use dimensions m=2, 3, and 4. For T=500, we go up to m=5. We replicate these two sample sizes 5000 times. For T=1000, we go up to m=10, but we only replicate this sample size 2000 times.

   The first issue we address is what region of ϵ yields BDS statistics that are well approximated by the asymptotic distribution, and whether that region expands as the sample size increases. We answer this by examining the Monte Carlo results for m=2, described in Tables 1 through 6 in Appendix A, which contain the size of the BDS statistic. They show that the finite sample property is quite poor for samples of T=100. The uniform and bimodal yield the worst results, rejecting the null hypothesis much too frequently for all values of ϵ. The normal and $\chi^2(4)$ are only slightly better, rejecting about 2 to 4 times more often than they should. The t(3) and the double exponential are the only distributions that are close to the correct size for ϵ=1, 1.5, and 2. To obtain some measure of the accuracy of these size estimates, we use a normal approximation to the binomial distribution, and obtain standard errors of 0.71% for 5000 replications [T=100 and 500], and 1.12% for 2000 replications [T=1000].

As we increase the sample size, the distribution of the BDS statistic becomes more normal. At T=500, the bimodal still yields the worst results, where $\epsilon=2$ is the only value for which the size of the test looks reasonable. The uniform is the next worst, where only $\epsilon=1.5$ and 2 provide sensible sizes. The normal, t(3), double exponential, and $\chi^2(4)$ all seem to achieve normality for $\epsilon=0.5$, 1, 1.5, and 2.

Normality holds for an even wider range of ϵ at T=1000. Here, t(3) yields good sizes for all values of ϵ between .25 and 2; the normal, double exponential, and $\chi^2(4)$ also give good results for ϵ between 0.5 and 2. The uniform provides sensible sizes for ϵ between 1 and 2. The bimodal is still the worst, giving reasonable results only for ϵ of 1.5 and 2.

These results at m=2 clearly demonstrate that, as sample size grows, the asymptotic normality is achieved for an increasing range of ϵ. In particular, it appears that values of ϵ between 0.5 and 2 work well for the normal, t(3), double exponential, and $\chi^2(4)$ for T=500 or higher. When the sample is small (less than 500), the asymptotic distribution is a poor approximation of the sampling distribution of the BDS statistic. We suggest either using the quantiles from our simulations or bootstrapping (as in Efron 1982) the distribution as guidance to the actual sizes of the BDS statistics.

Next, we examine the effect of increasing the dimension m. If we hold the sample size fixed, we expect the finite sample property to worsen as m increases. The reason is that the number of nonoverlapping observations is reduced as m grows. It is no surprise to find that the finite sample property is very poor at m>2 for T=100. We only report the results for T=500 and 1000. At T=500, the normal, t(3), double exponential, and chi-square all yield reasonable sizes at ϵ between .5 and 2 when m=5. The uniform gives good sizes only at ϵ=1.5 and 2, and the bimodal gives good sizes only at ϵ=2. These results remain the same when T=1000.

When we increase m to 10, the normal, t(3), double exponential, and $\chi^2(4)$ all give reasonable sizes for ϵ between 1 and 2, the uniform for ϵ between 1.5 and 2, and the bimodal only at ϵ equal to 2.

The reason for the failure of the BDS statistic to achieve normality at small ϵ for higher dimensions is that there are too few observations. For example, $C_1(.25)$ = 0.14 for the normal, and so at dimension 6, $C_6(.25)$ = 0.14^6 = 0.0000075, which means that the expected number of 6-histories within ϵ=.25 of each other is less than 1 out of 1000 observations. Typically, the estimate of $C_6(.25)$ for 1000 observations will be identically 0. Hence the BDS statistics all turn out to be negative and large.

We suspect that the number of nonoverlapping data points, i.e., (T/m), should exceed 200 for the asymptotic distribution to hold. This can be seen by the remarkable similarity of the sizes of the test when m=2 and T=500, and when m=5 and T=1000. If T/m is less than 200, we again suggest bootstrapping the sizes of the BDS statistics.

In summary, the Monte Carlo simulations suggest that the asymptotic distribution can approximate the finite sample distribution of the BDS statistic for 500 or more observations. The dimension should be 5 or lower, and ϵ should be between 0.5 to 2 standard deviations of the data. Furthermore, the approximation appears not to be affected by skewness or heavy tails, but rather by bimodality or thin tails.

If the data distribution is very different from the four distributions, e.g., normal, t(3), $\chi^2(4)$, and double exponential, or if a researcher has any doubts about the asymptotic approximation for IID data, we suggest using a bootstrap.

Next, we simulate the ability of the BDS to detect nonlinearity.

2.3 The Power of BDS against Various Alternatives

Now that we have derived the asymptotic distribution of the BDS statistic and simulated its finite sample distribution under the null hypothesis of IID, we deal with the natural question: how well can BDS detect nonlinearity? In statistical jargon, what is the power of the BDS test against specific alternatives? In this section, we consider seven popular alternatives to IID: first order autoregression (AR(1)), first order moving average (MA(1)), the tent map, threshold autoregression (TAR), nonlinear moving average (NMA), the autoregressive conditional heteroskedasticity (ARCH) model, and the generalized ARCH (GARCH) model. The AR(1) and MA(1) are linear models, the tent map is a chaotic (i.e., nonlinear deterministic) model, while the TAR, NMA, ARCH, and GARCH are nonlinear stochastic models. We provide the answer both in terms of theoretical asymptotic power and in terms of Monte Carlo simulation for finite samples. We show that BDS can detect all these models, which means that we must remove any linear dependence in our data before we can use BDS to test for nonlinearity.

2.3.1 Asymptotic Power against Seven Alternative Models

In terms of theoretical asymptotic power, Section 2.1 showed that the statistic:

$$w_{m,T}(\epsilon) - [C_m(\epsilon)-C(\epsilon)^m]/\sigma_m(\epsilon) \tag{2.3.1}$$

is asymptotically normally distributed with mean zero and variance $[\omega_m(\epsilon)/\sigma_m(\epsilon)]^2$. Under any specific alternative, as long as $C_m(\epsilon) \neq C(\epsilon)^m$, and $0 < \omega_m(\epsilon), \sigma_m(\epsilon) < \infty$, the BDS test will reject the null hypothesis of IID (which implies $C_m(\epsilon)=C(\epsilon)^m$) with probability one. This turns out to be true for all seven alternatives considered here, as we will demonstrate below for the case of m=2. This will not be true, however, if the data is not IID but $C_m(\epsilon)=C(\epsilon)^m$, which can happen in pathological cases (see examples given in Dechert 1988).

The first two alternatives are linear models with autocorrelated data.

First Order Autoregression

One of the simplest linear stochastic process is the first order autoregressive model (AR(1)):

$$x_t = \rho\, x_{t-1} + u_t, \tag{2.3.2}$$

where u_t is IID standard normal. If $|\rho| < 1$, the unconditional distribution of x_t is stationary with finite variance.

We shall concentrate on the case when $\rho=0.5$. Figure 2.1 plots $C_2(\epsilon)-C(\epsilon)^2$, which is positive for any ϵ between 0 and 4.5σ. Since $C_2(\epsilon) \neq C(\epsilon)^2$, the power of the BDS test approaches unity as the sample size increases. We note that the power of the BDS test declines as $|\rho|$ declines towards zero, but it increases as $|\rho|$ increases towards 1.

First Order Moving Average

Another simple linear stochastic process is the first order moving average model (MA(1)):

$$x_t = \theta u_{t-1} + u_t, \qquad (2.3.3)$$

where u_t is IID standard normal. As in the case of the AR(1), the unconditional distribution of the MA(1) is normal for all values of θ. The standard deviation is $s=(1+\theta^2)$.

We shall concentrate on the case for $\theta=.5$. Figure 2.2 plots $C_2(\epsilon)-C(\epsilon)^2$, which is positive for all values of ϵ between 0 and 4σ. Since $C_2(\epsilon) \neq C(\epsilon)^2$, the power of the BDS test will approach unity as sample size grows. Note that the power of the BDS test decreases as $|\theta|$ declines to zero, but it increases as $|\theta|$ increases to unity.

The next five models are nonlinear models, chosen so that they have no linear structure. This allows us to compare the power of the BDS statistic with other nonlinear tests in the Monte Carlo experiments.

Tent Map

The tent map is one of the simplest chaotic (nonlinear deterministic) systems. For almost all values of x_0 in the interval $(0,1)$, the sequence $\{x_t\}$ generated by:

$$x_t = 2 x_{t-1}, \qquad \text{if } x_{t-1} < .5$$
$$x_t = 2 - 2 x_{t-1}, \qquad \text{if } x_{t-1} \geq .5 \qquad (2.3.4)$$

is uniformly distributed over $(0,1)$.

To determine the asymptotic distribution of the BDS statistic at dimension two, we need to calculate $C(\epsilon)$, $C_2(\epsilon)$, $\sigma_2(\epsilon)$, and $\omega_2(\epsilon)$. Figure 2.3 plots $[C_2(\epsilon)-C(\epsilon)^2]$ as a function of ϵ. It begins at 0 when $\epsilon=0$, climbs to a peak at around $\epsilon=.64\sigma$, and turns back down. It crosses 0 at around $\epsilon=1.732\sigma$, goes negative for larger values of ϵ, reaches a bottom near $\epsilon=2.13\sigma$, and turns back up, hitting 0 again at the largest value of ϵ, 3.464σ. (For $\epsilon>3.464\sigma$, both $C(\epsilon)$ and $C_2(\epsilon)$ are identically 1.) We can see that, except for values of ϵ near 1.732σ, $C_2(\epsilon)\neq C(\epsilon)^2$, which means that the power of the BDS test goes to unity as sample size increases.

When $\epsilon=1.732\sigma$, $C_2(\epsilon)=C(\epsilon)^2$, so the test will not reject IID with probability 1. (This is confirmed by Monte Carlo simulation.) To deal with this problem, we must modify the testing procedure. One way is to compute the slope of $[C_2(\epsilon)-C(\epsilon)^2]$ as ϵ changes. Under the null hypothesis of IID, the slope is zero everywhere (since $C_2(\epsilon)=C(\epsilon)^2$ for all ϵ). Under the tent map alternative, $[C_2(\epsilon)-C(\epsilon)^2]$ has nonzero slope except at two extremum points. In particular, its slope is negative at $\epsilon=1.732\sigma$. We can then use the Denker and Keller method to derive the asymptotic distribution of the test statistic

$$\{\, [C_2(\epsilon+\delta)-C(\epsilon+\delta)^2]-[C_2(\epsilon-\delta)-C(\epsilon-\delta)^2]\,\} \,/\, 2\delta.$$

Threshold Autoregressive Model

Threshold autoregressive models (TAR) have been proposed in Tong and Lim 1980. A simple TAR model is given by:

$$x_t = -.5\, x_{t-1} + u_t, \qquad \text{if } x_{t-1} \leq 1,$$

$$x_t = .4\, x_{t-1} + u_t, \qquad \text{if } x_{t-1} > 1, \tag{2.3.5}$$

where u_t is IID standard normal.

Figure 2.4 plots $C_2(\epsilon) - C(\epsilon)^2$, which begins at 0 for $\epsilon = 0$, rises to a maximum near $\epsilon = \sigma$, crosses 0 slightly to the right of $\epsilon = 2\sigma$, reaches a minimum slightly to the right of $\epsilon = 3\sigma$, and turns back up to zero for large values of ϵ. This shape is similar to that of the tent map, but the absolute value of $C_2(\epsilon) - C(\epsilon)^2$ is smaller. The implication is that, except for a small number of points close to $\epsilon = 3\sigma$, the power of the BDS test will approach unity as sample size grows.

Nonlinear Moving Average

Nonlinear moving average (NMA) models have been proposed by Robinson 1977. A simple NMA model is given as follows:

$$x_t = u_t + \gamma\, u_{t-1}\, u_{t-2}, \tag{2.3.6}$$

where u_t is IID standard normal. For any finite value of γ, x_t has a stationary distribution with finite variance. The unconditional distribution of the NMA is nonnormal, with standard deviation $(1+\gamma^2)$. We shall concentrate on the case when $\gamma = 0.8$.

Figure 2.5 plots $C_2(\epsilon) - C(\epsilon)^2$, which is nonpositive for all values of ϵ between 0 and 5σ. This means that the power of the BDS test approaches unity as the sample size increases.

Autoregressive Conditional Heteroskedasticity

Engle 1982 proposes the autoregressive conditional heteroskedasticity (ARCH) model. A simple ARCH model is given by:

$$x_t = h_t u_t ,$$

$$h_t^2 = h_0^2 + \phi\, x_{t-1}^2, \tag{2.3.7}$$

where u_t is IID standard normal. If ϕ is between 0 and 1, x_t has an unconditional stationary distribution (which is typically nonnormal), with variance $h_0^2/[1-\phi]$. We shall concentrate on the case when $\phi=0.5$.

Figure 2.6 plots $C_2(\epsilon)-C(\epsilon)^2$, which is positive for ϵ between 0 and 5σ. This means that the power of the BDS test will approach unity as the sample size increases.

Generalized ARCH

Bollerslev 1986 proposes the generalized autoregressive conditional heteroskedasticity (GARCH) model. A simple GARCH model is given by:

$$x_t = h_t u_t,$$

$$h_t^2 = h_0^2 + \phi\, x_{t-1}^2 + \psi\, h_{t-1}^2, \tag{2.3.8}$$

where u_t is IID standard normal. If $[\psi+\phi]$ is between 0 and 1, x_t has an unconditional stationary distribution (which is typically nonnormal), with variance $h_0^2/[1-\psi-\phi]$. We shall concentrate on the case when $\phi=0.1$ and $\psi=0.8$.

Figure 2.7 plots $C_2(\epsilon)-C(\epsilon)^2$, which is mostly positive for ϵ between 0 and 5σ. This means that the power of the BDS test will approach unity as the sample size increases.

We have completed the discussion of the asymptotic power of the BDS statistic. We have shown that the BDS test will asymptotically reject

IID for all seven alternative models, particularly in the recommended
rate of ϵ between 0.5σ and 2σ, with the possible exception of a small
range in the case of the tent map (near $\epsilon=1.732\sigma$) and the TAR (near
$\epsilon=2\sigma$). We now turn to the power of the BDS test in finite samples.

2.3.2 Monte Carlo Simulations and Power Comparisons

In terms of finite sample properties, we use Monte Carlo simulation
to explore the power of the BDS statistic in detecting departures from
IID in the seven alternative models. The results are presented in
Tables 1 through 14 in Appendix B. They show that BDS can reject
the IID null hypothesis in both linear and nonlinear models. In order
to use BDS as a nonlinear test, one must first remove any linear
dependence in the data. If the resulting BDS statistic still rejects IID,
we will have reason to suspect the presence of nonlinearities.

We also compare the power of the BDS statistic to that of other
nonlinear tests, such as Tsay 1986 and Engle 1982, in the five
nonlinear alternatives: tent map, TAR, NMA, ARCH, and GARCH.

Tsay Test for Nonlinearity

Tsay 1986 proposes to test for nonlinearity by testing for the statistical
significance of the cross-terms $(x_{t-i}x_{t-j})$ on the series x_t after purging
any linear dependence. The Tsay test is computed in four steps.

1.   Regress x_t on the lagged vector $w_t = [1\ x_{t-1} \ldots x_{t-M}]'$. Save the
        residuals u_t.

2.   Build the vector z_t using the distinct elements of the matrix
        $[x_{t-1} \ldots x_{t-M}]'\ [x_{t-1} \ldots x_{t-M}]$. For M=2, $z_t = [x_{t-1}^2\ x_{t-1}x_{t-2}\ x_{t-2}^2]$.
        Regress z_t on w_t and save the residual vector a_t.

3.   Regress u_t on a_t and save the residuals e_t.

4.   Calculate:

$$F = (\Sigma a_t u_t)(\Sigma a_t' a_t)^{-1} (\Sigma u_t a_t')(T-M-r-1) / (\Sigma e_t^2)r, \qquad (2.3.9)$$

where $r=M(M+1)/2$.

Tsay shows that if x_t is an autoregressive process of order M, F is asymptotically distributed as $F(r, T-M(M+3)/2-1)$. For our comparisons, we will use M=2 and M=3.

Engle Test for ARCH

Engle 1982 proposes a test for ARCH, computed as follows. Take the residuals of a fitted linear model, u_t. Engle shows that the statistic TR^2 of the regression of u_t^2 on p lags of itself and a constant term under the null hypothesis of IID is asymptotically $\chi^2(p)$. Although Engle interprets this as a Lagrange multiplier test for ARCH, his test actually has power against many types of nonlinearity. This is noted in McLeod and Li 1983, who show that the autocorrelation function of u_t^2 can be used to identify nonlinearity. For our purpose, we shall use p=1 and 2.

The results are tabulated in Table 2.1. They indicate that all three nonlinear tests have good power against the tent map, NMA, and TAR. All three also have poor power against GARCH. The main difference lies in the ARCH model, where both BDS and Engle's test have good power, but the Tsay test has much lower power. The reason is that the Tsay test is looking for nonzero terms in the third order cumulants of a zero mean time series $\{x_t\}$, given by:

$$c_{xxx}(i,j) = E[x_t x_{t-i} x_{t-j}], \qquad (2.3.10)$$

for i,j>0. For ARCH and GARCH models, these third order cumulants are identically zero, which explains the low power of the Tsay test. We also note that the Tsay test is the time domain analogue of the Hinich 1982 bispectrum test for nonlinearity. The bispectrum is the double Fourier transform of the third order cumulants. Hinich shows that if $\{x_t\}$ is linear, its bispectrum is constant at all frequencies. He proposes a nonlinearity test that looks for nonconstancy of the bispectrum. This test also has low power against ARCH and GARCH models, since the bispectrum of data generated by ARCH and GARCH models is identically zero.

On the face of the Monte Carlo evidence, the Engle test appears to be the winner, since it is easier to compute than the BDS test, while it has the same power against the five nonlinear alternatives. We need, therefore, to justify why we want to use the BDS test. It is simply this. As a test against ARCH, the Engle test may be optimal. The Engle test is looking for linear dependence in the conditional variance of $\{x_t\}$, i.e., nonzero autocovariances of $\{x_t^2\}$, given by:

$$\mu_{x^2x^2}(k) \;=\; E[(x_t-\mu_x)^2(x_{t-k}-\mu_x)^2], \qquad (2.3.11)$$

for k>0. Thus, the Engle test will have low power against nonlinear models for which $\mu_{x^2x^2}(k)$ are identically zero for all k>0. This happens in the following class of models. Suppose x_t is normally distributed, with mean zero and variance h_t^2, where h_t^2 depends on its own past in a nonlinear manner. If, for example, h_t^2 follows a tent map, BDS should be able to detect the nonlinearity in x_t but the Engle test will not. (Neither does the Tsay test, for that matter.) In all fairness to Engle 1982, however, he never proposed to use his test for general types of nonlinearity.

2.4 Specification Test: Scalar Case

A general approach to specification testing in time series econometrics has been given by White 1987 and his references, especially to Newey 1985 and Tauchen 1985. In Pagan and Hall 1983 there is a review of diagnostic tests and specification tests that are based upon estimated residuals. In this section, we deal with using BDS as a specification test. For certain cases (as shown in Section 2.3), BDS has good power against a wide class of alternatives to the null model. It is a *general* test for model misspecification, not designed to test the null model against a specific alternative.

The price to be paid for this test is that the null model must have IID innovations or it must be transformed (if possible) into such a model where the transformation can be estimated $T^{\frac{1}{2}}$-consistently. The class of null models is not all that restrictive. The breadth of the class of models that can be treated with our methods will be discussed at the end of the section.

The reason to test for adequacy of the transformability of the null model into a model with IID innovations is because the BDS test is a nonparametric test for independence that appears to have good properties. It has good performance on size (Section 2.1), and has power against a wide class of alternatives (including some which are uncorrelated, but not independent) as well as against nonstationary alternatives (Section 2.3). Also, for a fairly large class of null models, the test has the same first order asymptotics whether it is evaluated using the estimated residuals of a null model with IID innovations or with the true residuals. This "nuisance parameter free" property is useful in actual practice for testing the adequacy of null models. One simply estimates the model and tests the estimated residuals for IID. The small sample performance of this procedure is evaluated by Monte Carlo methods in Section 2.5.

Here we address the following types of problems of testing for specification errors in a time series model. First, consider the stationary time series model:

$$y_t = f(y_{t-1}, y_{t-2}, \ldots) + u_t \equiv f(Y_{t-1}) + u_t, \qquad (2.4.1)$$

where $\{y_t\}$ is a scalar time series, $\{u_t\}$ is an IID sequence of innovations with zero mean and finite variance, which we set equal to unity without loss of generality, f is a function to be estimated, and $Y_{t-1} \equiv (y_{t-1}, y_{t-2}, \ldots)$. Suppose that the correct specification for the model is given by equation (2.4.1), but one estimates instead the following model:

$$y_t = g_T(Y_{t-1}) + v_{t,T}, \qquad (2.4.2)$$

from a sample of length T. If the estimator $g_T(\cdot)$ converges almost surely to some function $g(\cdot)$ as $T \to \infty$, then $v_{t,T} \to v_t$ where

$$v_t = f(Y_{t-1}) - g(Y_{t-1}) + u_t \equiv h(Y_{t-1}) + u_t. \qquad (2.4.3)$$

We would like a convenient method to test whether or not f = g, i.e., the model is correctly estimated. It is obvious that f = g implies $\{v_t\}$ is IID. It would be nice to show that $\{v_t\}$ IID implies f = g. It turns out that this is true for linear cases that satisfy some regularity conditions. We have the following result:

Theorem 2.2. If $f(Y_{t-1}) = \Sigma_{j=1}^{\infty} a_j y_{t-j}$, and $g(Y_{t-1}) = \Sigma_{j=1}^{\infty} b_j y_{t-j}$, with $\| a \|_2 < \infty$ and $\| b \|_2 < \infty$, then $\{v_t\}$ with $E[v_t^2]<\infty$ IID implies $a = b$.

Proof. By hypothesis on f and g, and by definition of $\{v_t\}$ in equation (2.4.3),

$$v_t = \Sigma_{j=0}^{\infty} c_j u_{t-j}, \tag{2.4.4}$$

where $c_0 = 1$ and $\| c \|_2 < \infty$. Since the $\{v_t\}$ are IID (uncorrelated is sufficient), $\forall k > 0$,

$$0 = E[v_t v_{t+k}] = E[\Sigma_{m=0}^{\infty}\Sigma_{n=0}^{\infty} c_m c_n u_{t-m} u_{t+k-n}]$$
$$= \Sigma_{n=0}^{\infty} c_{n+k} c_n, \tag{2.4.5}$$

where we have used the fact that $E[u_t u_{t+k}] = 0$ if $k > 0$ and $E[u_t u_{t+k}] = 1$ if $k = 0$. Similarly,

$$E[v_t^2] = \Sigma_{n=0}^{\infty} c_n^2 < \infty. \tag{2.4.6}$$

Let H be the Hilbert space of square summable sequences, and e^0, e^1,..., be the unit vectors, $e_t^n = \delta_{nt}$, which span H. For $x \in H$, define the right shift operator R as:

$$(Rx)_t = 0 \text{ if } t=0, \ (Rx)_t = x_t \text{ if } t\geq1, \tag{2.4.7}$$

and define R^n by $R^0 x = x$, and

$$R^n x = R(R^{n-1} x) \quad n \geq 1. \tag{2.4.8}$$

Equation (2.4.13) can then be written as:

$$\langle c, R^n c \rangle = 0 \quad n \geq 1. \tag{2.4.9}$$

Let (x) denote the subspace spanned by x, and define its orthogonal complement by:

$$(x)^{\perp} = \{ y \in H | \langle y, x \rangle = 0 \}, \tag{2.4.10}$$

and let

$$M = \bigcap_{n \geq 1} (R^n c)^{\perp}. \tag{2.4.11}$$

In this notation, equation (2.4.17) implies that $c \in M$. For any $x \in H$, solve the following for $\alpha_0, \alpha_1, ...$:

$$x_0 = \alpha_0$$
$$x_1 = \alpha_0 c_1 + \alpha_1$$
$$\vdots$$
$$x_n = \alpha_0 c_n + \alpha_1 c_{n-1} + ... + \alpha_n$$
$$\vdots \tag{2.4.12}$$

Notice that $\forall k \geq 0$,

$$\langle x - \Sigma_{n=0}^{\infty} \alpha_n R^n c, e^k \rangle = x_k - (\alpha_0 c_k + \alpha_1 c_{k-1} + ... + \alpha_k) = 0, \qquad (2.4.13)$$

and therefore

$$x = \Sigma_{n=0}^{\infty} \alpha_n R^n c. \qquad (2.4.14)$$

Now for $n > m$, $\langle R^n c, R^m c \rangle = \langle c, R^{n-m} c \rangle = 0$, and using this in equation (2.4.20), we get that

$$\langle x, R^m c \rangle = \Sigma_{n=0}^{\infty} \alpha_n \langle R^n c, R^m c \rangle = \alpha_m \| R^m c \|^2 = \alpha_m \| c \|^2. \qquad (2.4.15)$$

Therefore, any $x \in H$ has the representation:

$$x = (\langle x, R^n c \rangle / \| c \|^2) R^n c. \qquad (2.4.16)$$

In particular,

$$e^0 = (\langle e^0, R^n c \rangle / \| c \|^2) R^n c = c / \| c \|^2, \qquad (2.4.17)$$

which implies that $c = e^0$.   Q.E.D.

This theorem shows that for the linear case, testing the sequence of residuals is a method of testing for the correct specification of the model. In particular, one of the implications of this theorem is that when the true model is a linear autoregressive process the *limiting* residual errors will be IID only when the correct number of lags have been estimated.

As a generalization of Theorem 2.2 to nonlinear models, we have the following result:

Theorem 2.3. Suppose $\{v_t\}$ is IID with mean zero, finite variance and satisfies:

$$v_t = h(u_{t-1}, u_{t-2}) + u_t, \qquad (2.4.18)$$

where $\{u_t\}$ is an IID with mean zero and finite moments, $E[|u_t|^n] < \infty$. If $h : R^2 \to R$ is measurable with respect to the product measure μ_2 induced on R^2 by $F(u) = P(u_t < u)$, then $h = 0$, μ_2 almost surely.

Proof. First, consider the case that h is a function only of u_{t-1}. Without loss of generality, $E[h(u_{t-1})] = 0$, and so $E[v_t] = 0$. By independence, $E[v_{t+1}v_t^n] = E[v_{t+1}]E[v_t^n] = 0$, and therefore:

$$0 = E[((h(u_t) + u_{t-1}))(h(u_{t-1}) + u_t)^n]$$

$$= E[h(u_t) \Sigma_{k=0}^n \binom{n}{k} h(u_{t-1})^k u_t^{n-k}$$

$$+ E[u_{t+1}]E[(h(u_{t-1}) + u_t)^n]$$

$$= \Sigma_{k=0}^n \binom{n}{k} E[h(u_{t-1})^k] E[u_t^{n-k} h(u_t)]. \qquad (2.4.19)$$

Now for $n = 1$, this implies that $E[u_t h(u_t)] = 0$, and since

$$\Sigma_{k=0}^{n+1} \binom{n+1}{k} E[h(u_{t-1})^k] E[u_t^{n+1-k} h(u_t)]$$

$$= E[u_t^{n+1} h(u_t)] + \Sigma_{k=1}^{n+1} \binom{n+1}{k} E[h(u_{t-1})^k] E[u_t^{n+1-k} h(u_t)], \qquad (2.4.20)$$

it follows by induction that $\forall n$, $E[u_t^n h(u_t)] = 0$. Thus,

$\int u^n h(u)dF(u) = 0 \quad \forall n \geq 0.$ (2.4.21)

The set of square integrable functions, $\int f^2 dF < \infty$, forms a Hilbert space in which the span of $(1, u, u^2, ...)$ is dense. Since $h(\cdot)$ is orthogonal to these functions, $h \equiv 0$. A similar proof works for the case that $v_t = h(u_{t-1}, u_{t-2}) + u_t$, for which it can be shown that:

$\int u^n v^m h(u,v)dF(u)dF(v) = 0 \quad \forall n,m \geq 0.$ (2.4.22)

This then implies that $h(\cdot,\cdot) \equiv 0$.   Q.E.D.

We do not know how to generalize the proof to handle the case when $h(\cdot)$ is a function of more than two lags of u_t, since the computations become increasingly tedious. We can only offer the following conjecture:

Conjecture. Suppose $\{v_t\}$ is IID with mean zero, finite variance and satisfies:

$v_t = h(u_{t-1},...,u_{t-q}) + u_t,$ (2.4.23)

where $\{u_t\}$ is an IID process with mean zero and finite moments. Let $h : R^q \to R$ be measurable with respect to the product measure μ_q induced on R^q by $F(u) = P(u_t < u)$. Then $h = 0$, μ_q almost surely.

The conjecture above if true, would imply that residual functions of a finite number of lagged u's must be zero. A possible extension is that (under an appropriate condition on the vanishing dependence of h on the qth lag of u as $q \to \infty$) all residual functions of lagged u's must be zero. We have already shown that certain classes of functions, h, must be zero provided that $\{v_t\}$ is IID. Of course $\{v_t\}$ IID is consistent with h being zero, i.e. the specification is correct. In current research we are looking for a useful set of conditions on the data generator (2.4.1) and the model (2.4.2), so that the IID property of the estimated residuals as sample size goes to infinity guarantees that the correct model for the data generator has been estimated.

What Theorems 2.2 and 2.3 show is that, under appropriate restrictions, the *limiting* residuals of a correctly specified model are IID, if the true disturbances themselves are IID. Thus, the BDS test can be used as a specification test.

Since we do not observe actual disturbances, we must rely on the estimated residuals. It was shown in Brock 1988 that the estimated residuals may be used to test for the adequacy of the null model. For example, suppose that the null model is:

$$y_t = by_{t-1} + u_t, \ |b|<1, \ \{u_t\} \ \text{IID}, \tag{2.4.24}$$

and one estimates:

$$y_t = b_n y_{t-1} + u_{t,T} \tag{2.4.25}$$

using a sample of length T. Then if the data are generated by model (2.4.24), the asymptotic distribution of the BDS statistic still holds, even though it is evaluated at the *estimated* residuals, $\{u_{t,T}\}$. In fact, this "nuisance parameter free" property of the BDS statistic is quite general. Appendix D gives sufficient conditions.

The reason why the BDS test works well as a model specification test is because the condition that $W_{m,T} \to 0$ almost implies that the underlying sequence of innovations is IID. In Dechert 1988 a variant on the BDS test statistic was used to show that for a stationary Gaussian process, independence is equivalent to the statistic converging to zero. The power of the test comes about because it is extremely sensitive to departures from either independence or stationarity.

In fact, the BDS test can be used to detect a lack of stationarity in time series. Consider the following model with a simple time trend:

$$y_t = a_0 + a_1 t + u_t. \tag{2.4.26}$$

If one estimates the model without the trend:

$$y_t = b_T + v_{t,T}, \tag{2.4.27}$$

then as $b_T \to b_0$, $v_{t,T} \to v_t$ and the $\{v_t\}$ satisfy:

$$v_t = a_0 - b_0 + a_1 t + u_t. \tag{2.4.28}$$

If $\{v_t\}$ are IID, then $E[v_t] = a_0 + a_1 t$, and for $E[v_t] = E[v_s]$ it is necessary that $a_1 = 0$. The BDS test applied to the estimated residuals in equation (2.4.27) strongly rejects the hypothesis that $a_1 = 0$ whenever it is nonzero. The analysis also extends to trends that are polynomials in t.

Another class of models that can be detected with the BDS test are those with trends in variance:

$$y_t = a_0 + (1 + b_0 t)u_t. \tag{2.4.29}$$

If one estimates the stationary model:

$$y_t = c_T + v_{t,T}, \tag{2.4.30}$$

then $c_T \to c_0$ and $v_{t,T} \to v_t$, where v_t satisfies:

$$v_t = a_0 - c_0 + (1 + b_0 t)u_t. \tag{2.4.31}$$

In this case, $\text{Var}(v_t) = (1 + b_0 t)^2$, and for $\{v_t\}$ to be identically distributed, it is necessary that $b_0 = 0$. The BDS test also strongly rejects the hypothesis that $b_0 = 0$ in this type of model.

All of the data generating models treated above had IID innovations. This strong assumption can be relaxed, as done in Appendix D.

2.5 Finite Sample Distribution with Nuisance Parameters

The important remaining issue is whether the finite sample properties of the BDS statistic examined in Section 2.3 for the IID case continues to apply in the presence of nuisance parameters. To answer this question, we report several sets of simulations: regression residuals from a univariate autoregressive model and a moving average model, and standardized residuals from ARCH and GARCH models.

2.5.1 Residuals from an AR(1) Model
We generate $\{x_t\}$ from an AR(1) process:

$$x_t = \rho\, x_{t-1} + u_t, \qquad\qquad\qquad (2.5.1)$$

where u_t is IID, $N(0,1)$. Perform ordinary least squares (OLS), regressing x_t on x_{t-1} and a constant term, and apply the BDS test on the residuals. Tables 1 and 2 in Appendix E report the results for $\rho=.5$ and .95, respectively, at $\epsilon/\sigma=.5$, 1, 1.5, and 2, for T=100, 500, and 1000. We find that the size of the BDS test on these residuals is very similar to that on the IID standard normal data, as given in Table 1 in Appendix A. They indicate that the finite sample distribution of the BDS statistic on regression residuals can be well approximated by the asymptotic distribution when there are more than 500 observations.

2.5.2 Residuals from an MA(1) Model

We generate $\{x_t\}$ from an MA(1) process:

$$x_t = \theta\, u_{t-1} + u_t, \qquad\qquad\qquad (2.5.2)$$

where u_t is IID, $N(0,1)$. Perform maximum likelihood (conditional on $u_0=0$), and apply the BDS test on the residuals. Tables 3 and 4 in Appendix E report the results for $\theta=.5$ and .95, respectively, at $\epsilon/\sigma=.5$, 1, 1.5, and 2, for T=100, 500, and 1000. We find that the size of the BDS test on these residuals is very similar to that on the IID standard normal data, as given in Table 1 in Appendix A. They indicate that the finite sample distribution of the BDS statistic on regression residuals can be well approximated by the asymptotic distribution when there are more than 500 observations.

2.5.3 Standardized Residuals from an ARCH(1) Model

We generate $\{x_t\}$ from the following ARCH(1) model:

$$x_t = h_t^{\frac{1}{2}} u_t, \tag{2.5.3}$$

$$h_t = 1 + \phi x_{t-1}^2, \tag{2.5.4}$$

where u_t is IID, $N(0,1)$. Perform maximum likelihood estimation of ϕ, and apply BDS to the standardized residuals:

$$z_t = x_t/\hat{h}_t^{\frac{1}{2}}, \tag{2.5.5}$$

where $\hat{h}_t$ is the fitted value of h_t. Tables 5 and 6 in Appendix E report the results for $\phi=.5$ and $.95$, respectively, at $\epsilon/\sigma=.5$, 1, 1.5, and 2, for T=100, 500, and 1000. We find that the size of the BDS statistic on these standardized residuals is very different from that of the BDS statistic on IID data. The reason is that the ARCH model does not satisfy the assumptions of the theorems in Section 2.4.

2.5.4 Standardized Residuals from a GARCH(1,1) Model

We generate $\{x_t\}$ from the following GARCH(1,1) model:

$$x_t = h_t^{\frac{1}{2}} u_t, \tag{2.5.6}$$

where u_t is IID, $N(0,1)$, and

$$h_t = 1 + \phi x_{t-1}^2 + \psi h_{t-1}. \tag{2.5.7}$$

Perform maximum likelihood estimation of ϕ and ψ, and apply BDS to the standardized residuals:

$$z_t = x_t/\hat{h}_t^{\frac{1}{2}}, \tag{2.5.8}$$

where $\hat{h}_t$ is the fitted value of h_t. Table 7 report the results for $\phi=.1$ and $\psi=.8$, at $\epsilon/\sigma=.5$, 1, 1.5, and 2, for T=100, 500, and 1000. We find that the size of the BDS statistic on these standardized residuals is similar to that from the ARCH(1) model. Again the GARCH model does not satisfy the assumptions of the theorems in Section 2.4.

2.5.5 Standardized Residuals from the NMA Model

We generate $\{x_t\}$ from the following NMA model:

$$x_t = u_t + \gamma\, u_{t-1}\, u_{t-2}, \tag{2.5.9}$$

where u_t is IID and N(0,1). Perform maximum likelihood estimation of γ, and apply BDS to the residuals. Table 8 report the results for $\gamma=0.5$, for T=100, 500, and 1000. We find that the size of the BDS statistic on these residuals is similar to that from the AR(1) model, indicating that the finite sample distribution of the BDS statistic on residuals of nonlinear regressions may be well approximated by the asymptotic distribution when there are more than 500 observations.

2.6 Further Discussion

In this last section of Chapter 2, we deal with some of the remaining issues that arise in using the BDS statistic. One, the BDS test is only a test of IID against all alternatives. In a lot of situations, we are not

concerned with some of these alternatives. To be specific, consider
the following regression:

$$y_t = x_t'\beta + u_t, \quad t=1,...,T. \tag{2.6.1}$$

Write this compactly as:

$$y = X\beta + u. \tag{2.6.2}$$

Let $\hat{\beta}$ be the least squares estimate of β, and $\hat{u} = y - x'\hat{\beta}$ be the vector
of residuals. We know that $\hat{\beta}$ is a consistent estimate of β, if
$\text{plim}_{T\to\infty} X'u/T = 0$ and $\text{plim}_{T\to\infty} X'X/T$ is positive definite.
However, if u is heteroskedastic and we run BDS on $\hat{u}$, we will reject
IID.

If we are not concerned with efficiency of estimation, we may
still want to use $\hat{\beta}$, since it is a consistent estimate of β. Does it mean
that the BDS test should not be used on residuals of linear regressions?
We argue that the BDS statistic is still useful. A rejection of IID
indicates that the standard method of calculating the covariance matrix
of $\hat{\beta}$,

$$V_{OLS} = s^2 [X'X]^{-1}, \tag{2.6.3}$$

may not be correct. Inference based on this covariance matrix can be
misleading. If u is heteroskedastic, a heteroskedasticity-consistent
covariance estimator, given by:

$$V_{HC} = [X'X]^{-1} [\Sigma\hat{u}_t^2 x_t x_t'] [X'X]^{-1}, \tag{2.6.4}$$

can be used instead. If u is autocorrelated, we may use a Hansen 1982 or a Newey and West 1987 estimator.

Two, a rejection of IID by the BDS statistic does not tell us what is wrong with the model. Researchers may feel that it is better to forget the BDS test and just perform a number of tests designed against specific alternative hypotheses. First, we point out that other specification tests, such as the Hausman 1978 test and the White 1982 information test, have the same problem. Second, BDS has good power against a large number of alternatives. If BDS rejects IID, we know something is wrong with the model, and we would naturally conduct further tests to diagnose the misspecification. The problem with performing only a series of diagnostic tests with power against specific alternatives is that we do not know when to stop testing. Third, nonlinear time series models are usually estimated with maximum likelihood assuming that the disturbances are IID. (See the discussion in the bilinear models of Granger and Andersen 1978, for example.) A rejection by the BDS is evidence against the null model.

In summary, we do not advocate using only the BDS test. There is no "perfect" diagnostic test. BDS should be one of many routinely used diagnostics. If the test finds misspecification, the researcher will need to do more work to locate the problem. There is, however, one warning. Our Monte Carlo experiments have found that the asymptotic distribution does not approximate very well the BDS statistic applied to standardized residuals of ARCH, GARCH, and EGARCH models. We recommend that readers use the tables in Appendix C as a guideline, or bootstrap the null distribution, or estimate directly the needed correction term to the asymptotic variance as detailed in the appendix on residuals.

Table 2.1

Power Comparisons

(500 observations; 5000 replications)

	Tent	NMA	TAR	ARCH	GARCH
W_2	1.00	0.89	0.94	1.00	0.42
W_3	1.00	0.98	0.89	1.00	0.54
W_4	1.00	0.98	0.78	0.99	0.56
T_2	0.95	1.00	1.00	0.57	0.27
T_3	0.90	1.00	1.00	0.56	0.30
E_2	1.00	0.95	1.00	1.00	0.62
E_3	1.00	0.98	0.96	1.00	0.44

W_2:   BDS test, dimension 2, $\epsilon/\sigma = 0.50$

W_3:   BDS test, dimension 3, $\epsilon/\sigma = 0.50$

W_4:   BDS test, dimension 4, $\epsilon/\sigma = 0.50$

T_2:   Tsay test, M=2

T_3:   Tsay test, M=3

E_2:   Engle test, p=2

E_3:   Engle test, p=3

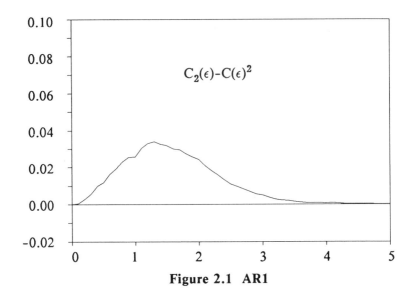

Figure 2.1   AR1

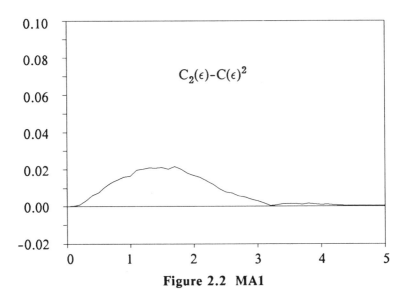

Figure 2.2   MA1

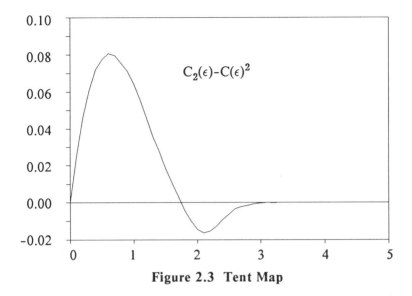

Figure 2.3 Tent Map

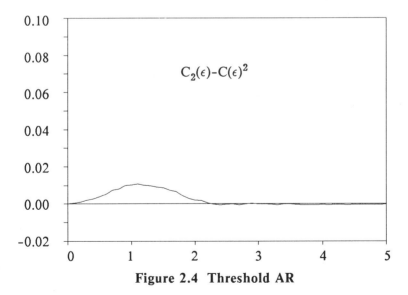

Figure 2.4 Threshold AR

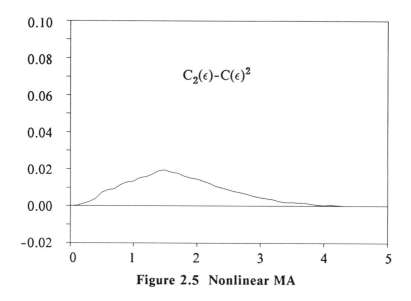

Figure 2.5 Nonlinear MA

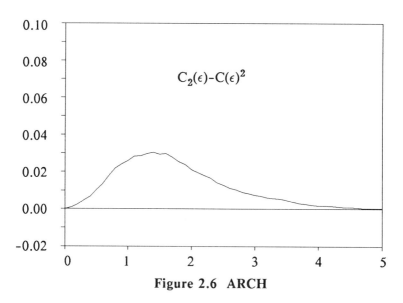

Figure 2.6 ARCH

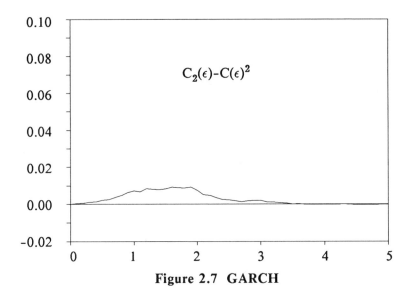

Figure 2.7 GARCH

Chapter 3
The Changing Structure of Stock Returns

In this chapter, we test for nonlinear structure in stock returns. Stock prices are long believed to follow a geometric random walk with uncorrelated innovations. (See Fama 1970 for summaries of empirical evidence.) Let p_t denote the logarithm of the stock price at time t. The geometric random walk states that p_t evolves according to: $p_t = p_{t-1} + \mu + u_t$. Here, u_t is an independent and identically distributed (IID) random variable with mean zero and finite variance, and μ is a constant (possibly nonzero) drift. This model implies that stock returns, as measured by p_t-p_{t-1}, be IID random variables.

Before the days of nonlinear dynamics, tests for the random walk usually relied on checking that autocorrelation coefficients were not statistically different from zero. Now, we know that the lack of linear dependence (i.e., autocorrelation) does not rule out nonlinear dependence, which, if present, would contradict the random walk

---

This chapter is based upon LeBaron 1988b. The Standard and Poors 500 stock index is the one used in French, Schwert, and Stambaugh 1987.

model. Specifically, Granger and Andersen 1978 and Sakai and Tokumaru 1980 have shown that simple nonlinear models may exhibit no serial correlation while containing strong nonlinear dependence. This has led several authors to look for nonlinear structure in stock returns. Among these are Granger and Andersen 1978, Hinich and Patterson 1985, and Scheinkman and LeBaron 1989b.

Before going to complicated nonlinear models, we already know two reasons why stock returns deviate from the random walk model. One, the variance of stock returns is not constant over time. This was pointed out by Mandelbrot 1963, who noted that although stock returns appeared uncorrelated, large changes tended to be followed by large changes, and small changes tended to be followed by small changes. This fact has led to the development of the ARCH and GARCH models of Engle 1982 and Bollerslev 1986 respectively. These models attempt to capture the changing variance in a time series. They will be used in this chapter to see if they can eliminate dependence seen in the time series. Two, there are the calendar anomalies discovered by many authors. Returns differ by small (although statistically significant) amounts during different periods (i.e., day of the week, week of the month, and month of the year).

We proceed as follows. Section 3.1 presents the tests to be used. Section 3.2 applies these tests to some simulated models. Section 3.3 applies the tests to the stock returns data, and Section 3.4 concludes.

3.1 Test Descriptions

We shall use six methods to test for nonlinearity of stock returns. Three have already been mentioned in Chapter 2: the BDS statistic, the

Engle 1982 test for ARCH, and the Tsay 1986 test for nonlinearity. There is no need to repeat them here. In this section, we will give simple and intuitive explanations of the remaining three tests. More detailed treatment is available in Brock 1986, Eckmann and Ruelle 1985, and Brock, Dechert, and Scheinkman 1987.

Dimension Plots

The dimension plots of Grassberger and Procaccia 1983a are intended to get information about the dynamics of deterministic systems. Let $\{x_t\}$ be a scalar time series of length T. Compute the correlation integral,

$$C_{m,T}(\epsilon) = \Sigma_{t<s} \, I_\epsilon(x_t^m, x_s^m) \times [2/T_m(T_m-1)], \qquad (3.1.1)$$

where, $T_m=T-(m-1)$, $x_t^m=(x_t,...,x_{t+m-1})$, and $I_\epsilon(x_t^m, x_s^m)$ is an indicator function which equals 1 if $\| x_t^m - x_s^m \| < \epsilon$ and equals 0 otherwise.

The correlation integral $C_{m,T}(\epsilon)$ is an estimator of the probability that two vectors of the time series of length m are within a distance ϵ of each other, using the sup-norm, i.e., the L^∞-norm, as a distance measure. In general this may be replaced by other norms, but the sup-norm is chosen here to be consistent with the BDS statistic.

The dimension plots consist of graphing $\log C_{m,T}(\epsilon)$ versus $\log \epsilon$. For deterministic systems, these slopes are used in estimating the correlation dimension of the system, defined in equations (1.1.9) and (1.1.10). This number can give some idea of the complexity of a deterministic system.[1] However, a lot of data may be needed to give accurate estimates of the correlation dimension. Brock and Baek 1987 and Denker and Keller 1986 have shown that standard errors and confidence intervals can be estimated for correlation dimension estimates for data sets of the length available in economics and finance, provided that the correlation dimension is low enough. But correlation dimension estimates for stock returns data range from six to eight and even higher. Also Ramsey and Yuan 1989 point out that the quantity of economic data is so low (or the period of plausibility for the stationarity assumption is so short) that correlation dimension estimates are severely biased. Furthermore Brock 1988 and LeBaron 1988b showed that the correlation dimension estimates change quite dramatically over the two halves of the Scheinkman and LeBaron 1989b data set. So, in order to avoid these problems, we will not even compute correlation dimension estimates. Instead, we compare the GP plot of the observed data with the GP plots of bootstrapped data, which are truly IID and have the same distribution. If the GP plot of the observed data differs substantially from those of the bootstrapped data, it is evidence against the IID hypothesis.

Intuitively, the GP plots for the data and its scrambled counterpart are closely related to the BDS statistic. At each ϵ, the GP plot for the data is an estimate of $\log C_m(\epsilon)$, while the GP plot for the scrambled data is an estimate of $\log C_1(\epsilon)^m$. Their difference is therefore a test of the null hypothesis: $\log C_m(\epsilon) = \log C_1(\epsilon)^m$. While this is not identical to BDS, which tests the null hypothesis that $C_m(\epsilon) = C_1(\epsilon)^m$, it is measuring the same phenomenon, namely, how different are $C_m(\epsilon)$ and $C_1(\epsilon)^m$. So one can usefully think of the GP plot as a graphical representation of the BDS test.

Sign Scrambling Plots

In financial time series much of the nonlinear dependence occurs in volatility. This is generally believed to arise from adjustments to new information. During turbulent times, the market is reacting to the inflow of new information, so beliefs are relatively heterogeneous and volatility is high. During quiet times, beliefs are more homogeneous and much of the volatility comes from liquidity trading. While volatility is correlated, the actual price changes remain uncorrelated.

What is needed is a test for this type of process without specifying how the variance should move. To do so, we strengthen the assumption about volatility by assuming that all that can be learned about today's price change from previous price changes comes from the information contained in the size (not the sign) of previous price changes. Strengthen this even further to assume that the conditional density of the price change is symmetric, i.e.,

$$f(x_t, x_{t-1}, ...) = f(-x_t, -x_{t-1}, ...). \tag{3.1.2}$$

To test (3.1.2), let u_t be an IID discrete random variable that takes on the values +1 and -1 with equal probability. Generate the "sign scrambled" series:

$$y_t = u_t x_t, \quad t=1, ..., T. \tag{3.1.3}$$

Under the null hypothesis (3.1.2), the joint distribution of $\{y_t\}$ is the same as that of $\{x_t\}$. Let $\hat{C}_{m,T}(\epsilon)$ be the correlation integral of $\{y_t\}$. From symmetry of $\{x_t\}$,

$$E[\hat{C}_{m,T}(\epsilon)] = E[C_{m,T}(\epsilon)]. \tag{3.1.4}$$

This implies that the GP plot of sign scrambled data, $\{y_t\}$, should be similar to that of the original data, $\{x_t\}$. If not, we conclude that $\{x_t\}$ has asymmetry, which is not consistent with the explanation that nonlinear dependence of $\{x_t\}$ arises solely from changing variances.

Note that the sign scrambling test should detect the nonlinear structure in the threshold autoregressive model in equation (1.2.2), and the bilinear model in equation (1.2.3), while it is designed not to find the nonlinear structure in the GARCH model.

One problem with the sign scrambling test is that it detects any deviation from the assumption of symmetry in the time series. There may be many deviations from this strong assumption that are not very interesting. For example, x_t may be IID but the distribution is skewed. However, the stock returns in this chapter have very little skewness, so this should not be a problem.

Recurrence Plots
Structural changes in the data can be detected by the recurrence plot of Eckman, Kamphorst, and Ruelle 1987. It is a graph, where each axis represents the time length being studied. Let t and s be two time periods. The point (t,s) on the graph is turned on (darkened) if

$$d(x_t^m, x_s^m) < \epsilon, \tag{3.1.5}$$

for a distance measure d, an imbedding dimension m, and a distance ϵ. Here the sup-norm is used as the distance measure.

The recurrence plot is related to the correlation integral, and thus to the BDS test, in the following way. When (t,s) is darkened in the recurrence plot, x_t^m and x_s^m are within ϵ of each other. If x_t is an IID series, the probability that (t,s) is darkened is just the correlation integral, $C_m(\epsilon)$. In fact, an IID null implies that the probability of any (t,s) being darkened is the same for all t and s, i.e., that the recurrence plot should have uniform shade. Large dark areas on the recurrence plot indicate that many of the close points are occurring within a small segment of time. Light areas on the recurrence plot indicate that distant points are occurring within a small segment of time. This indicates violation of independent and identical distribution.

We can infer the type of violation of IID by the patterns of light and dark areas in the recurrence plot. If (t,s) is darkened implies that (t+1,s+1) is likely to be darkened, the recurrence plots will have streaks parallel to the diagonal, which means that near neighbors can help to forecast future values. When time trends are present, the recurrence plot tends to fade out from the diagonal. During a period of reduced volatility, the recurrence plot contains darker squares symmetric about the diagonal. Finally, when the dynamics change abruptly between two periods, the recurrence plot displays an abrupt change of shading, making the recurrence plot a good indicator of structural shifts in economic and financial data.

3.2 Simulations

Before applying the nonlinear tests to actual data, we want to know their finite sample behavior. To do so, we generate data from stochastic and deterministic models. The sample size is 600, roughly equal to that of the weekly stock returns data used in Section 3.3.

Stochastic Models

We begin by generating IID standard normal data. In Figure 3.1, the "∗" symbol represents the Grassberger and Procaccia (GP) plot, which graphs log $C_{m,T}(\epsilon)$ versus log ϵ. For these experiments the imbedding dimension m is set to 10 (comparisons are done on 10 vectors). Since the base of the logarithm does not matter, it is taken to be 2. On the x-axis the ϵ's are scaled by the sample standard deviation of the series, so 0.00 corresponds to one standard deviation, 1.00 to two standard deviations, and -1.00 to half a standard deviation. The "+" and "-" symbols are, respectively, the largest and smallest values of log $C_{m,T}(\epsilon)$ from 50 bootstraps (as in Efron 1982) of the original series. We shall refer to them as the "high-low" bands because they provide estimates of the variability of the GP plot if the data were IID. We see that the "∗" symbols all lie within the high-low bands, since the simulated data are IID.

In Figure 3.2, the "∗" series is again the GP plot of the original data, identical to that in Figure 3.1. However, the high-low bands are now the largest and smallest values of log $C_{m,T}(\epsilon)$ from 50 sign scramblings of the original series. They provide estimates of the variability of the GP plot if the data were symmetric. Again, we see that the "∗" symbols all lie within the high-low bands, since the normal distribution is symmetric.

Next we generate data from a low-order autoregressive process with a periodic dummy variable,

$$x_t = \alpha_1 x_{t-1} + \alpha_2 x_{t-2} + \alpha_3 x_{t-3} + \beta D_t + u_t, \qquad (3.2.1)$$

where D_t is a dummy variable that is one if t is divisible by 4, and u_t is an IID standard normal random variable. This process is intended to simulate the type of low-level linearities present in weekly stock returns. The dummy variable represents a week-of-the-month seasonal found in stock returns (Ariel 1987). For this simulation $\alpha_1=0.05$, $\alpha_2=-0.009$, $\alpha_3=0.093$, and $\beta=0.003$, numbers that roughly correspond to those for weekly stock returns. The GP plots in Figures 3.3 and 3.4 are similar to those for the IID normal numbers in Figures 3.1 and 3.2. This means that the GP plots are unable to detect low order linear structure.

It is well known that variances are changing over time in many financial series. So our third simulation is a GARCH(1,1) model:

$$x_t \sim N(0,h_t),$$

$$h_t = \alpha + \beta\, h_{t-1} + \gamma\, x^2_{t-1}. \tag{3.2.2}$$

We set $\alpha=0.00001$, $\beta=0.8$, and $\gamma=0.1$, numbers that are close to those estimated for stock returns. The GP plot in Figure 3.5 could not detect the nonlinear structure in the data, even though the nonlinearity is very strong (as found by the nonlinear diagnostics, discussed below). The sign scrambled GP plot in Figure 3.6 detects no asymmetry in the data, as expected, for the GARCH model is symmetric in its signs.

Although this graphical analysis is useful, it does not present solid statistical evidence. Table 3.1 contains the nonlinear diagnostics for the simulated GARCH data. The first column gives the BDS statistics for dimensions 2 through 6, setting ϵ at half the standard deviation of the data. These are asymptotically distributed $N(0,1)$ under the null of independent and identical distribution. Using the method of bootstrapping (discussed in Chapter 2), we find that the BDS statistic is rejecting the null of IID at the 10% and the 2% levels for all dimensions except 5, where it only rejects at the 10% level.[2]

This column also presents the Tsay and Engle statistics. The Tsay statistic is approximately distributed $F(3,600)$ under the null that the series is coming from a linear filter of strict white noise. The critical value for the 5% level for this statistic is 2.6. For this example the Tsay statistic does not find any evidence of nonlinearity. This is because the GARCH models all have zero third order cumulants, i.e., $E[x_t x_{t-i} x_{t-j}]=0$, for all $i \neq j$. The Tsay test is designed to pick up deviations in these terms, so for the GARCH models this test will have low power. The Engle statistic is asymptotically $\chi^2(1)$ with a 5% critical value of 3.8. This statistic clearly rejects the null hypothesis of no ARCH.

The second column tests for nonlinearity in the standardized residuals of a fitted GARCH model. This model was estimated using maximum likelihood, and the estimated parameter values are in Table 3.3. The standardized residuals are:

$$z_t = x_t / \hat{h}_t^{\frac{1}{2}}, \tag{3.2.3}$$

where $\hat{h}_t$ is the in-sample estimate of h_t. It is clear that the fitted GARCH model has removed all the series' structure from the standpoint of all these tests. This is what should be expected since we are taking residuals of a correctly specified model.

One criticism of using GARCH to model changes in volatility is that it is too smooth. In real life, volatility may take large discrete jumps that the smooth, linear (in variance) GARCH model does not capture. We therefore generated data from a two-state variance process. During the high variance state (H) the data generated will be $3u_t$. During the low variance state (L) the data will be u_t. Here u_t is IID standard normal. The system remains in the same state with probability 0.95, and transits to the other state with probability 0.05. These numbers are chosen so that the process generates kurtosis in the range of weekly stock returns in Section 3.3. However, no formal parameter estimation is performed. The GP plots in Figures 3.7 and 3.8 show very little evidence of nonlinear structure or asymmetry. However, the BDS and Engle statistics are able to detect the change in variance.

Out of curiosity, we fit a GARCH(1,1) model to the two-state variance process. After GARCH residuals have been taken, all the statistics indicate that there is no remaining structure. This may indicate that the simple GARCH model does a good job of modeling conditional variance even when it is misspecified, or that the GARCH model has destroyed the ability of the diagnostics to detect an incorrect model.

Deterministic Models

We shall apply the same methods to two deterministic models, the tent map and the Mackey and Glass 1977 equation. We do this for two reasons. The first is to see whether the nonlinear tests can detect deterministic chaos with sample sizes in the same range, 600. The second is to see whether fitting GARCH models will generate standardized residuals that appear random.

The tent map is a simple difference equation:

$$x_{t+1} = 2x_t, \qquad \text{if } x_t \leq .5$$

$$x_{t+1} = 2 - 2x_t, \qquad \text{if } x_t \geq .5. \tag{3.2.4}$$

The tent map is shown in Figure 3.9. It generates a time series that is uncorrelated. One such time series is shown in Figure 3.10.

The GP plot of the tent map is in Figures 3.11 and 3.12. There is clear evidence of nonlinear structure, as the GP plot lies outside the high-low band in Figure 3.11. In addition, its slope is about 1, which is the true correlation dimension of the tent map. There is also clear evidence of asymmetry, as the GP plot lies outside the high-low bands in Figure 3.12, which is very different from that of the previous (stochastic) models.

The nonlinearity in the tent map also shows up in Table 3.1, where the BDS, Tsay, and Engle statistics are extremely large. An interesting result is that the BDS and Tsay statistics can detect remaining nonlinearity in the standardized residuals from fitting a (misspecified) GARCH model to the tent map data. This means that the GARCH model does not always destroy the ability of the diagnostic statistics to detect an incorrect model. Note, however, that the Engle test does not reject the absence of ARCH in the standardized residuals, which means that the distribution of this statistic must be affected by the GARCH model. (This is analogous to the fact that the sampling distribution of autocorrelation coefficients is different when applied to the residuals of an autoregression.)

The Mackey and Glass 1977 equation is a more complicated chaotic deterministic system from a delay differential equation:

$$x(t) = \alpha x(t-\tau) / [1 + x(t-\tau)^{10}] - \beta x(t), \qquad\qquad (3.2.5)$$

where $\alpha=0.2$, $\beta=0.1$, $\tau=100$. This follows the simulations in Grassberger and Procaccia 1983a. The Mackey and Glass equation is formally an infinite dimensional system, but its attracting set dimension varies as the delay parameter τ is changed. For $\tau=100$, the dimension is about 7 or greater. After the data are generated, their linear structure is removed by an AR(10) linear filter.

The GP plots for the (linearly filtered) Mackey and Glass data are in Figures 3.13 and 3.14, which are very similar to those of the tent map in Figures 3.11 and 3.12, in that the GP plots typically lie outside the high-low bands, detecting both nonlinearity and asymmetry. The main difference here is that the slope changes are not as pronounced. This is due to the fact that the Mackey and Glass system is a much higher dimensional system than the tent map. The nonlinear tests on the original data and the standardized residuals from a GARCH(1,1) model are in Table 3.1. As in the case of the tent map, the BDS, Tsay, and Engle statistics for the Mackey and Glass data are very large. Also the BDS and Tsay test detect nonlinearity in the GARCH standardized residuals, while the Engle test does not.

3.3 Stock Returns

We now turn to the results of the nonlinear tests applied to stock returns. The data are continuously compounded weekly returns on the CRSP value weighted index and the S&P 500 index. The CRSP index includes dividends while the S&P 500 index does not. The data are graphed in Figures 3.15 and 3.16. We first remove any linear dependence by a linear filter, the results of which are presented in Table 3.2. For stock returns these include testing for two anomalies: the January effect, and the week-of-the-month affect (Ariel 1987). The January effect is not significant for any of the series, which is not surprising since it is mainly a small firm effect (Keim 1983). The week-of-the-month effect is significant for some of the time periods and not for others. We fit a different linear model to each time period. Also GARCH(1,1) models are estimated for each series, and the results are reported in Table 3.3.

CRSP Value Weighted Index

The first part of Table 3.4 repeats the results of Scheinkman and LeBaron 1989b. The data column presents the BDS statistics for this series with ϵ set to be one-half the sample standard deviation. The small sample distribution of the BDS statistic can be obtained from Appendix E, since the data are residuals of a linear regression. The comparison shows that all the BDS statistics reject IID.

The GARCH residual column presents the BDS statistics for residuals of a fitted GARCH(1,1) model. This reduces greatly the values of the BDS statistics. Here, BDS is applied to residuals of a fitted GARCH model, which can change its finite sample distribution, as shown in Appendix F. To counter this problem, we simulate a new distribution of BDS statistics, by first generating a true GARCH(1,1) process, then estimating a correctly specified model on the generated data, and then calculating the BDS statistics of the standardized residuals. This should generate the appropriate distribution for the BDS statistic under the maintained hypothesis that the data follow a true GARCH process. For this simulation 250 GARCH(1,1)'s are used with α=0.00001, β=0.8, and γ=0.1, the same parameter values used in Section 3.2. The bootstrap p-value is the fraction of the simulation runs that gave a BDS statistic greater in absolute value than that generated by the GARCH residuals on the original data. These again show all the BDS statistics in the GARCH residual column rejecting IID. So for this data set the GARCH model was unable to correctly eliminate all the nonlinear structure.

Also presented are the Tsay and Engle statistics. Under the null of linearity the Tsay statistic is approximately distributed F(3,600) with a 5% critical value of 2.62. The Engle statistic is asymptotically $\chi^2(1)$ with a 5% critical value of 3.84 under the null of no ARCH effects. These both indicate the presence of some nonlinearity in the original time series. However, after GARCH residuals are taken, they show no indication of further nonlinearity. Since these statistics are not designed to be used on residuals of fitted models, their use here as a residual diagnostic cannot be totally trusted. Also, the Engle statistic is looking for just the ARCH-GARCH type of structure, exactly the structure that is removed by fitting a GARCH model to the data.

In beginning to look for nonlinear systems in the data, one would like to know how stable these results are over time. Figure 3.17 presents the recurrence plot for the value weighted series. This picture shows a large amount of clumping in the lower left-hand corner representing the early part of this time series. This may indicate two things. First, it could be that the series is just much quieter during the earlier period. Second, much of the nonlinear structure may be coming from this period. Either way, this is a troubling lack of uniformity and should be further explored by splitting the series. We therefore proceed along this line.

In Table 3.4, under VW1, are the results for the first half of the CRSP value weighted weekly returns series, July 1962 through April 1974. The BDS, Tsay, and Engle statistics all clearly indicate that nonlinear structure is present in the data. In the second column the tests are run on the standardized residuals of a fitted GARCH(1,1) model. The BDS statistics continue to indicate unusual structure for all m, as indicated by the bootstrap p-values. The Tsay and Engle statistics indicate no structure after the GARCH model has been fit.

The GP plot for the first half of the CRSP value weighted series is in Figures 3.18 and 3.19. It shows strong nonlinear structure, lying above the high-low bands in Figure 3.18, and its slope is rising at a different rate than those of the high-low bands. It also shows slight evidence of asymmetry, lying outside the high-low bands for several epsilons in Figure 3.19, but its slope is not perceptibly different from those of the high-low bands. Compare this with the simulated results for the tent map and the Mackey and Glass equation. Stock returns show some asymmetry, but much less than the deterministic chaotic models. This may indicate that much of the structure is in variance and not means.

In Table 3.4, under VW2, are the results for the second half of the CRSP value weighted series, May 1974 through December 1985. The BDS statistics are similar to those of VW1. The numbers are smaller, but they are all in the tails of the simulated distribution. The results change when the GARCH residuals are checked. For VW2 the GARCH model has removed all the structure seen by the BDS statistics. The Tsay and Engle statistics repeat their results for the previous series, showing structure on the original data, but none on the GARCH residuals.

The GP plot for the second half of the CRSP value weighted series is in Figures 3.20 and 3.21. There is still nonlinear structure, since a large fraction of the GP plot is above the high-low bands in Figure 3.20. But there is little asymmetry, since the GP plot barely leaves the high-low band in Figure 3.21.

We are led to the conclusion that VW1 contains nonlinear structure not attributable to GARCH, while VW2 probably contains mainly variance changes.

This change in structure indicates that it may be interesting to look at a longer range series to see which of these two periods is more representative of the history of stock returns. Unfortunately, the CRSP value weighted series at weekly frequency does not go back any farther than 1962. So we turn to the S&P 500 index, which is also a value weighted index, but does not include dividend income as the CRSP value weighted series does. This omission may be a problem, but at weekly frequency dividend income will most likely not play a major role in the dynamics. For the 1962 to 1985 period the correlation between the weekly CRSP value weighted returns and the S&P 500 returns after linear filtering is 0.993.

S&P 500 Index

Figure 3.22 presents the recurrence plot for the S&P 500 weekly returns series from 1928 to 1985. One can see some important structural changes. For example, the depression, a very turbulent time for this series, shows up as a large white space. Also, the early 1960s, an extremely stable period, shows up as a dark black box. The changes from light to dark in this plot may indicate that either dark periods were extremely quiet times, or they were periods in which there is more nonlinear structure.

For the S&P index, we examine two subperiods: SP1, from 1928 to 1939, and SP2, from 1950 to 1962. (We dropped the 1940s, due to the Second World War.) The results for the periods corresponding to those used for the CRSP value weighted series will not be repeated here, since they are very similar.

The GP plot for the first subperiod of the S&P series from 1928 to 1939 is in Figures 3.23 and 3.24. It is similar to that of the 62-74 CRSP value weighted series. There is evidence of nonlinear structure in Figure 3.23. However, there is only slight evidence of asymmetry in Figure 3.24. In Table 3.4, under SP1, are the nonlinear tests for this series. They all reject IID. GARCH appears to capture most of the nonlinearity, with evidence of some structure at dimensions 3 and 4. This is similar to the first half of the CRSP value weighted series, but here this indication is not as strong.

The GP plot for the second subperiod of the S&P series from 1950 to 1962 is in Figures 3.25 and 3.26. There is no strong evidence of nonlinear structure or asymmetry. In Table 3.4, under SP2, are the nonlinear tests for this series. The BDS and Engle statistics for this period show evidence of some structure. This period is also the only time for which the Tsay test is unable to reject linearity on the data series, but the GARCH model appears to remove all of the nonlinearity.

GARCH-M Models

So far, the GARCH model is able to explain most of the nonlinear structure in two of the four time periods: VW2 (April 1974 to December 1985), and SP2 (January 1950 to June 1962), but is unable to do so in the other two: VW1 (July 1962 to March 1974), and SP1 (January 1928 to December 1939). Since there is strong asymmetry in VW1 and SP1, the simple GARCH model can be modified to account for this. This has led to the GARCH-M (i.e., GARCH-in-the-mean) model, used by Bollerslev, Engle, and Wooldridge 1988 and French, Schwert, and Stambaugh 1987, which allows the mean to change with the variance. A simple form of this model is as follows:

$$x_t \sim N(y_t, h_t),$$

$$h_t = \alpha + \beta\, h_{t-1} + \gamma\, x^2_{t-1}, \qquad\qquad\qquad (3.3.1)$$

$$y_t = \phi\, h_t.$$

In this simple model the mean is proportional to the variance at time t.

Table 3.5 presents the estimation results for a form of this model for both time periods: VW1 and SP1. We use the Schwarz 1978 criterion as an identification tool, and found a more complicated model containing dummy variables for the week of the month, and some autoregressive terms. These are now fit to the original data and not the linearly filtered data. In the case of GARCH, the parameter estimates are consistent even after linear filtering of the data, but in the case of the GARCH-M, this no longer holds and the two-stage procedure is not possible. Note that in the estimation for the SP1 series the changing mean parameter is not significantly different from zero. However, for the VW1 series it is. This agrees with the results of French, Schwert, and Stambaugh 1987 who find the mean parameter changing over time.

Table 3.6 presents the BDS statistics for the residuals of these fitted models. Note that the bootstrap p-value represents the comparison with the actual fitted GARCH residuals. This may not be quite correct here since the model being tested is a GARCH-M model. It is not known how the small sample estimation properties change as one moves from the GARCH model to the GARCH-M model. Assuming that the finite distribution of GARCH-M residuals is similar to that of GARCH residuals, this table shows that the GARCH-M model does not explain more nonlinearity over and above the GARCH model.

It should be noted that the GARCH-M may be difficult to justify in theoretical general equilibrium models with changing risk structure. The response of expected asset returns to changes in beliefs about future volatility are not necessarily monotonic in the expected volatility. Another problem here is that the use of nominal returns may now effect the results as changing expected returns are be compared across time.[3]

3.4 Forecasting

An important question remaining here is that if stock returns are exhibiting some kind of nonlinear structure, then how forecastable could this structure be. This section will perform some rather crude tests on the returns data, and compare these with some of the simulated deterministic models mentioned earlier.

Forecasting a time series of possibly very complicated nonlinear structure without presupposing a model is not easy. There have been several attempts in this area. Yakowitz 1987 uses a nearest neighbor method. Farmer and Sidorowich 1987 propose a local linearization technique where close vectors are used to locally linearize the system, and this linear system is used for forecasting. Diebold and Nason 1989 use weighted nearest neighbors to forecast exchange rate changes. Other techniques involve the area of neural nets, and kernel density estimation. These are used by Lapedes and Farber 1987, White 1988, and Prescott and Stengos 1988.

First we try the nearest neighbor method of Yakowitz 1987. To forecast a point x_{t+1}, a nearest neighbor for the history $x_t, x_{t-1}, ..., x_{t-m+1}$ is sought using the sup norm. If $x_\tau, x_{\tau-1}, ..., x_{\tau-m+1}$ is the nearest neighbor, then $x_{\tau+1}$ will be the forecast. Neighbors are only sought in the time series up to t (the forecast does not use information not known at time t). Forecasting begins halfway through each series. This gives the forecasting program some amount of historical information with which to work. Forecasting is evaluated by regressing the true value on the forecast. Results of these regressions are presented in Table 3.7. β is the regression coefficient and t-stat is its t-statistic, and m is the amount of lagged forecasting information used.

The forecasting technique shows some ability at forecasting during the first half of the value weighted series, VW1, but for the second half, VW2, the forecasting ability becomes insignificant. For both these series the R^2 of the forecasts are very low, indicating that there is little nonlinear information. For the two S&P series there is also little nonlinear forecastability. As a comparison the deterministic models presented earlier are also forecasted. The tent map contains no possible linear forecasting information, and the Mackey and Glass data are first filtered by an AR(10) to remove most of the linear dependence. Both these models exhibit very good nonlinear forecasting properties using nearest neighbor techniques, as indicative of the large β's and statistically significant t-statistics. The tent map is clearly very easy to forecast, as we should expect from its very simple shape. The Mackey and Glass equation looks much more difficult to forecast, but still the system seems to be picking up a good amount of forecastable structure.

The more complicated Farmer and Sidorowich technique was also tested on stock returns with no significant improvement. We have therefore omitted those results. Such experiments indicate that there is no easily observed forecastable structure in the stock returns. More complicated forecasting techniques may yield improvements, but this remains to be seen.

Frank and Stengos 1989 have found that the abilities of the nearest neighbor type of forecasting quickly degrade as the system becomes more complex. More specifically, there is an abrupt reduction in forecasting performance as one moves to a tent map iterated 3 times. The poor forecasting results are consistent with the view that the stock returns data may just be too small for any useful forecasting.

3.5 Additional Remarks

The results of such a large number of new tests on simulated and actual data do not present us with the possibility of quick and easy summary, but an overview of these results is certainly necessary.

The two goals of this chapter were to find what might be causing indications of nonlinearities in stock returns, and to check the stability of these results over time. In both cases we have made some advances, but have opened up new questions.

In searching for simple causes for dependencies seen in the data, the first place to look was calendar anomalies. These have been ruled out, both by removing them from the series tested, and by simulating series containing calendar anomalies of the same size as those found in the data. In the first case the results were unaffected, and in the second case this type of dependence could not be detected by the tests used. This does not mean that these effects are not interesting to study, just that the BDS types of tests have low power against these alternatives.

Looking for simple GARCH-ARCH types of changes in variance as a cause of these results has been more successful. Of the four time periods tested, two periods, January 1950 to June 1962, and April 1974 to December 1985, appeared IID to the all the tests after GARCH residuals were taken. Of the other two, one period covers the 1929 crash and the depression, a period in which one would have little hope of fitting any stationary model. The last period, July 1962 to March 1974, remains very difficult to explain. It shows some evidence of nonlinear forecastable structure, it does not appear symmetric to the sign scrambling test, and the GP plots for this time period indicate the most structure.

These results do not give a clear indication that the GARCH model is the correct specification here. One should be very careful when running diagnostics on residuals of fitted models, because an incorrect model may be garbling delicate nonlinear structure. There are two indications that GARCH is not the correct specification. First, the Tsay statistic should be insensitive to GARCH-ARCH models, since it looks at third order cumulants $E[x_t x_{t-i} x_{t-j}]$. (This can be seen by looking at the simulated GARCH series.) For all the periods tested, the Tsay statistic indicates nonlinear structure except January 1950 to June 1962. Second, the sign scrambling tests indicate a lack of sign symmetry in all periods except the most recent one (VW2). This might be caused by unconditional skewness in the series, but such skewness is inconsistent with GARCH models. Most of these lack-of-symmetry and cumulant results agree with those of Hinich and Patterson 1986, who reject a martingale structure for daily stock returns. The GARCH-ARCH models with no changes in conditional means are martingales.

As attempts to find the nature of the nonlinear structure, both sign scrambling and forecasting tests were performed. Both of these indicate very little evidence of forecastable (in mean) structure. The sign scrambling plots for all the stock returns show no evidence of the kind of structure seen in the deterministic chaotic systems tested. Forecasting nearest neighbors was also ineffective in three out of the four subperiods tested. These forecasting tests are rather crude, and it remains to be seen whether more sophisticated techniques will improve the results. The sign scrambling results suggest that much of the structure picked up in the original GP plots is probably coming from changes in variance rather than a strong forecastable nonlinear pattern.

In general rational expectations asset pricing models of Lucas 1978 and Brock 1982, nonlinearities in the returns series are quite common. Both models require strong assumptions to rule out the possibility of nonlinear relations in return series. Recent models using rational expectations equilibria have begun to study some of the possible explanations for deviations from strict martingale behavior in asset markets. Some of these are Abel 1988, Gennotte and March 1986, Giovannini 1989, and for exchange rates Hsieh 1988b. The first two models look at changes in the variability of dividend income streams. The third looks at the precautionary demand for money balances as uncertainty is changed. The fourth studies changes in central bank intervention policies over time causing changes in conditional moments of the observed time series. Testing for all these types of effects will require combining information on nonstationarities and nonlinearities into a more unified framework, and implementing more multivariate techniques.

Conclusions about the underlying dynamics of economic state variables may still be difficult with the univariate techniques used here. In theory one can observe only one state variable of a dynamical system and still recover its properties, but having more observables can't hurt. With the rather short and noisy economic series, it might be necessary to use several series.

In the high frequency asset market data, there may be other effects being picked up. These are noise and information dynamics of traders (Black 1986). If trading on noise drives asset prices far from their equilibrium values then tests of short-range dynamics may pick up more noise movements than movements generated by changes in underlying fundamentals. One problem is that it seems unlikely that this type of trading may generate any recognizable pattern that could be detected by these tests, but this will require more specific testing and modeling of noise trading types of behavior. To study these types of effects, data of different frequencies will have to be used. High frequency data may give us new insights into the structure of the trading process itself, and the processing of new information by the market. Such information will be important in understanding the dynamics of market relations, such as the stock market—futures market connection.

To summarize these many varied results in a few sentences will be difficult. They seem to suggest to the world of nonlinear researchers to proceed with caution. These tests have not been able to find uniform results between time periods. Also, much of the structure seems to be coming from changes in variance. Although simulated GARCH-type models do not generate the same types of graphs or test results, they seem to fit the data pretty well for several time periods, as their fitted residuals indicate. This research indicates that the nature of the nonlinearities may not remain stationary long enough for researchers to reliably detect them.

Notes

1.   See Eckmann and Ruelle 1985 and references therein for detailed work on correlation dimension and other related measures.

2.   This agrees with the simulation using 2000 replications in Appendix F.

3.   For an example of this see Abel 1988, who showed that the movement in returns of risky assets depends on preference parameters.

Table 3.1
Nonlinear Diagnostic Statistics
Simulated Data

Model	Test	Data	GARCH Residuals
GARCH	W_2	3.68	0.62
	W_3	4.14	-0.08
	W_4	3.64	-0.32
	W_5	3.84	-0.02
	W_6	3.97	0.74
	T_2	0.23	0.54
	E_2	21.64	0.33
Two State	W_2	5.60	0.50
	W_3	8.86	1.45
	W_4	10.62	0.66
	W_5	12.12	-0.05
	W_6	13.07	-0.41
	T_2	1.65	0.65
	E_1	8.42	0.22
Tent	W_2	789	777
	W_3	1099	1085
	W_4	1580	1563
	W_5	2392	2368
	W_6	3781	3744
	T_2	3010	2906
	E_1	18	0
Mackey-G	W_2	26	25
	W_3	34	34
	W_4	41	42
	W_5	47	48
	W_6	53	54
	T_2	158	141
	E_1	32	1

Notes: GARCH, Two State, Tent, and Mackey-G are, respectively, the GARCH(1,1) model, the two state variance Markov process, the tent map, and the Mackey and Glass equation. W_i is the BDS test with m=i, ϵ=0.5 standard deviation. T_2 is the Tsay test with M=2, and E_1 is the Engle test with p=1.

Table 3.2
Linear Filtering and Summary Statistics

	SP1	SP2	VW1	VW2
α_1	–	0.055	0.134	-0.002
		(0.039)	(0.040)	(0.040)
α_2	–	0.118	–	-0.016
		(0.039)		(0.040)
α_3	–	–	–	0.151
				(0.040)
WOM1	–	0.006	0.003	–
		(0.002)	(0.001)	

Residual Summary Statistics

Std. Dev.	0.046	0.015	0.017	0.022
Skewness	-0.144	-0.609	-0.152	-0.078
Kurtosis	5.154	4.530	4.453	5.463

Residual ACF's

ACF(1)	0.010	0.007	-0.001	0.005
ACF(2)	0.062	0.001	-0.005	0.009
ACF(3)	0.008	-0.027	0.011	-0.012
ACF(4)	0.046	-0.003	-0.048	-0.009
ACF(5)	-0.045	-0.020	0.020	-0.072
ACF(6)	0.023	-0.031	0.038	0.052
ACF(7)	0.022	0.029	0.013	-0.042
ACF(8)	0.026	0.017	-0.023	-0.034
ACF(9)	-0.046	0.052	-0.080	0.065
ACF(10)	0.023	-0.044	0.051	-0.046

Notes: α_i is the parameter for an AR at lag i. WOM1 is a dummy variable for the first week of a month. The numbers in parenthesis are standard errors. AR's of different orders were fitted to different periods. The minus signs indicate that a parameter was not estimated. ACF(i) represents the autocorrelation coefficient at lag i for the estimated residuals. The periods are: SP1 = S&P 1928-39, SP2 = S&P January 1950–June 1962, VW1 = VW July 1962–March 1974, VW2 = VW April 1974–December 1985.

Table 3.3
Estimated GARCH(1,1) Parameters

	α	se(α)	β	se(β)	γ	se(γ)
Simulated data:						
GARCH	1.1 E-5	(5.8 E-6)	0.76	(0.085)	0.12	(0.038)
Two State	1.13	(0.35)	0.74	(0.033)	0.22	(0.030)
Tent	0.08	(0.55)	0.56	(2.920)	0.00	(0.320)
Mackey-G	0.07	(0.04)	0.00	(0.469)	0.15	(0.055)
Stock returns:						
SP1	2.0 E-5	(9.3 E-6)	0.89	(0.018)	0.10	(0.025)
SP2	1.7 E-5	(9.5 E-6)	0.84	(0.054)	0.10	(0.027)
VW1	1.1 E-5	(4.5 E-6)	0.78	(0.038)	0.20	(0.040)
VW2	3.3 E-5	(1.4 E-6)	0.82	(0.058)	0.11	(0.034)

Notes: Parameters are for GARCH(1,1) model as follows:

$x_t \sim N(0, h_t)$,

$h_t = \alpha + \beta h_{t-1} + \gamma x_{t-1}^2$,

Estimation is by maximum likelihood. Numbers in parenthesis are asymptotic standard errors. The periods are: SP1 = S&P 1928–39, SP2 = S&P January 1950–June 1962, VW1 = VW July 1962–March 1974, VW2 = VW April 1974–December 1985. GARCH, Two State, Tent, and Mackey-G are, respectively, the simulated GARCH(1,1) series, the two state variance Markov process, the tent map, and the Mackey and Glass equation, used in Section 3.2.

Table 3.4
Nonlinear Diagnostic Statistics
Stock Return Data

Series	Test	Raw Data	GARCH Residuals	Bootstrap p-value
VW	W_2	8.44	2.29	0.09
	W_3	11.07	2.68	0.07
	W_4	15.81	4.28	0.07
	W_5	21.95	5.89	0.06
	T_2	9.71	0.97	
	E_1	46.80	0.03	
VW1	W_2	8.32	3.08	0.04
	W_3	12.04	5.15	0.03
	W_4	18.48	8.94	0.02
	W_5	25.80	10.72	0.02
	T_2	5.52	1.55	
	E_1	53.97	0.07	
VW2	W_2	4.68	-0.27	0.83
	W_3	4.94	-0.46	0.74
	W_4	4.86	-1.20	0.44
	W_5	5.16	-1.42	0.47
	T_2	5.55	1.54	
	E_1	18.02	0.12	
SP1	W_2	8.48	1.43	0.30
	W_3	13.11	2.73	0.06
	W_4	16.37	3.41	0.08
	W_5	19.96	3.66	0.13
	T_2	8.20	2.04	
	E_1	21.30	0.02	
SP2	W_2	1.08	-1.24	0.38
	W_3	2.29	-0.56	0.67
	W_4	2.80	0.45	0.78
	W_5	3.91	1.54	0.43
	T_2	0.38	1.21	
	E_1	5.72	0.07	

Notes: See Table 3.3. VW = July 1962—December 1985.

Table 3.5
Estimated GARCH-M(1,1) Parameters
Stock Return Data

	SP1		VW1	
α	2.11 E-5	(9.6 E-6)	1.11 E-5	(3.5 E-6)
β	0.10	(0.020)	0.14	(0.024)
γ	0.89	(0.179)	0.834	(0.025)
ρ	0.61	(0.778)	5.330	(1.680)
ϕ	–		2.00 E-3	(7.2 E-4)
ψ	–		0.088	(0.032)

Notes: Parameters are for GARCH-M(1,1) model as follows:

$$x_t \sim N(y_t, h_t),$$

$$h_t = \alpha + \beta\, h_{t-1} + \gamma\, (x_{t-1} - y_{t-1})^2,$$

$$y_t = \rho\, x_{t-1} + \phi\, h_t + \psi\, D_{wom},$$

where D_{wom} is a dummy variable for the first week of the month. Estimation is by maximum likelihood. Numbers in parenthesis are asymptotic standard errors. The periods are: SP1 = S&P 1928–39, VW1 = VW July 1962–March 1974.

Table 3.6
Estimated GARCH-M(1,1) Residual BDS Statistics

Series	Test	GARCH Residuals	Bootstrap p-value
VW1	W_2	1.25	0.37
	W_3	2.98	0.05
	W_4	5.70	0.03
	W_5	7.16	0.04
SP1	W_2	1.43	0.29
	W_3	2.71	0.06
	W_4	3.50	0.08
	W_5	3.82	0.12

Notes: The periods are: SP1 = S&P 1928–39, VW1 = VW July 1962–March 1974.

Table 3.7
Performance of Nearest Neighbor Forecasts
Regression of Actual Outcomes on Forecasts

Series	m	β	t-stat	R^2
VW1	1	0.16	2.53	0.02
	2	0.24	3.85	0.04
	3	0.19	3.03	0.03
	4	0.11	1.69	0.01
VW2	1	0.00	-0.07	0.00
	2	-0.03	-0.49	0.00
	3	-0.01	-0.19	0.00
	4	0.02	0.29	0.00
SP1	1	0.01	0.11	0.00
	2	0.00	0.10	0.01
	3	0.02	1.62	0.01
	4	0.01	0.31	0.00
SP2	1	-0.01	-0.23	0.00
	2	-0.07	-1.34	0.01
	3	-0.01	-0.12	0.00
	4	-0.03	-0.54	0.00
Tent	1	0.99	1303	1.00
	2	0.99	704	1.00
	3	0.99	365	1.00
	4	0.98	184	0.99
Mackey-G	1	0.25	4.71	0.07
	2	0.46	9.67	0.24
	3	0.55	11.61	0.32
	4	0.54	10.84	0.29

Notes: m is the amount of lagged information used in forecasting. β is the regression coefficient of the actual data on the nearest neighbor forecast. t-stat is the t-statistic for the null hypothesis that $\beta=0$. The periods are: SP1 = S&P 1928—39, SP2 = S&P January 1950—June 1962, VW1 = VW July 1962—March 1974, VW2 = VW April 1974—December 1985. Tent is the simulated tent map, and Mackey-G is AR(10) residuals of simulated Mackey and Glass data.

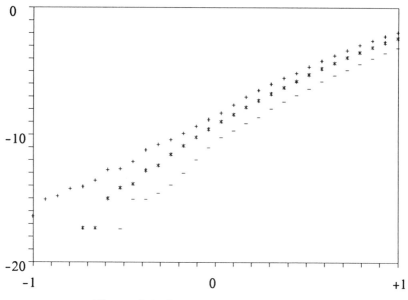

Figure 3.1 GP Plot: Scrambled Normal

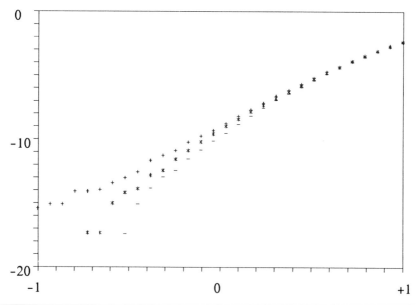

Figure 3.2 GP Plot: Sign Scrambled Normal

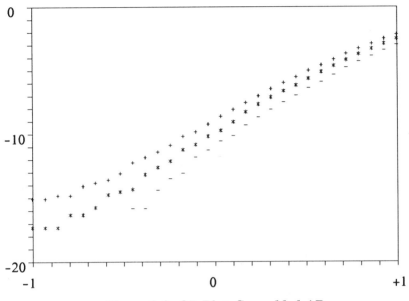

Figure 3.3 GP Plot: Scrambled AR

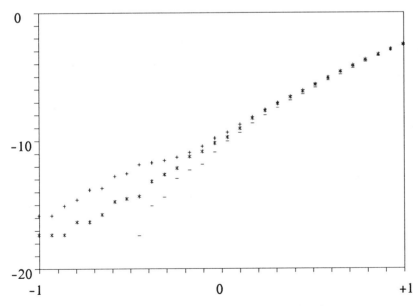

Figure 3.4 GP Plot: Sign Scrambled AR

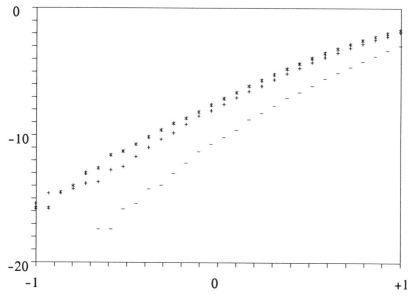

Figure 3.5 GP Plot: Scrambled GARCH

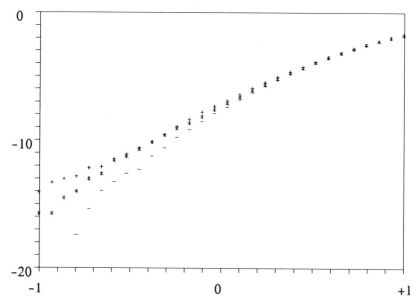

Figure 3.6 GP Plot: Sign Scrambled GARCH

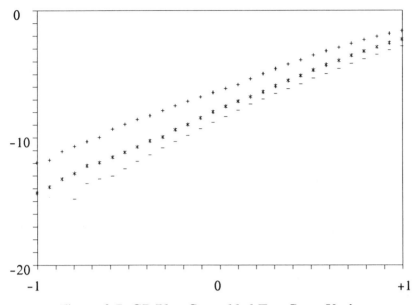

Figure 3.7 GP Plot: Scrambled Two State Variance

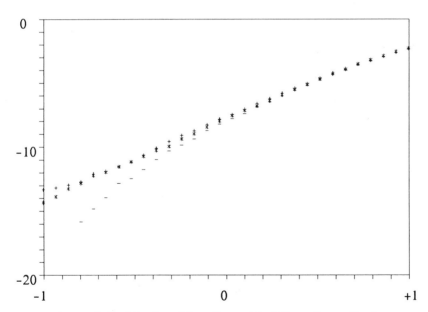

Figure 3.8 GP Plot: Sign Scrambled Two State Variance

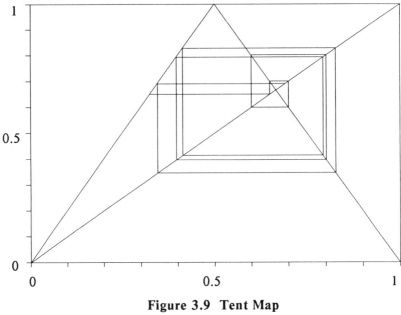

Figure 3.9 Tent Map

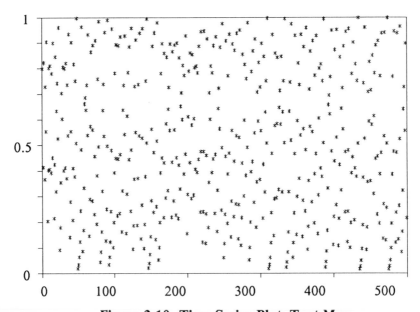

Figure 3.10 Time Series Plot: Tent Map

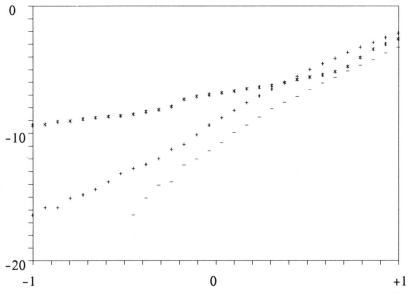

Figure 3.11 GP Plot: Scrambled Tent Map

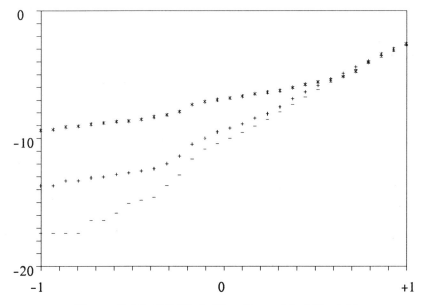

Figure 3.12 GP Plot: Sign Scrambled Tent Map

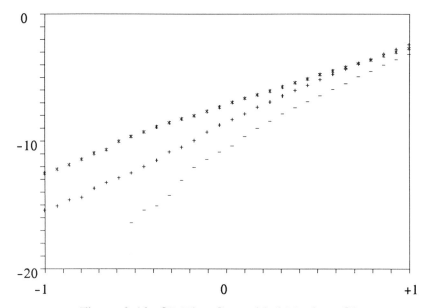

Figure 3.13 GP Plot: Scrambled Mackey-Glass

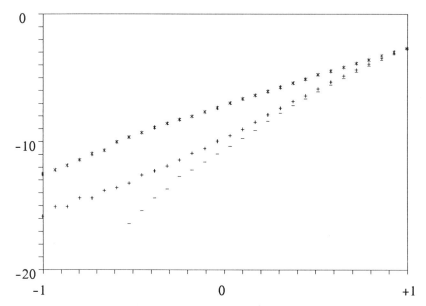

Figure 3.14 GP Plot: Sign Scrambled Mackey-Glass

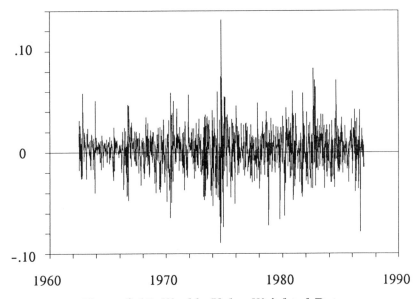

Figure 3.15 Weekly Value Weighted Returns

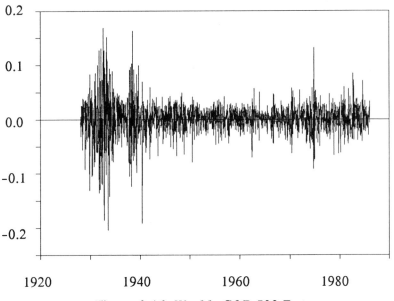

Figure 3.16 Weekly S&P 500 Returns

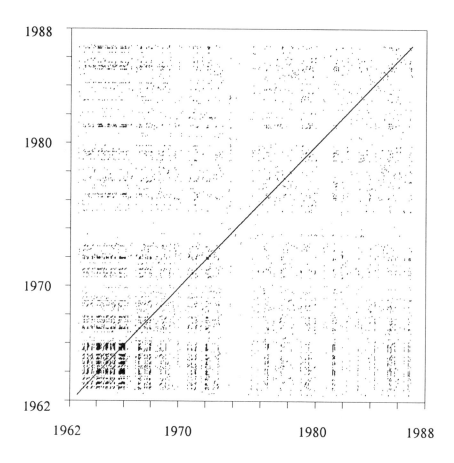

Figure 3.17 Recurrence Plot: VW (1962-1986)

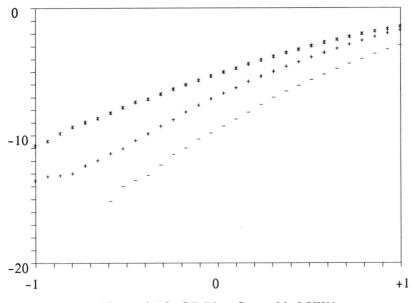

Figure 3.18 GP Plot: Scrambled VW1

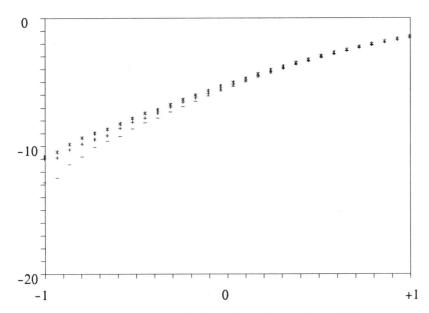

Figure 3.19 GP Plot: Sign Scrambled VW1

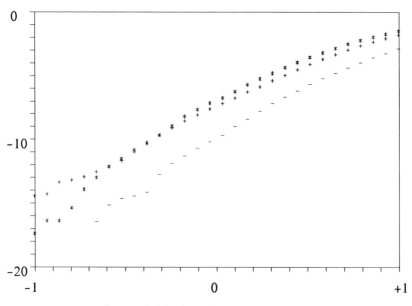

Figure 3.20 GP Plot: Scrambled VW2

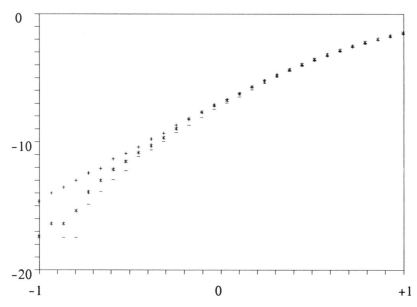

Figure 3.21 GP Plot: Sign Scrambled VW2

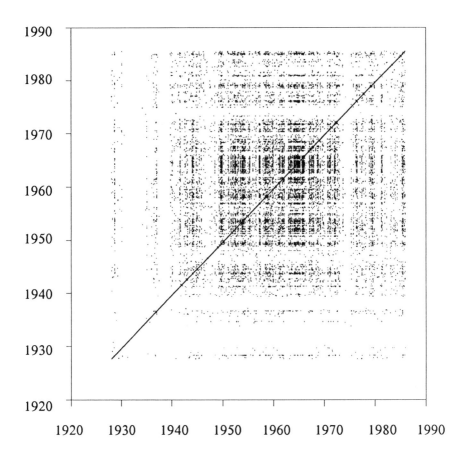

Figure 3.22 Recurrence Plot: S&P (1928-1985)

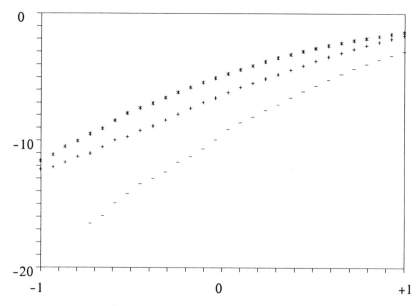

Figure 3.23 GP Plot: Scrambled SP1

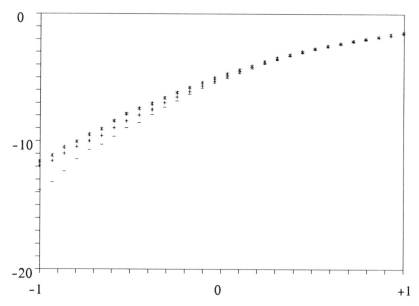

Figure 3.24 GP Plot: Sign Scrambled SP1

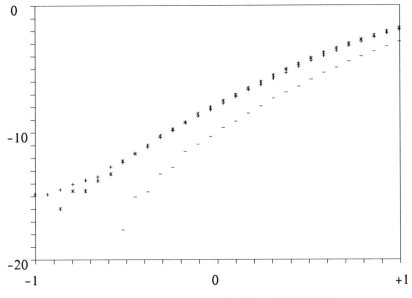

Figure 3.25 GP Plot: Scrambled SP2

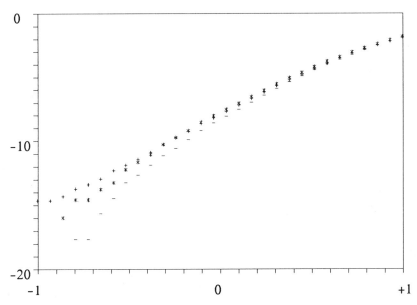

Figure 3.26 GP Plot: Sign Scrambled SP2

Chapter 4
Nonlinearity in Foreign Exchange

In this chapter, we investigate whether changes in foreign exchange rates exhibit nonlinear dependence. While Chapter 3 emphasizes the GP plots and recurrence plots in detecting nonlinearity in stock returns, this chapter focuses more on the BDS statistic in applications to foreign exchange. The reason for this is simple. The computation times for the GP plots and graphical software for the recurrence plots are currently inadequate to handle datasets with much more than 1,000 observations. The daily exchange rate data we use contain 2,510 observations. To fix the notation, let S_t denote the U.S. dollar price of a unit of foreign currency at date t; $s_t = \log(S_t)$ is the natural logarithm of S_t; and $x_t = s_t - s_{t-1}$ is the continuous time rate of change of the exchange rate.

A prevalent view in the literature is that s_t follows a random walk.[1] Thus far, there has been no strong statistical evidence confirming or refuting this view. At best, exchange rate changes are uncorrelated, i.e., *linearly independent*. More recently, there is

---

This chapter is based on Hsieh 1989a.

evidence that exchange rate changes are *nonlinearly dependent*. Hsieh 1988a rejects the null hypothesis that x_t is IID for daily price changes of five currencies from 1974 to 1983, and finds that this rejection can be attributed to changing means and variances. Manas–Anton 1986 shows that $|x_t|$ and x_t^2 are serially correlated, even though x_t itself is not. This chapter applies the BDS statistic to test for nonlinearity in exchange rates.

4.1 Testing Nonlinearity in Foreign Exchange Rates

Our data consist of daily closing bid prices of five major currencies in U.S. Dollars: British Pound (BP), Canadian Dollar (CD), Deutsche Mark (DM), Japanese Yen (JY), and Swiss Franc (SF). There are a total of 2,510 daily observations, from January 2, 1974 to December 30, 1983. The rates of change are calculated by taking the logarithmic differences between successive trading days. They are displayed in Figures 4.1 through 4.5.

Table 4.1 provides summary statistics of the data distribution. All five currencies have coefficients of kurtosis substantially in excess of 3, indicating heavy tails. Table 4.2 tests for linear structure. Standard errors of the autocorrelation coefficients and the Box and Pierce Q-statistics are adjusted for heteroskedasticity according to Diebold 1988. They show little serial correlation. The runs test also fails to detect any linear dependence. This is consistent with findings in the literature.[2]

Next, we examine the graphical depictions of nonlinearity in exchange rates. In Figures 4.6 through 4.10, the "*****" symbols are the GP plots, while the "**+**" and "**-**" symbols are, respectively, the largest and smallest values of the GP plot from 50 bootstraps of the original data. Figures 4.11 through 4.15 are the recurrence plots for the five exchange rates. All ten figures indicate that there is substantial departure from independent and identical distribution in exchange rates.

This is confirmed in the statistical analysis. Table 4.3 tests for nonlinear dependence using the BDS statistics for ϵ/σ = 1.5, 1.25, 1.0, .75, and .50 and m = 2,3,...,10 for the raw data. It is clear that the BDS statistics all lie in the extreme positive tail of the standard normal distribution, thus strongly rejecting the null hypothesis of independence and identical distribution. Note that the BDS statistics for low dimensions (e.g., m=2,3,4) are not sensitive to the choice of ϵ/σ, but those for higher dimensions (e.g., m=8,9,10) are. The reason is that, while we have 1250 non-overlapping 2-histories at dimension 2, we only have 250 non-overlapping 10-histories at dimension 10.

The large BDS statistics can arise in two ways: either the finite sample distribution under the null hypothesis of independent and identical distribution is poorly approximated by the asymptotic normal distribution, or the BDS statistics are large when the null hypothesis of independent and identical distribution is violated.

We use three kinds of Monte Carlo evidence to demonstrate that the finite sample distribution of the BDS test is well approximated by the asymptotic distribution. First, our Monte Carlo simulations in Chapter 2 show that the BDS statistic is well approximated by its asymptotic distribution for sample sizes of 500 or more (especially when the underlying distribution is unimodal and heavy tailed). Second, the finite sample distribution from bootstrapping the exchange rate data corroborate this finding. Table 4.4 summarizes the distribution of the BDS statistics for 625 random permutations of the ordering of the data. (The bootstrap results are essentially the same if we sample with replacement.) The mean BDS statistic is close to 0, and the standard deviation is close to 1. At low dimensions, it is normally distributed. The observed BDS statistics in Table 4.3 are clearly larger than those from all 625 random permutations. Third, our Monte Carlo simulations in Chapter 2 (Section 2.3 and Appendix B) show that the average magnitude of the BDS statistics under a number of alternative models is large. For these three reasons, we believe that the asymptotic distribution of the BDS statistic is applicable and that the large BDS statistics in Table 4.3 provide strong evidence of nonlinearity in exchange rate changes.

Since BDS has power against linear dependence (such as an AR process), we prefilter the data by the following autoregression:

$$x_t = \beta_0 + \beta_M D_{M,t} + \beta_T D_{T,t} + \beta_W D_{W,t} + \beta_R D_{R,t} + b_H HOL_t$$
$$+ \Sigma_{i=1}^{r} \beta_i x_{t-i} + u_t \qquad (4.1.1)$$

where $D_{M,t}$, $D_{T,t}$, $D_{W,t}$, $D_{R,t}$ are dummy variables for Monday, Tuesday, Wednesday, and Thursday, and HOL_t is the number of holidays (excluding weekends) between two successive trading days. For each currency, we use the AR(r) model for which the adjusted $Q_x(50)$ test is not significant at the 10% level. This identifies r to be 0, 5, 6, 10, and 6, respectively, for the BP, CD, DM, JY, and SF. An alternative procedure uses 10 lags for all five currencies. These procedures do not affect the first order asymptotic distribution of the BDS statistic. Since our sample size is large we believe that the asymptotic results are applicable.

Table 4.5 reports the BDS test of the two sets of filtered data for ϵ set to be 1 standard deviation of the data. They do not differ substantially from those using the raw data, which suggests that the BDS test is not merely picking up linear dependence, but is in fact detecting strong nonlinear dependence in the data. BDS could be picking up omitted but forecastable nonstationarity or nonforecastable nonstationarity, i.e., conditional moments could be time-dependent in such a way as to be nonforecastable given the information set of past rates.

Table 4.6 gives the results of other tests of nonlinearity of the raw data. The autocorrelation coefficients of the squared data, $\rho_{xx}(k)$, and the Ljung-Box $Q_{xx}(K)$ of the squared data are both substantially larger than the corresponding $\rho_x(k)$ and $Q_x(K)$ in Table 4.2, corroborating the BDS inference that the data contain important nonlinearity. Interestingly, the Tsay test (described in Chapter 2, Section 2.3) picks up little nonlinearity when M=2 or 4, except for the CD. But at M=8 and 10, the Tsay test is able to detect some nonlinearity.

4.2 Distinguishing Between Nonlinearities

In this section, we try to characterize the type of nonlinearity in the exchange rate data. The first step is to distinguish between nonlinear deterministic chaos and nonlinear stochastic models. We have already commented that there is no practical difference between high-dimensional chaos or low-dimensional "irregular" chaos on the one hand and true randomness on the other hand. We are therefore only interested in seeing whether there is low-dimensional "regular" chaos in exchange rates.

Notice that the strong rejection of independent and identical distribution by the BDS statistics is *consistent* with the presence of low-dimensional "regular" chaotic dynamics in exchange rates. But many other types of behavior, such as nonlinear stochastic dynamics, are also consistent with the strong rejection of independent and identical distribution. We cannot use the rejection of independent and identical distribution as evidence of chaotic behavior. We need corroborating evidence. If exchange rates are governed by low-dimensional "regular" chaotic dynamics, it should be predictable over short time periods. This work in fact has been done by Diebold and Nason 1990, who found that weighted nearest neighbor methods could not outperform a random walk model in out-of-sample forecasting for ten currencies using weekly data. Similar results are reported in Table 4.7 for daily data. In three of the five currencies, the root mean squared forecast errors of the weighted nearest neighbor method are larger than that of the simple random walk (RW) method. In the other two cases, the weighted nearest neighbor method can only outperform the random walk method by less than 2%. There is certainly no evidence in favor of low-dimensional "regular" chaotic dynamics. We therefore proceed to consider nonlinear stochastic models.

Since the class of nonlinear stochastic model is extremely large, we restrict our attention to two classes, which encompass all nonlinear stochastic models discussed in the time series literature:

Mean-Nonlinearity: $\qquad x_t = A(J_t) + u_t,$ $\qquad\qquad$ (4.2.1)

Variance-Nonlinearity: $\qquad x_t = B(J_t)u_t,$ $\qquad\qquad$ (4.2.2) where $J_t = [x_{t-1},...,x_{t-k},u_{t-1},...,u_{t-k}]'$. Here u_t is an IID random variable with zero mean and independent of past x's and u's, and A and B are arbitrary nonlinear functions of J_t. These two classes contain all of the nonlinear time series models discussed in Section 1.2. Priestley's 1980 state-dependent model, the nonlinear moving average, the threshold autoregression, and the bilinear model are examples of mean-nonlinearity, while ARCH and GARCH models are examples of variance-nonlinearity. Note that the ARCH-M (i.e., ARCH-in-the-mean) model, used in Domowitz and Hakkio 1985 and Diebold and Pauly 1988, is a hybrid, since nonlinearity enters both the mean and the variance:

$$x_t = A(J_t) + B(J_t)u_t. \tag{4.2.3}$$

Both mean- and variance-nonlinearity imply that x_t^2 is not IID. However, they differ in the following way. Define:

$$F(J_t) = E[x_t|x_{t-1},...,x_{t-k}]. \tag{4.2.4}$$

Variance-nonlinearity implies that $F(J_t)=0$, while mean-nonlinearity typically yields that $F(J_t) \neq 0$.

This provides a test to discriminate between the two types of nonlinearity. The null hypothesis is F=0, versus the composite alternative that $F \neq 0$. The idea is this. Suppose F is at least twice continuously differentiable. We can approximate it by a second order Taylor series expansion around 0, and obtain terms $x_{t-i}x_{t-j}$. Variance-nonlinearity implies that x_t is not correlated with these terms, while mean-nonlinearity implies that x_t is typically correlated with at least some of these terms.[3]

To implement this test, we define the third order moments of x_t:

$$\rho_{xxx}(i,j) = E[x_t x_{t-i} x_{t-j}]/\sigma_x^3. \tag{4.2.5}$$

The null hypothesis that $F(\ )=0$ implies $\rho_{xxx}(i,j) = 0$ for all $i,j>0$. We estimate $\rho_{xxx}(i,j)$ using sample moments, i.e.,

$$r_{xxx}(i,j) = [\ \Sigma\ x_t x_{t-i} x_{t-j} / T\ ] / [\ \Sigma\ x_t^2 / T\ ]^{3/2}. \tag{4.2.6}$$

Under the null hypothesis of $\rho_{xxx}(i,j) = 0$ and auxiliary restrictions about the behavior of $\{x_t\}$, $T^{\frac{1}{2}} [\ \Sigma\ x_t x_{t-i} x_{t-j} / T\ ]$ is asymptotically normally distributed, with mean zero and variance:

$$\omega(i,j) = \text{plim}_{T\to\infty}\ \Sigma\ x_t^2\ x_{t-i}^2\ x_{t-j}^2 / T, \tag{4.2.7}$$

provided that the probability limit exists. Then $r_{xxx}(i,j)$ is asymptotically normally distributed, with mean zero and variance $\omega(i,j)/\sigma_x^6$, which can be consistently estimated by:

$$[\ \Sigma\ x_t^2\ x_{t-i}^2\ x_{t-j}^2 / T\ ] / [\ \Sigma\ x_t^2 / T\ ]^3. \tag{4.2.8}$$

An asymptotic test of $\rho_{xxx}(i,j) = 0$ can then be obtained. We call this the "third moment" test.

This procedure is very similar to the Tsay 1986 test for nonlinearity. We test $\rho_{xxx}(i,j) = 0$ individually, while Tsay 1986 tests jointly for $\rho_{xxx}(i,j) = 0$ for $0<i,j<k$. There is, however, an important difference. Tsay 1986 assumes that x_t is IID, while we assume that $E[x_t|x_{t-1},...,x_{t-k}]=0$ along with sufficient moment conditions to guarantee the asymptotic normality of $r_{xxx}(i,j)$ and consistent estimation of its variance. The reason is that the Tsay 1986 test is designed to detect any type of nonlinearity. Our test is designed to reject only in the presence of mean-nonlinearity but not variance-nonlinearity. However, it should be clear that the Tsay test will have low power against variance-nonlinearity (when $\rho_{xxx}(i,j)=0$ for all i,j).

To check that the third moment test has power against mean-nonlinearity, we apply this test to several models. The results are reported in Table 4.8. The statistic, $T^{\frac{1}{2}} r_{xxx}(i,j) / [\omega(i,j)/\sigma_x^6]$, is used to test whether third order moments are different from zero, up to the fourth lag. A rejection is registered if the absolute value of this statistic is larger than 2.576, constituting a two-tailed test at the 1% significance level. The test rejects the null hypothesis of zero third order moments at approximately the nominal size of 1% for the AR1, the MA1, and the ARCH models, which have no mean-nonlinearity. The test also rejects the null hypothesis of zero third order moments at about 99% for the nonlinear moving average (at $i=2$, $j=1$), the threshold autoregression (at $i=1$, $j=1$), and the tent map (at $i=1$, $j=1$, and $i=2$, $j=2$), which have mean-nonlinearity. This shows that the third moment test has good size characteristics and has good power against mean-nonlinearity. In addition, the third order moment test is able to detect mean-nonlinearity in a hybrid model, rejecting 64% for the ARCH-M (at $i=1$ and $j=1$). Although this rejection rate is low, the power rises to 84% when the sample size increases to 2,500 observations.

Table 4.9 applies the third moment test to our exchange rate data. We use the residuals from the tenth order autoregression with dummies for days of the week and holidays. None of them are significantly different from zero at the 1% level. Although the table reports only the results for $i=j=5$, none of the third moments up to $i=j=10$, other than $\rho_{xxx}(5,6)$ for the CD, $\rho_{xxx}(2,10)$ for the JY, and $\rho_{xxx}(6,10)$ for the SF, are significantly different from zero at the 1% level. We obtain similar results for the raw data, or the filtered data from the Box and Jenkins 1976 identification procedure (i.e., lags of 0, 5, 6, 10, and 6 for the BP, CD, DM, JY, and SF). The evidence supports the view that changing variances is responsible for the rejection of independence and identical distribution in exchange rate changes.

4.3 GARCH Models for Exchange Rates

To capture variance-nonlinearity, we use Engle's 1982 ARCH model and Bollerslev's 1986 GARCH model. Applications of ARCH and GARCH to exchange rates can be found in Bollerslev 1987, Diebold 1988, Diebold and Nerlove 1989, Diebold and Pauly 1988, Engle and Bollerslev 1986, Hsieh 1989b, Manas-Anton 1986, and Milhøj 1987. Here we estimate a simple GARCH model, which is specified as follows:

$$x_t = \beta_0 + \beta_M D_{M,t} + \beta_T D_{T,t} + \beta_W D_{W,t} + \beta_R D_{R,t} + \beta_H HOL_t +$$

$$\Sigma_{i=1}^{r} \beta_i x_{t-i} + u_t, \tag{4.3.1}$$

where r is 0, 5, 6, 10, and 6, respectively, for the BP, CD, DM, JY, and SF, and u_t (conditional on past data) is normally distributed, with zero mean and variance h_t, such that:

$$h_t = \phi_0 + \phi_M D_{M,t} + \phi_T D_{T,t} + \phi_W D_{W,t} + \phi_R D_{R,t} + \phi_H HOL_t +$$

$$\phi h_{t-1} + \psi u_{t-1}^2. \tag{4.3.2}$$

After estimation, we perform diagnostic tests on the standardized residuals:

$$z_t = u_t / \hat{h}_t^{\frac{1}{2}}, \tag{4.3.3}$$

where u_t is the residual of the mean equation and $\hat{h}_t$ its estimated variance.

The diagnostic tests are given in Table 4.10. The runs test and $Q_x(50)$ find no first order dependence, while $Q_{xx}(50)$ finds second order dependence only in the DM. On the basis of these two tests, other researchers have concluded that GARCH fits most of these currencies. We have added three more diagnostics: the Tsay test, the BDS test, and the Pearson goodness-of-fit test. The Tsay test finds no evidence of nonlinearity in any of the currencies. The BDS test also finds no evidence of nonlinearity in the CD, JY, and SF, some nonlinearity (at dimensions 8, 9, and 10) for the DM, and strong nonlinearity for the BP. The goodness-of-fit test rejects conditional normality in all five currencies.

We must point out that this procedure is often biased in favor of accepting the model. Tauchen 1985 shows that diagnostics of maximum likelihood models may have a different asymptotic distribution than those applied to the raw data, and gives examples of diagnostics that are biased towards accepting the model when no adjustments are made to account for the presence of estimated parameters.

For some diagnostics, there are standard methods to adjust the asymptotic distribution for the estimated parameters. For $Q_x(50)$, the degrees of freedom are reduced by the number of coefficients in the mean equation (4.3.7). For $Q_{xx}(50)$, the degrees of freedom are reduced by the number of coefficients in the variance equation (4.3.8). For the goodness of fit, the degrees of freedom are not reduced, since there are no parameters to estimate in the standard normal.

For the BDS statistic applied to standardized residuals of GARCH models, Monte Carlo evidence in Chapter 2 (Section 2.5) shows that some correction must be made to the asymptotic distribution. Exactly what the correction is has not been worked out, and is one important topic of future research. Instead, we have been using simulations to determine the critical values of the BDS statistic. Ideally, one simulation should be performed for each model using the estimated parameters. In our case, this would call for 15 different simulations, a rather cumbersome procedure. We have instead used one set of results. This is given in Table 4 in Appendix F, providing the size and distribution of the BDS statistic applied to GARCH residuals for $\psi=.1$ and $\phi=.8$, which is close to most of the estimated parameter values.

To allow for conditional nonnormal distributions, we use the Student-t and the generalized error distribution.[4] The results are provided in Tables 4.11 and 4.12. None of the Pearson $\chi^2(50)$

goodness-of-fit tests are significant at the 1% level for these two distributions. Note that the degrees of freedom are reduced by 1, since there is one parameter to estimate in the Student-t and the generalized error distribution. This is a conservative adjustment, as discussed in Kendall and Stuart 1970 (Chapter 30). The diagnostic tests on their standardized residuals are reported in Tables 4.10 and 4.11.

The GARCH(1,1) Student-t model is not rejected by any diagnostic test for the SF. For the other four exchange rates, there is evidence of leftover nonlinearity. The runs test also picks up some dependence in the JY. The $Q_{xx}(50)$ appears to be unusually low for the BP and unusually high for the JY. There may be some problem with the $Q_{xx}(50)$ test and the Tsay test, since the Student-t has low degrees of freedom for the BP and JY (just below 3), which means that fourth moments do not exist. In addition, the standardized residuals for both the BP and JY have enormous coefficients of kurtosis (314.67 and 43.25, respectively). This is consistent with the estimated models, since a Student-t distribution with 3 degrees of freedom has infinite kurtosis. However, this is certainly contrary to the spirit of ARCH and GARCH models, particularly in light of the fact that the original data in Table 4.1 exhibit substantially lower kurtosis. Furthermore, (unreported) simulations of GARCH models with the estimated parameters yield data that are so extremely ill-behaved that we have no doubt that exchange rate data could not have been generated by such a model. One possible explanation for these negative results is that the densities of the BP and JY data have very high peaks at zero, which are driving the degrees of freedom of the standardized Student-t distribution to low levels.

The GARCH(1,1) generalized error distribution also gives similar results. It is not rejected by any diagnostic test for the SF. For the other four exchange rates, there appears to be leftover nonlinearity. The $Q_{xx}(50)$ appears to be unusually small for the BP and quite high for the JY. In addition, the kurtosis is very large for both currencies.

4.4 Additional Remarks

This chapter shows that daily exchange rate changes are not independent of past changes. Although there is little linear dependence in the data, there is strong evidence against independence and identical distribution. While this is consistent with the presence of low-dimensional chaos, there is no corroborating evidence in terms of short-term predictability of exchange rates. We therefore turn our attention to nonlinear stochastic models. Evidence from third order moments indicates that the nonlinearity is likely to enter through variances rather than through means. This is consistent with the presence of conditional heteroskedasticity.

GARCH models with normal and nonnormal conditional distributions are estimated to try to account for conditional heteroskedasticity. Conditional normality is strongly rejected in all currencies, in favor of conditional nonnormal distributions. In fact, the GARCH(1,1) using either the Student-t or generalized error distribution can describe the SF very well. But there is reason to believe that the GARCH models cannot model all the nonlinearity in the CD, DM, JY, and SF.

An important lesson in this exercise is that the asymptotic distribution of the BDS statistic is affected when using standardized residuals from GARCH models. Simulations in Chapter 2 show that it is biased *in favor* of the GARCH specification. Bootstrapping is therefore very important. Recent improvements in the speed of microcomputers and the available fast algorithms for computing the BDS statistics will aid greatly in this effort.

Notes

1. See Mussa 1979 and Meese and Rogoff 1983.

2. See Giddy and Dufey 1975, Burt, Kaen and Booth 1977, Cornell 1977, Logue and Sweeney 1977, Logue, Sweeney and Willett 1978, Rogalski and Vinso 1978, Manas-Anton 1986, and Hsieh 1988a.

3. Pemberton and Tong 1981 give examples of nonlinear models in which x_t is uncorrelated with all $x_{t-i}x_{t-j}$, for all i,j>0, and yet $F( )\neq0$.

4. The generalized error distribution is used in Nelson 1988. The density function is given by:

$$g(x) = .5 \, \nu \, \Gamma(3/\nu) \, Q(1/\nu)^{-1.5} \exp(-.5 \, |x/\lambda|^\nu), \text{ where}$$

$$\lambda = \Gamma(1/\nu)^{.5} \, \Gamma(3/\nu)^{-.5} \, 2^{-2/\nu} .$$

When $\nu=2$, $g(x)$ is the standard normal density. When $\nu=1$, $g(x)$ is the double exponential density. When $\nu=0$, $g(x)$ is the uniform density.

Table 4.1
Summary Statistics of Log Price Changes: 1974-1983
($x_t \times 100$)

	BP	CD	DM	JY	SF
Mean	-0.0184	-0.0089	0.0005	0.0077	0.0171
Median	0.0000	0.0098	0.0000	0.0000	0.0000
Std Dev	0.5921	0.2234	0.6372	0.6260	0.7889
Skewness	-0.4136	-0.3149	-0.4249	-0.2044	-0.2835
Kurtosis	8.90	8.61	12.79	11.27	10.22
Maximum	3.7496	1.5492	3.6686	3.5703	4.4466
Minimum	-4.6623	-1.8677	-7.0967	-6.2566	-7.0054
Runs test	1.96	-0.86	2.38	0.64	0.77
N(0,1)	(0.0500)	(0.3898)	(0.0173)	(0.5222)	(0.4413)

Marginal significance level (two-tailed test) in parentheses.

Table 4.2
Autocorrelation Coefficients of Log Price Changes: 1974–1983
[Heteroskedasticity-Consistent Standard Errors]

Lags	BP	CD	DM	JY	SF
$\rho_x(1)$	-.0216	.0406	-.0638*	-.0569	-.0410
	[.0286]	[.0354]	[.0274]	[.0254]	[.0311]
$\rho_x(2)$	-.0025	.0201	.0021	.0237	.0046
	[.0279]	[.0267]	[.0351]	[.0260]	[.0289]
$\rho_x(3)$	-.0075	.0176	.0240	.0344	.0050
	[.0248]	[.0274]	[.0261]	[.0245]	[.0265]
$\rho_x(4)$	-.0064	.0317	-.0244	.0055	-.0229
	[.0237]	[.0282]	[.0261]	[.0249]	[.0270]
$\rho_x(5)$	.0224	.0740*	.0265	.0386	-.0074
	[.0275]	[.0254]	[.0289]	[.0265]	[.0290]
$\rho_x(6)$	-.0021	.0212	.0373	.0140	.0561
	[.0254]	[.0254]	[.0251]	[.0240]	[.0252]
$\rho_x(7)$	-.0124	.0306	.0113	-.0094	-.0070
	[.0221]	[.0268]	[.0235]	[.0218]	[.0241]
$\rho_x(8)$	-.0155	-.0065	.0128	.0093	-.0290
	[.0226]	[.0240]	[.0248]	[.0235]	[.0233]
$\rho_x(9)$	.0586*	.0483	.0391	.0739*	.0385
	[.0218]	[.0237]	[.0232]	[.0238]	[.0257]
$\rho_x(10)$	.0017	.0266	.0333	.0715*	.0296
	[.0253]	[.0221]	[.0225]	[.0245]	[.0273]
$\rho_x(20)$	.0247	-.0238	-.0061	.0067	-.0099
	[.0214]	[.0216]	[.0239]	[.0252]	[.0241]
$\rho_x(30)$	-.0033	-.0405	-.0203	.0095	-.0004
	[.0237]	[.0217]	[.0249]	[.0234]	[.0222]
$\rho_x(40)$	.0197	-.0083	.0271	.0566*	-.0053
	[.0236]	[.0239]	[.0221]	[.0230]	[.0233]
$\rho_x(50)$	.0170	.0170	.0206	-.0267	.0029
	[.0224]	[.0212]	[.0222]	[.0216]	[.0258]
Adjusted Box-Pierce $Q_x(50)$	39.71 (.8512)	54.35 (.3123)	44.85 (.6796)	70.27 (.0308)	44.72 (.6846)

Marginal significance levels in parentheses.

Heteroskedasticity-consistent standard errors in brackets.

* Significantly different from zero at the 1% level (one-tailed test).

Table 4.3
BDS Test: Raw data

m	ϵ/σ	BP	CD	DM	JY	SF
2	1.50	8.71	11.12	9.41	8.64	9.34
3	1.50	11.68	13.91	12.52	11.47	12.62
4	1.50	13.41	16.27	15.16	13.73	15.31
5	1.50	14.99	18.26	17.37	15.89	17.46
6	1.50	16.61	20.18	19.62	18.42	19.55
7	1.50	18.21	22.09	21.43	20.70	21.43
8	1.50	19.65	24.10	23.40	23.11	23.33
9	1.50	21.12	26.06	25.46	25.57	25.45
10	1.50	22.89	28.08	27.65	28.25	27.93
2	1.25	9.76	11.89	9.53	9.92	9.88
3	1.25	13.17	14.87	12.84	13.63	13.73
4	1.25	15.38	17.47	15.88	16.52	17.00
5	1.25	17.60	19.80	18.71	19.50	20.00
6	1.25	19.93	22.42	21.70	23.05	22.87
7	1.25	22.43	25.26	24.38	26.66	25.77
8	1.25	25.08	28.40	37.45	30.89	29.11
9	1.25	27.95	31.74	30.81	35.69	33.01
10	1.25	31.50	35.42	34.66	41.37	37.88
2	1.00	10.73	12.61	9.86	10.95	10.82
3	1.00	14.74	15.75	13.70	15.60	15.24
4	1.00	17.93	18.75	17.32	19.72	19.38
5	1.00	21.57	21.78	21.11	24.61	23.44
6	1.00	25.65	25.59	25.50	30.74	28.07
7	1.00	30.44	30.06	29.97	38.05	33.25
8	1.00	36.42	35.28	35.48	47.62	39.92
9	1.00	43.75	41.36	42.11	59.81	48.50
10	1.00	53.30	48.65	50.36	75.96	59.93
2	0.75	11.63	12.95	10.34	13.09	11.69
3	0.75	16.76	16.07	14.83	19.73	16.89
4	0.75	21.69	19.53	19.46	26.66	22.44
5	0.75	28.16	23.57	25.07	36.25	28.62
6	0.75	36.57	28.95	32.55	49.38	36.64
7	0.75	48.26	35.57	41.62	67.95	46.96
8	0.75	65.76	43.87	54.11	95.26	62.00
9	0.75	91.92	54.55	71.52	135.91	83.66
10	0.75	131.14	68.65	95.66	195.80	115.51
2	0.50	14.69	12.65	10.84	17.23	12.81
3	0.50	22.67	15.70	16.62	27.81	19.45
4	0.50	33.16	19.91	23.24	42.66	27.88
5	0.50	50.21	25.02	32.93	67.55	37.24
6	0.50	78.63	32.20	48.67	110.04	52.89
7	0.50	131.65	41.97	72.22	184.82	76.23
8	0.50	231.40	55.74	112.48	321.97	113.37
9	0.50	433.09	74.92	186.11	580.91	173.69
10	0.50	843.42	105.57	317.35	1062.04	279.16

Table 4.4
Distribution of BDS Statistics at $\epsilon/\sigma=1$
(625 random samples of 2510 points without replacement)

m		BP	CD	DM	JY	SF
2	Mean	-0.04	-0.04	-0.01	0.07	-0.04
	Std dev	1.05	1.01	1.04	0.96	1.07
	Skewness	0.15	-0.14	-0.07	0.00	0.09
	Kurtosis	2.92	2.98	2.91	2.72	2.79
3	Mean	-0.07	-0.05	-0.05	0.07	-0.05
	Std dev	1.05	0.99	1.01	0.94	1.03
	Skewness	0.06	-0.10	-0.11	0.15	0.07
	Kurtosis	2.87	2.86	2.97	2.94	2.75
4	Mean	-0.06	-0.03	-0.05	0.06	-0.07
	Std dev	1.05	0.99	1.01	0.94	1.04
	Skewness	0.11	0.04	-0.07	0.22	0.07
	Kurtosis	3.00	2.97	2.82	3.00	2.79
5	Mean	-0.04	-0.02	-0.04	0.05	-0.06
	Std dev	1.05	0.98	1.02	0.95	1.04
	Skewness	0.24	0.12	-0.08	0.24	0.06
	Kurtosis	3.43	2.96	2.85	3.06	2.76
6	Mean	-0.04	-0.01	-0.03	0.05	-0.05
	Std dev	1.05	0.98	1.02	0.95	1.05
	Skewness	0.36	0.20	-0.05	0.23	0.10
	Kurtosis	3.81	2.89	2.78	3.14	2.70
7	Mean	-0.03	-0.01	-0.03	0.05	-0.06
	Std dev	1.04	0.97	1.02	0.96	1.05
	Skewness	0.49	0.25	0.03	0.24	0.15
	Kurtosis	4.21	2.93	2.67	3.15	2.70
8	Mean	-0.02	-0.01	-0.02	0.05	-0.05
	Std dev	1.04	0.97	1.02	0.97	1.06
	Skewness	0.62	0.31	0.11	0.31	0.24
	Kurtosis	4.74	2.93	2.62	3.28	2.75
9	Mean	0.00	-0.01	0.00	0.05	-0.04
	Std dev	1.05	0.97	1.01	0.97	1.07
	Skewness	0.74	0.39	0.17	0.42	0.32
	Kurtosis	5.30	3.01	2.63	3.47	2.81
10	Mean	0.02	-0.02	0.00	0.06	-0.04
	Std dev	1.06	0.99	1.01	0.97	1.08
	Skewness	0.85	0.46	0.24	0.47	0.40
	Kurtosis	5.96	3.12	2.66	3.51	2.88

Table 4.5
BDS Test: Filtered Data

m	ϵ/σ	BP	CD	DM	JY	SF
lags =		0	5	6	10	6
2	1.00	11.09	12.37	8.60	10.60	10.28
3	1.00	15.00	15.43	12.82	15.29	14.73
4	1.00	18.06	18.06	16.42	19.72	18.78
5	1.00	21.56	20.85	20.32	24.77	22.82
6	1.00	25.56	24.32	24.69	30.78	27.35
7	1.00	30.01	28.21	29.25	37.94	32.46
8	1.00	35.63	32.59	34.78	47.33	38.98
9	1.00	42.65	37.59	41.37	59.31	47.21
10	1.00	51.57	43.75	49.57	75.21	58.20
lags =		10	10	10	10	10
2	1.00	10.51	12.35	8.63	10.60	10.26
3	1.00	14.71	15.40	12.83	15.29	14.75
4	1.00	18.01	18.03	16.55	19.72	18.87
5	1.00	21.63	20.68	20.49	24.77	22.92
6	1.00	25.63	24.02	24.83	30.78	27.46
7	1.00	30.35	27.73	29.34	37.94	32.63
8	1.00	36.19	31.93	34.81	47.33	39.27
9	1.00	43.20	36.81	41.37	59.31	47.63
10	1.00	52.20	42.85	49.53	75.21	58.79

All test statistics are significant at the 0.1 percent level.

Table 4.6
Some Standard Tests of Nonlinearity: Raw Data

Lags	BP	CD	DM	JY	SF
Autocorrelation Coefficients of Squared Log Price Changes:					
$\rho_{xx}(1)$	0.1333	0.2806	0.0753	0.0603	0.1549
$\rho_{xx}(2)$	0.1200	0.1024	0.1773	0.0674	0.1192
$\rho_{xx}(3)$	0.0677	0.1160	0.0609	0.0494	0.0835
$\rho_{xx}(4)$	0.0522	0.1290	0.0607	0.0538	0.0899
$\rho_{xx}(5)$	0.1137	0.0804	0.0931	0.0746	0.1218
$\rho_{xx}(6)$	0.0776	0.0805	0.0490	0.0433	0.0647
$\rho_{xx}(7)$	0.0291	0.1041	0.0328	0.0192	0.0492
$\rho_{xx}(8)$	0.0355	0.0588	0.0464	0.0371	0.0390
$\rho_{xx}(9)$	0.0240	0.0534	0.0302	0.0412	0.0721
$\rho_{xx}(10)$	0.0756	0.0288	0.0228	0.0495	0.0948
Ljung-Box	365.84*	593.36*	215.06*	206.09*	531.87*
$Q_{xx}(50)$	(0.0000)	(0.0000)	(0.0000)	(0.0000)	(0.0000)
Tsay test for nonlinearity:					
M=2	2.19	4.13*	0.62	0.74	1.46
$F(\ 3,2504)$	(0.0857)	(0.0064)	(0.6061)	(0.5315)	(0.2221)
M=4	2.04	4.95*	1.96	1.74	1.17
$F(10,2495)$	(0.0261)	(0.0000)	(0.0338)	(0.0666)	(0.3062)
M=6	1.55	4.64*	2.30*	2.05*	1.71
$F(28,2474)$	(0.0524)	(0.0000)	(0.0007)	(0.0034)	(0.0231)
M=8	1.67*	3.25*	2.05*	2.05*	1.42
$F(36,2465)$	(0.0076)	(0.0000)	(0.0002)	(0.0002)	(0.0194)
M=10	2.15*	2.51*	2.09*	2.24*	1.64*
$F(55,2444)$	(0.0000)	(0.0000)	(0.0000)	(0.0000)	(0.0023)

Marginal significance levels in parentheses.
* Significantly different from zero at the 1% level (one-tailed test).

Table 4.7
Root Mean Squared Forecast Errors

Near neighbors as Fraction of Sample	1	Lags 2	3
BP (RW: 0.33117)			
.1	0.33258	0.33264	0.33189
.2	0.33136	0.33142	0.33093
.3	0.33125	0.33131	0.33101
.4	0.33101	0.33108	0.33088
.5	0.33067	0.33073	<u>0.33061</u>
CD (RW: <u>0.01347</u>)			
.1	0.01368	0.01371	0.01367
.2	0.01353	0.01354	0.01352
.3	0.01359	0.01360	0.01358
.4	0.01360	0.01360	0.01360
.5	0.01361	0.01362	0.01360
DM (RW: <u>0.26143</u>)			
.1	0.26833	0.26896	0.26835
.2	0.26561	0.26627	0.26578
.3	0.26377	0.26444	0.26415
.4	0.26269	0.26337	0.26328
.5	0.26175	0.26241	0.26232
JY (RW: 0.22248)			
.1	0.21848	<u>0.21840</u>	0.21908
.2	0.22027	0.22020	0.22062
.3	0.22021	0.22015	0.22056
.4	0.22028	0.22021	0.22058
.5	0.22037	0.22031	0.22055
SF (RW: <u>0.30766</u>)			
.1	0.31697	0.31701	0.31712
.2	0.31480	0.31480	0.31471
.3	0.31411	0.31407	0.31386
.4	0.31249	0.31244	0.31217
.5	0.31109	0.31104	0.31076

Note:
The lowest root mean squared forecast error is underlined.

Table 4.8
Power of Third Moment Tests for Different Models
(2000 replications of 1000 points)

Lag i j	AR1 $\rho=0.5$	MA1 $\theta=0.5$	Nonlinear MA	ARCH $\phi=0.5$	Threshold AR	Tent Map	ARCH–M $\phi=.5, \gamma=1$
Percent of Replications Rejected At 1% Level (Two-tailed test)							
1 1	0.05	0.00	0.05	0.10	100.00	100.00	64.00
2 1	0.80	0.50	99.85	0.25	1.30	1.05	0.45
2 2	0.15	0.25	0.25	0.10	0.55	99.80	10.50
3 1	1.65	0.85	1.05	0.65	1.35	1.45	0.50
3 2	1.55	0.85	1.05	0.40	1.10	1.00	0.45
3 3	0.35	0.25	0.05	0.40	0.15	3.20	0.95
4 1	1.15	0.75	1.00	0.75	1.20	0.70	0.50
4 2	1.80	1.35	1.70	0.85	1.15	1.30	0.75
4 3	1.80	0.50	1.20	1.00	0.80	1.05	0.55
4 4	0.30	0.25	0.25	0.25	0.15	0.05	0.20

Notes:
The figures in the table are the percentage of test statistics
with absolute value greater than 2.576. One standard error bound is 1.12%.

AR1: $x_t = \rho\, x_{t-1} + u_t$

MA1: $x_t = \theta\, u_{t-1} + u_t$

Nonlinear MA: $x_t = u_t + .8u_{t-1}u_{t-2}$

ARCH: $x_t = [1+\phi x_{t-1}^2]\, u_t$

Threshold AR: $x_t = -.5\, x_{t-1} + u_t$, if $x_{t-1} \leq .5$

                 $= .4\, x_{t-1} + u_t$, if $x_{t-1} > .5$

Tent: $x_t = 2\, x_{t-1}$,   if $x_{t-1} \leq .5$

                $= 2 - 2\, x_{t-1},$ if $x_{t-1} > .5$

ARCH-M: $x_t = \delta h_t^{\frac{1}{2}} + u_t$, $V[u_t] = h_t = 1+\phi u_{t-1}^2$

Table 4.9
Third Order Moments of Filtered Data

Lags i	j	BP	CD	DM	JY	SF
1	1	-0.124	-0.132	-0.086	-0.060	-0.103
		(0.105)	(0.150)	(0.081)	(0.073)	(0.110)
2	1	0.008	-0.054	-0.008	0.024	0.021
		(0.050)	(0.065)	(0.053)	(0.035)	(0.048)
2	2	-0.109	-0.030	0.008	0.004	0.009
		(0.104)	(0.094)	(0.176)	(0.074)	(0.101)
3	1	-0.003	-0.112	0.048	-0.011	-0.016
		(0.042)	(0.046)	(0.052)	(0.033)	(0.052)
3	2	-0.012	0.006	-0.030	-0.013	-0.015
		(0.042)	(0.055)	(0.052)	(0.032)	(0.047)
3	3	-0.001	0.176	-0.014	0.031	-0.069
		(0.074)	(0.114)	(0.079)	(0.075)	(0.103)
4	1	-0.034	-0.104	-0.005	0.032	0.005
		(0.040)	(0.054)	(0.037)	(0.030)	(0.049)
4	2	0.040	0.017	0.067	-0.009	-0.055
		(0.045)	(0.041)	(0.061)	(0.041)	(0.057)
4	3	0.068	0.078	0.032	0.045	-0.044
		(0.031)	(0.079)	(0.031)	(0.032)	(0.038)
4	4	-0.026	0.171	-0.095	0.094	-0.069
		(0.067)	(0.109)	(0.106)	(0.092)	(0.091)
5	1	-0.019	-0.076	0.044	0.074	0.054
		(0.047)	(0.051)	(0.049)	(0.036)	(0.049)
5	2	-0.019	-0.020	-0.038	-0.065	-0.035
		(0.047)	(0.032)	(0.067)	(0.034)	(0.045)
5	3	0.009	-0.037	0.015	-0.019	-0.031
		(0.037)	(0.040)	(0.054)	(0.038)	(0.051)
5	4	-0.069	-0.025	0.048	0.036	-0.021
		(0.035)	(0.052)	(0.039)	(0.038)	(0.044)
5	5	-0.026	0.020	-0.014	0.016	0.080
		(0.093)	(0.068)	(0.085)	(0.073)	(0.119)

Standard errors in parentheses.

Table 4.10
Tests of Nonlinearity: Standardized Residuals
GARCH(1,1) Normal

m	ϵ/σ	BP	CD	DM	JY	SF
BDS Tests						
2	1.00	2.94*	2.11*	-1.18	-1.03	-0.28
3	1.00	3.93*	2.03*	-0.85	-1.11	0.17
4	1.00	4.47*	1.96*	-0.18	-0.65	0.46
5	1.00	5.19*	1.86*	0.67	-0.32	0.40
6	1.00	6.03*	1.93*	1.53*	0.28	0.40
7	1.00	7.17*	1.96*	2.03*	0.70	0.15
8	1.00	8.46*	1.95*	2.60*	1.25	0.02
9	1.00	10.26*	1.75*	3.13*	1.85*	-0.09
10	1.00	12.42*	1.55	3.79*	2.38*	-0.03
Runs test		0.74	-0.86	-1.10	0.46	-1.14
$N(0,1)$		(0.2297)	(0.1949)	(0.1357)	(0.3228)	(0.1271)
$Q_x(50)$		58.25	54.30	56.64	51.56	50.05
		(0.0736)	(0.0526)	(0.0263)	(0.0273)	(0.0913)
$Q_{xx}(50)$		41.86	40.78	75.94*	38.97	49.13
		(0.4771)	(0.5245)	(0.0010)	(0.6047)	(0.2091)
Tsay test for nonlinearity:						
M=2		0.90	0.24	0.46	2.99	0.55
F(3,2504)		(0.4424)	(0.8684)	(0.7142)	(0.0295)	(0.6524)
M=4		0.79	1.67	0.45	1.34	0.90
F(10,2495)		(0.6386)	(0.0820)	(0.9218)	(0.2029)	(0.5323)
M=6		0.76	1.23	0.48	1.04	0.84
F(21,2482)		(0.7719)	(0.2140)	(0.9774)	(0.4095)	(0.6719)
M=8		0.85	0.83	0.64	0.83	0.72
F(36,2465)		(0.7220)	(0.7529)	(0.9528)	(0.7678)	(0.8915)
M=10			0.94	0.81	0.73	0.78.92
F(55,2444)		(0.6011)	(0.8402)	(0.9320)	(0.8804)	(0.6425)
Skewness		-0.13	-0.06	0.002	-0.40	0.18
Kurtosis		9.91	4.79	6.68	13.23	5.92
Goodness						
of fit		357.73*	97.37*	75.71*	355.29*	138.96*
$\chi^2(50)$		(0.0000)	(0.0001)	(0.0109)	(0.0000)	(0.0000)

* Significant at the 1.0 percent level.

Table 4.11
Tests of Nonlinearity: Standardized Residuals
GARCH(1,1) Student-t

m	ϵ/σ	BP	CD	DM	JY	SF
BDS Tests						
2	1.00	1.79	2.00*	-0.69	1.77	0.26
3	1.00	1.66*	1.86*	-0.43	2.19*	0.98
4	1.00	1.45*	1.70*	0.13	2.59*	1.28
5	1.00	1.03	1.51*	0.61	2.66*	1.18
6	1.00	0.74	1.54*	1.21	2.88*	0.95
7	1.00	0.65	1.50*	1.49*	2.83*	0.56
8	1.00	0.37	1.44*	1.85*	2.88*	0.29
9	1.00	0.23	1.24	2.22*	2.92*	0.05
10	1.00	0.17	1.04	2.65*	2.92*	-0.03
Runs test		1.86	-1.02	-2.14	-2.57*	-1.54
N(0,1)		(0.0314)	(0.1539)	(0.0162)	(0.0051)	(0.0618)
$Q_x(50)$		47.50	52.00	60.52	39.21	47.73
		(0.3320)	(0.0757)	(0.0115)	(0.2476)	(0.1337)
$Q_{xx}(50)$		0.76	38.75	43.11	389.07*	55.93
		(1.0000)	(0.6144)	(0.4236)	(0.0000)	(0.0736)
Tsay test for nonlinearity:						
M=2		4.52*	0.24	0.84	24.79*	0.53
F(3,2504)		(0.0039)	(0.8684)	(0.4743)	(0.0000)	(0.6659)
M=4		0.96	1.62	0.59	2.25	1.16
F(10,2495)		(0.4765)	(0.9477)	(0.8234)	(0.0130)	(0.3133)
M=6		0.55	1.21	0.41	1.94*	0.88
F(21,2482)		(0.9505)	(0.2308)	(0.9916)	(0.0064)	(0.6188)
M=8		0.62	0.82	0.59	1.36	0.70
F(36,2465)		(0.9632)	(0.7678)	(0.9754)	(0.0753)	(0.9100)
M=10		0.59	0.80	0.65	1.11	0.92
F(55,2444)		(0.9930)	(0.8544)	(0.9786)	(0.2704)	(0.6425)
Skewness		5.14	-0.38	-0.38	-2.11	0.12
Kurtosis		314.67	4.90	11.97	43.25	6.80
Goodness						
of fit		69.08	57.35	70.67	56.90	53.59
$\chi^2(50)$		(0.0381)	(0.2213)	(0.0287)	(0.2337)	(0.3383)

* Significant at the 1.0 percent level.

Table 4.12
Tests of Nonlinearity: Standardized Residuals
GARCH(1,1) Generalized Error Distribution

m	ϵ/σ	BP	CD	DM	JY	SF
BDS Tests						
2	1.00	2.32*	2.10*	-1.04	1.23	0.00
3	1.00	2.76*	1.93*	-0.86	1.44	0.58
4	1.00	2.83*	1.73*	-0.24	1.84*	0.82
5	1.00	2.77*	1.54*	0.27	1.92*	0.69
6	1.00	2.87*	1.58*	0.91	2.22*	0.44
7	1.00	3.21*	1.57*	1.24	2.21*	0.06
8	1.00	3.46*	1.56*	1.66*	2.33*	-0.16
9	1.00	3.93*	1.40	2.06*	2.42*	-0.36
10	1.00	4.43*	1.18	2.52*	2.48*	-0.41
Runs test		1.78	-1.26	-1.98	-2.18	-1.94
N(0,1)		(0.0375)	(0.1038)	(0.0239)	(0.0146)	(0.0262)
$Q_x(50)$		69.68*	53.32	61.65*	51.23	51.98
		(0.0081)	(0.0630)	(0.0090)	(0.0292)	(0.0649)
$Q_{xx}(50)$		13.14	39.84	59.05	84.37*	50.19
		(1.0000)	(0.5662)	(0.0422)	(0.0001)	(0.1806)
Tsay test for nonlinearity:						
M=2		0.80	0.22	0.56	7.52*	0.54
F(3,2504)		(0.4066)	(0.8818)	(0.6457)	(0.0001)	(0.6592)
M=4		0.99	1.60	0.50	1.80	1.11
F(10,2495)		(0.4497)	(0.1004)	(0.8910)	(0.0556)	(0.3503)
M=6		0.72	1.20	0.43	1.39	0.88
F(21,2482)		(0.8168)	(0.2396)	(0.9886)	(0.1106)	(0.6188)
M=8		0.85	0.81	0.61	1.01	0.72
F(36,2465)		(0.7220)	(0.7823)	(0.9677)	(0.4527)	(0.8915)
M=10		0.84	0.79	0.68	0.88	0.92
F(55,2444)		(0.7933)	(0.8678)	(0.9656)	(0.7217)	(0.6425)
Skewness		1.44	-0.06	-0.18	-1.31	0.17
Kurtosis		36.98	4.86	8.94	30.04	6.35
Goodness						
of fit		73.11	53.57	64.05	73.36	55.34
$\chi^2(50)$		(0.0182)	(0.3390)	(0.0874)	(0.0173)	(0.2802)

* Significant at the 1.0 percent level.

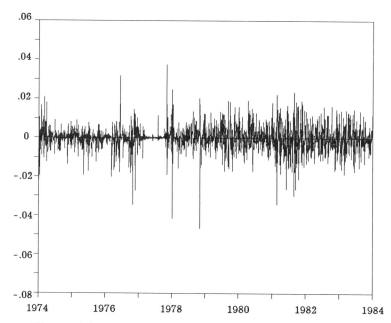

Figure 4.1 Rate of Change of $/BP Exchange Rate

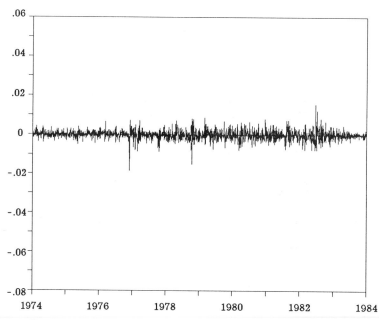

Figure 4.2 Rate of Change of $/CD Exchange Rate

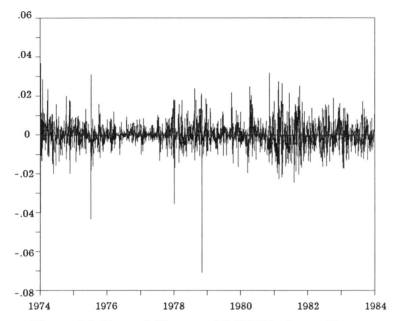

Figure 4.3 Rate of Change of $/DM Exchange Rate

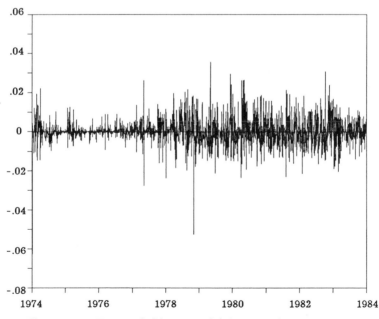

Figure 4.4 Rate of Change of $/JY Exchange Rate

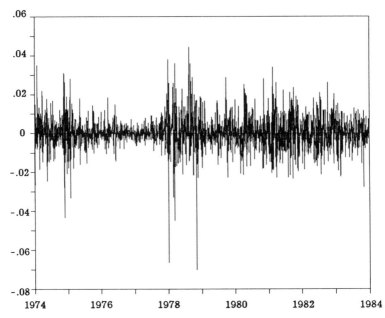

Figure 4.5 Rate of Change of $/SF Exchange Rate

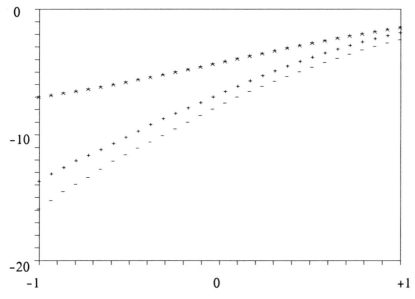

Figure 4.6 GP Plot: $/BP Exchange Rate

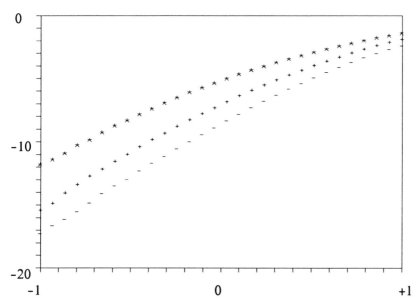

Figure 4.7 GP Plot: $/CD Exchange Rate

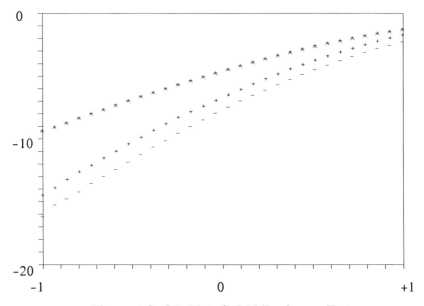

Figure 4.8 GP Plot: $/DM Exchange Rate

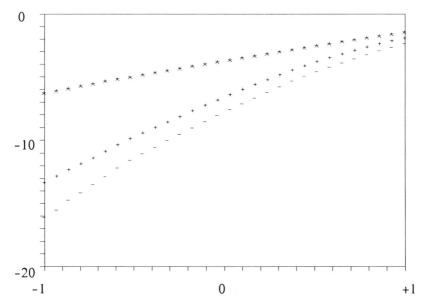

Figure 4.9 GP Plot: $/JY Exchange Rate

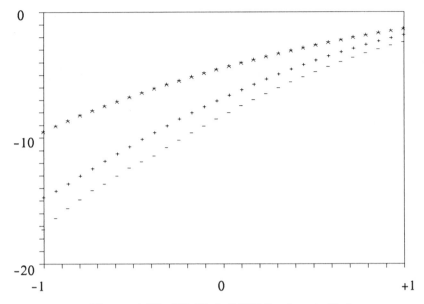

Figure 4.10 GP Plot: $/SF Exchange Rate

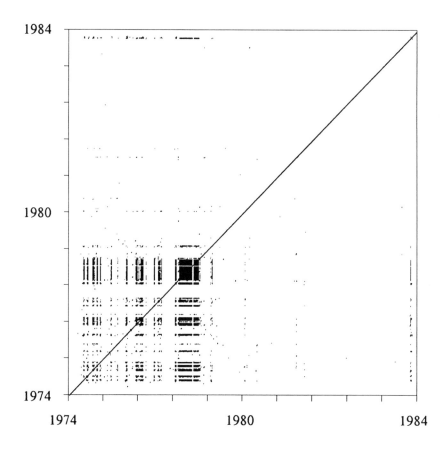

Figure 4.11   Recurrence Plot: $/BP Exchange Rate

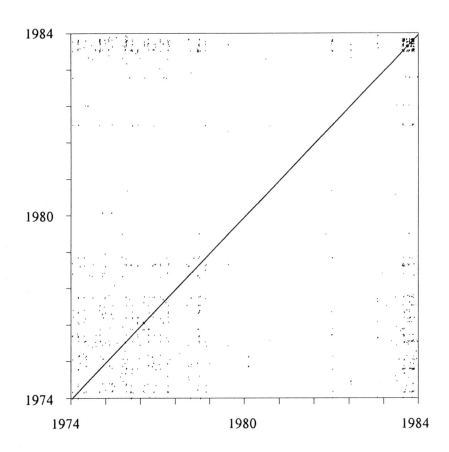

Figure 4.12 Recurrence Plot: $/CD Exchange Rate

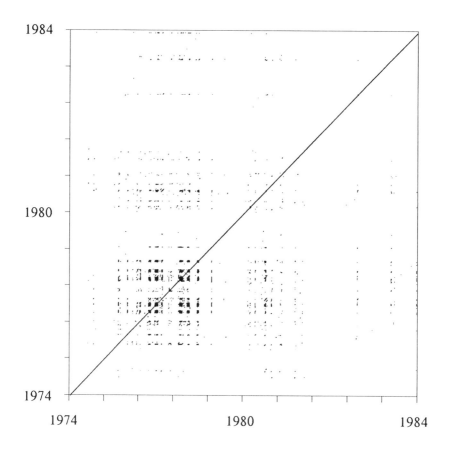

Figure 4.13   Recurrence Plot: $/DM Exchange Rate

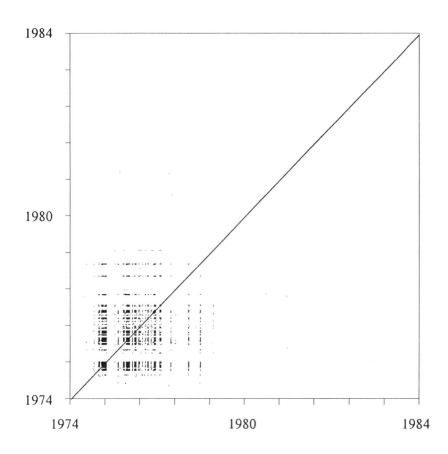

Figure 4.14 Recurrence Plot: $/JY Exchange Rate

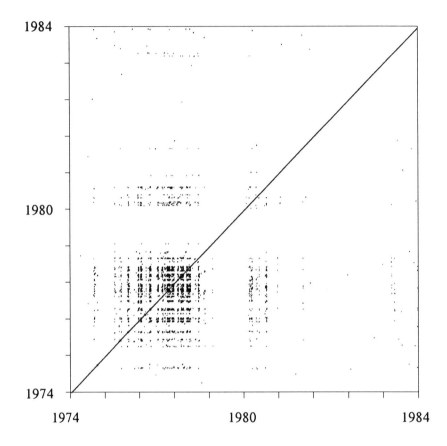

Figure 4.15 Recurrence Plot: $/SF Exchange Rate

Chapter 5

Summary, Relation to Other Work, and Future Horizons

This chapter will proceed through a list of unfinished business, relate our work to that of others, and pick up a basic summary of what we have done along the way.

5.1 Unfinished Business on Testing for Complex Dynamics

5.1.1 Null Class of Models Covered by the BDS Test

The work on the BDS test is incomplete because no theory was given for the choice of parameters m and ϵ. There are several standard ways to deal with this problem. A first approach is to do Monte Carlo work on size and power for a range of choices of m and ϵ for a range of distributions and alternatives. This we have done. Based on this work, we recommend a choice of ϵ between one-half and three halves of the standard deviation of the data, and a choice of m between 2 and

---

We thank Simon Potter for his helpful comments.

5 for small data sets (200 to 500 observations), and up to 10 for large data sets (at least 2,000 observations). Our simulations in Chapter 2 show that, for a range of m and ϵ values, the asymptotic distribution can approximate the finite sample distribution reasonably well if there are 500 or more observations, although we highly recommend doing some bootstrap experiments in actual applications, as we have done in Chapters 3 and 4, just to be on the safe side.

A second approach is to commit oneself to the null class of models, which are driven by IID innovations $\{e_t\}$ as in (5.1.1) below, and choose m and ϵ to maximize power against this class.

$$y_t = G(I_t, e_t, \gamma, t). \tag{5.1.1}$$

Here γ is a vector of parameters that is estimated at least $T^{\frac{1}{2}}$-consistently, $\{e_t\}$ is IID with zero mean and finite variance, G is invertible in e_t, the information set I_t can include past y's but not past e's, and e_t is independent of I_t for each t. In fact, we have explicitly treated the null class,

$$y_t = F(I_t, \alpha, t) + G(I_t, \beta, t) e_t. \tag{5.1.2}$$

Here α and β are vectors of parameters that can be estimated at least $T^{\frac{1}{2}}$-consistently. We place a "t" argument in F and G of (5.1.2) to remind the reader that deterministic trends can be included in these models. At the risk of being repetitive, we recall that the null class is tested by fitting a member of the class and using BDS to test the estimated innovations for independence and identical distribution.

Since (5.1.1) and (5.1.2) describe a very large class of models, it is not clear what to set up as the alternative class. This is especially so because null classes (5.1.1) and (5.1.2) include estimable trends. Indeed trends were treated in Section 2.4. Recall that in many natural applications, trends (e.g., polynomial trends) can be estimated with a degree of consistency greater than the $T^{\frac{1}{2}}$-consistency required for the first order asymptotics of the BDS statistic to be the same on the estimated $\{e_t\}$ as on the true $\{e_t\}$. If we reject the null models in (5.1.1) and (5.1.2) by applying BDS on the estimated residuals, it is not obvious what alternative models to consider. This brings us to:

Question 1. Can we characterize the economically and financially interesting class of models that are not in classes (5.1.1) and (5.1.2) above? If the BDS methods cannot be extended to test the innovations of these extra models, can we choose the parameters m and ϵ to maximize power against the economically and financially most interesting departures in this class of "extra" interesting models?

Of course we do not want to imply that the methods propounded in this book are the best way to do specification testing in dynamic modeling. While it would be a very useful task to compare and contrast the strengths and weaknesses of our method with methods surveyed by Gallant and White 1988, Pagan and Hall 1983, and White 1987, that daunting task is beyond the scope of this book. Indeed the whole area of specification testing is treacherous and difficult as a reading of Leamer 1987 and his references will attest. We recommend letting the test methodology propounded here play a role in nonlinear econometrics much like the role of the Durbin-Watson statistic and the Q statistic (cf. Box and Jenkins 1976, p. 291) in linear econometrics.

5.1.2 Local Alternatives and Power of BDS against Them

A third approach in statistical theory of test design is to investigate the power of a statistical test against a sequence of alternatives converging at the rate $T^{-\frac{1}{2}}$ to the null. One then looks for directions in alternative space where power is largest. The practical strategy is this. If the test statistic rejects the null, one then look in this direction first for the cause of the rejection. While Baek and Brock 1988b have made some progress on this question, much more remains to be done. A study of BDS along the lines of that done by Terasvirta 1990 for other linearity tests would be useful.

5.1.3 Comparison of BDS with Alternative Specification Tests

There has been some recent work besides ours on comparing BDS with other specification tests and tests for nonlinearity. A most interesting recent piece is that by Lee, White, and Granger 1989, hereafter LWG. LWG put forth a test for linearity in mean using neural network methods. We say that a stationary scalar valued stochastic process, $\{y_t\}$, is *linear in mean*, with respect to the vector information set I_t, if there is a vector of scalars, α, such that

$$\text{Prob}\{ E[y_t|I_t] = I_t \cdot \alpha \} = 1, \tag{5.1.3}$$

where "·" denotes scalar product. A typical application of this concept will put the information set $I_t = \{y_{t-1},...,y_{t-L}\}$ for some finite lag L.

LWG test for linearity in mean by running a linear regression of y_t on I_t to estimate α and then testing the orthogonality conditions of the residuals, $E[e_t|I_t]=0$, where e_t are the regression residuals. This implies, for any $h(\cdot)$, $E[h(I_t)e_t]=0$. This orthogonality condition is tested by using the estimated residuals $\hat{e}_t$ and an $h(\cdot)$ built up from neural network entities. The idea is that when linearity in mean is rejected in favor of the alternative, suggestions are made for construction of a nonlinear predictor on the residuals. The power of the neural network test is compared by LWG to tests by Kennan, Tsay, White (based on the information matrix), McLeod and Li (based on the autocorrelation function of the squared residuals), Ramsey's RESET, BDS (for m=2), and the bispectral test. The menu of alternatives includes threshold autoregressions, bilinear models, nonlinear autoregressions, etc. None of the alternatives are deterministic chaos. The sample sizes are typically small, between 50 and 200 observations.

On the whole, it is fair to say that, while BDS turns in a credible performance on the LWG menu of alternatives, the power is less than their neural network test. We should point out the following: (a) the LWG menu of alternatives does not include ARCH-GARCH models, and we suspect that their neural network test will have lower power against ARCH-GARCH models; (b) the power of BDS increases substantially when there are more than 500 observations, as shown in our simulations in Chapter 2; (c) even with 50 to 200 observations, BDS performs fairly well compared to the other tests and beats the McLeod and Li test; and (d) BDS has the advantage that its first order asymptotic distribution is the same for estimated residuals as for the true ones for a useful class of null models. This is not necessarily true of all the tests considered in LWG.

One apparent flaw of BDS is that when it rejects, unlike some of the other tests, it apparently gives no clue to the cause of rejection and no clue to how to construct a nonlinear predictor. This is more apparent than real. Under the strict assumption of stationarity (which is maintained by all nonlinear tests such as BDS and neural network, among others), there is a close connection between predictive potential by near neighbors at lag m and rejection by a BDS test at dimension m. Let us see why. Consider, for example, m=2,

$$C_2(\epsilon) = \Pr\{|x_t - x_s| < \epsilon, \, |x_{t-1} - x_{s-1}| < \epsilon\},$$
$$= C_{2|1}(\epsilon) \, C_1(\epsilon), \qquad\qquad (5.1.4)$$

where $C_{2|1}(\epsilon) = \Pr\{|x_t - x_s| < \epsilon$ given $|x_{t-1} - x_{s-1}| < \epsilon\}$. Under the null hypothesis of independent and identical distribution, the occurence of $|x_{t-1} - x_{s-1}| < \epsilon$ does not help to predict $|x_t - x_s| < \epsilon$, so $C_{2|1}(\epsilon) = C_1(\epsilon)$. Thus, $C_2(\epsilon) = C_1(\epsilon)^2$. So when BDS rejects at m=2, we know that $C_2(\epsilon)$ is statistically different from $C_1(\epsilon)^2$. Suppose $C_2(\epsilon) > C_1(\epsilon)^2$. This says that when x_{s-1} is close to x_{t-1}, chances are higher than average that x_s will be near the actual value x_t for s<t. In general when a BDS test at dimension (m+1) rejects independent and identical distribution, it is suggesting that there is predictive potential for the "forecast" x_s, s<t, of x_t by $(x_{s-1},...,x_{s-m})$ near to $(x_{t-1},...,x_{t-m})$. This is a type of near neighbor forecasting based on m lags. Deterministic chaos is an example of a type of dependence where near neighbors has high short-term forecasting potential. But the near neighbor method has potential to forecast in other processes besides chaotic processes.

Indeed, Savit and Green 1989 show how one can use generalizations of BDS-based tests to help discover at which lag there is direct dependence upon the past. A revised version of Brock and Baek 1987 shows how one can use a related idea to test when lagged values of one series incrementally help predict nonlinearly another series. To summarize the discussion at this point, we repeat that rejection of independent and identical distribution by a BDS test at dimension (m+1) tells the researcher that there is likely to be present some predictive potential using near neighbors with m lags, under the assumption of stationarity. This gives a clue in the search for a nonlinear predictor.

We should emphasis to the reader that the maintained hypothesis of stationarity is critical in the above discussion. Otherwise, a rejection of independent and identical distribution need not imply predictability. For example, nonstationarity can cause BDS (and other nonlinear tests such as the neural network) to reject independent and identical distribution. Let us turn now to comparison of BDS with some specification tests.

Baek and Brock 1988b have done some (very) small-scale Monte Carlo work comparing BDS-based tests with the Durbin-Watson test for autocorrelation and Ramsey's RESET specification test. In general, it is hard to beat the power of the Durbin-Watson test for the linear alternatives for which it was built. But BDS beats it for a set of nonlinear alternatives. RESET in general does better for the nonlinear alternatives. But the number of replications in the Monte Carlo work of Baek and Brock was too small to reliably estimate tail probabilities. More work needs to be done.

The recent burst of activity in nonparametric estimation techniques has led to development of new specification tests and new tests for independence. This raises the question of the value of BDS versus these other tests. Jeong 1990 and Robinson 1990 are two papers that are relevant here.

Suppose one wishes to test the null hypothesis, H_o, that the conditional mean $E[Y|I=x]=g(x)$ is in a given class of functions $M=\{m(x,\beta), \beta \text{ in } B\}$, against the alternative, H_1, that g is not in M. Jeong locates sufficient regularity conditions on g and M such that one can implement a test of H_o against H_1 by the following procedure. First, estimate β by a $T^{\frac{1}{2}}$-consistent method under the null, where T denotes sample length. Second, find an estimator for g such that if the alternative is true, the estimator converges to g as T converges to infinity.

Third, find a test statistic based upon $T^{\frac{1}{2}}$ times the difference of the average value of the squared forecast errors from the first estimator of g and the second estimator of g. This turns out not to work, but Jeong shows that a sample splitting technique and choosing the second estimator to be a nonparametric kernel estimator yield a nondegenerate asymptotically normal distribution under the null hypothesis. Furthermore this procedure yields an asymptotically consistent test against all members of the alternative. To put it another way, if a member of the alternative is true then Jeong's test will reject the null, asymptotically, with probability one.

With this background consider using BDS to test the class of models with parametric conditional mean function, with additive IID errors treated in Appendix D, e.g, (D.1), which we reproduce here for convenience,

$$y_t = f(I_t, \beta) + \sigma\, u_t. \tag{D.1}$$

As we have stressed many times in this book, Appendix D shows that the first order asymptotic null distribution of BDS is the same on the estimated residuals of (D.1) as it is for the true residuals, $\{u_t\}$. However, Dechert 1988 has shown that BDS is not an asymptotically consistent test for independent and identical distribution. To put it another way, he produced examples that are not IID and that BDS does not detect.

But consider using Jeong's test in the following way. Estimate $f(I_t, \beta)$ by a $T^{\frac{1}{2}}$-consistent method under H_o: $E[y|I] = f(I, \beta)$, β in B. Now estimate $E[y|I]$ by a nonparametric kernel estimator and implement Jeong's test. Since Jeong's regularity conditions necessary to get asymptotic consistency of his test are quite modest, therefore, it seems that Jeong's procedure would be automatically superior to using BDS. Furthermore Jeong does not require that $\{u\}$ be IID; he only requires the usual orthogonality condition, $E[I|u] = 0$.

There are three responses that we make to this. First, we know little about the power and size performance for tests like Jeong's even though they are asymptotically consistent. We know quite a lot about the size and performance of the BDS test because of the extensive Monte Carlo work reported in this book as well as in the papers of Lee, White, and Granger 1989 and Liu 1990.

Second, the lack of asymptotic consistency of BDS may be a theoretical result of little relevance to practice. Look at Figures 2.1 through 2.7. These show plots of $D = C_2 - C_1^2$ against ϵ for seven alternatives. Notice that except for the tent, $D > 0$ for all practical purposes. This means that BDS is asymptotically consistent against all alternatives for which D is nonzero for that value of ϵ, which is true almost all the time. The tent map presents little problem for BDS since D is zero for only one point in the relevant domain of ϵ.

Third, in order to implement a test based upon nonparametric regression under the alternative, one must commit to the form of I, the conditioning set. A mistake in the choice of I may lead to false acceptance of H_o that could be guarded against by using BDS as a portmanteau goodness-of-fit test on the estimated $\{u_t\}$. These three reasons lead us to believe that a test like BDS is a useful complement to tests like that of Jeong. Let us turn now to Robinson's 1990 test.

Robinson tests independence of X_t and X_{t-1} for a real valued strictly stationary process $\{X_t\}$ by using the Kullback-Liebler entropy-based measure of the difference between the joint distribution and the product of the two marginals. In order to get an asymptotically normal null distribution, Robinson introduces a sample weighting scheme (essentially a form of sample splitting), uses kernel estimators for the joint distribution and the marginals, and obtains an asymptotically consistent test. Robinson's test is also a one-sided test because the Kullback-Liebler measure is always positive unless the joint equals the product of the marginals. He points out that his test can be generalized to test independence of X_t, $X_{t-1},...,X_{t-k}$ for any integer k>0.

This suggests that Robinson's test would be a natural one to use to test the adequacy of model (D.1). All one should have to do is compute Robinson's test statistic for independence for various values of k just like we have done in this book using BDS. Several issues are raised. First, we know little about the size and power performance of independence tests based on the Kullback-Liebler measure. Monte

Carlo work is needed. Second, kernel estimators must be computed. This may require a great deal of computing power especially when k is large, but improvements in technology should get around this problem. Third, in practice, only estimated residuals are available to put to Robinson's test. We do not know whether the asymptotic null distribution of his test is changed by the use of estimated residuals. Fourth, as k grows, kernel density estimation of the joint distribution will face the curse of dimensionality that drove Wahba 1990 and others to more parametrically parsimonious methods.

For these reasons we offer BDS as a portmanteau goodness-of-fit test that is easy to compute for various values of m and ϵ to complement tests such as Jeong's and Robinson's. In summary, the work done in this book and the work of others suggest that BDS is a useful nonparametric test for independence that has good power against a wide range of other dependent alternatives besides having excellent power against chaos. It should be used as a general diagnostic test when sample sizes of 250 or more are available.

5.2 Instability Measures

We pointed out that instability is necessary but not sufficient for the presence of that rather special nonlinearity known as deterministic chaos. One needs the largest Lyapunov exponent to be positive for a deterministic chaos. This suggests testing for deterministic chaos by estimating the largest Lyapunov exponent of a time series.

Two major competing algorithms have been put forth by natural scientists to do this. The first one is by Eckmann, Kamphorst, and Ruelle 1987, and was applied to stock returns by Eckmann, Kamphorst, Ruelle, and Scheinkman in Anderson, Arrow, and Pines

1988. The second one is attributed to Wolf, Swift, Swinney, and Vastano 1985. Brock and Dechert 1988b derived theoretical sufficient conditions on the observer function $h(\cdot)$ and the underlying state dynamics $F(\cdot)$ for the Wolf, Swift, Swinney, and Vastano 1985 algorithm to converge to the largest Lyapunov exponent of $F(\cdot)$ when $x_{t+1}=F(x_t)$ must be observed through the observer function $a_t=h(x_t)$. Barnett and Chen 1988, and an early version of Brock and Sayers 1988 estimated the largest Lyapunov exponent for some macroeconomic data sets.

None of these studies, including those in the natural sciences, reported statistically rigorous standard errors for these estimates. This is not important for an experimental scientist, who can simply run his experiment long enough to drive the standard error as small as he wishes provided he can afford it. But standard errors are critical in data limited situations, especially when infected by nonstationarity, like those faced in economics. Furthermore, an early version of Brock and Sayers (reported in Brock 1986) indicated that, for short data sets, Lyapunov exponent estimation algorithms may generate spuriously positive estimates from IID processes and may have a hard time distinguishing linear stochastic processes from deterministic chaos. The issues revolve around the lack of standard errors for these estimates.

It also appeared theoretically from the work of Brock and Dechert 1988 that it may require a lot of regularity on the observer function $h(\cdot)$ and the underlying dynamics $F(\cdot)$ to be able to estimate the largest Lyapunov exponent from experimental and field data. In the case of experimental data or field data, one must observe the underlying dynamics through an observer apparatus. This is especially so for economic data where one observes the economy only indirectly through aggregative series collected by statisticians. Even returns on a stock is an aggregate in the sense that it represents the price of a claim on the aggregate of activities undertaken by a firm. This brings us to:

Question 2. How does one reliably infer instability in a short data set?

A plausible approach to this question would be to commit oneself to a particular null process, generate B replications, compute an estimate of the Lyapunov exponent for each replication, and compute the standard error of the B Lyapunov exponent estimates. While this procedure is in the spirit of Efron's 1982 bootstrapping, it raises statistical issues because bootstrapping theory is not worked out well for dependent processes. Particularly interesting would be an investigation along the above lines of whether Lyapunov exponent estimation algorithms can reliably distinguish between low-dimensional deterministic chaos and stochastic processes traditionally fitted by econometricians on sample lengths typical of those available in economics and finance over periods where stationarity is plausible. Brock and Baek 1987 develop some inference theory for Lyapunov-like measures. McCaffrey, Ellner, Gallant, and Nychka 1990 obtain a consistent estimator from time series data for the largest Lyapunov exponent. They do this by using nonparametric regression to obtain consistent estimators for the partial derivatives of the underlying law of motion.

5.3 Natural Nulls for Natural Scientists versus Natural Nulls for Economists

At least one of us has run into the following pair of divergent philosophies while on lecture tours. On the one hand, when talking to economists, especially in the United States, we have found that the burden of proof is on the scientist who is trying to establish evidence of low-dimensional determinstic chaos in the economic time series under scrutiny. Therefore, if one gets low dimension estimates, for example, one must rule out all plausible alternative explanations for the low dimension estimate before it will be convincingly accepted as evidence of low-dimensional deterministic chaos. This caveat especially holds for economics because near unit root processes can generate low dimension estimates and many economic time series are characterized as near unit root processes (Nelson and Plosser 1982). Ramsey, Sayers, and Rothman 1988 have criticized claims to have found low-dimensional deterministic chaos in economics.

On the other hand, when talking to some groups of natural scientists (and some economists, especially in parts of Europe), we have found that the burden of proof is on a scientist to demonstrate that the time series under scrutiny is *not* low-dimensional deterministic chaos. For example, see Barnett and Hinich 1990. While we believe that the work reported in this book has convincingly argued that evidence under any kind of standard is weak in economics and finance for the presence of low-dimensional deterministic chaos, the two views of burden of proof outlined above suggest an interesting class of null and alternative hypotheses.

Let us first exposit a simple example of what we have in mind. Suppose we observe a time series $\{x_t\}$. Let the null for economics be

$$A(L)x_t = e_t, \tag{5.3.1}$$

where $A(L)$ is a polynomial in the lag operator L, and e_t is IID, with mean zero and finite variance σ. We have in mind a difficult-to-distinguish alternative

$$A(L)x_t = c_t, \tag{5.3.2}$$

where c_t is a low-dimensional chaos that has "no autocorrelation," "mean zero," and "variance σ."

Obviously, linear time series methods will not be able to distinguish between (5.3.1) and (5.3.2). But the innovations c_t can be short-term forecastable by nonlinear methods such as nearest neighbors or more elaborate nonlinear methods such as Farmer and Sidorowich 1987 or Lapedes and Farber 1987. In contrast the innovations e_t are unforecastable.

The methods discussed in this book are capable (within limits) of distinguishing between (5.3.1) and (5.3.2) by prewhitening x_t and testing for nonlinearity in the estimated innovations. The BDS test should detect nonlinearity in (5.3.2) but not in (5.3.1), provided the chaos is "regular" enough, i.e., has bounded derivatives, or has a low enough dimension. No test would be able to detect a low-dimensional chaos which has large derivatives. An example of such a low-dimensional, but hard to detect, chaos would be the tenth iterate of the tent map. Here the absolute value of the derivative is very large at the points where the derivative exists. The size of the derivative is a measure of irregularity. No test procedure can be expected to detect a chaos if it is irregular enough, even though its dimension may be low.

In terms of forecastability of chaotic processes, the results are mixed. Chapter 3 has shown that prewhitened 7 dimensional Mackey and Glass 1977 data can be short-term forecasted to some extent using nonlinear techniques such as nearest neighbors. However, we have conducted experiments on tent map data where we take every q-th iterate of the tent map and have failed to detect that this data is nonrandom by the BDS test for q large enough, say 10. Note that, technically speaking, this data has a one-dimensional deterministic explanation. We suspect that, given a machine of finite resolution, one can always take the iteration number q large enough so that q-th iterate tent data look random to any test implemented on that machine. This occurs because the error caused by the finite resolution machine in truncating each number is magnified at an exponential rate in q.

In view of this fundamental difficulty of detecting highly irregular low-dimensional chaoses or detecting medium to high-dimensional less irregular chaoses, what does one do? Indeed, even though it is intuitively obvious that the q-th iterate of the tent map is a highly "irregular" map, how does one practically quantify "irregularity" for finite resolution computing machines, when these machines are the only means we have to test a time series for randomness? It seems at least one ingredient of a useful measure of irregularity is how much the output, f(x), of the law of motion changes when the input, x, changes. In the case of most pseudo random number generators, $f(\cdot)$ is a discontinuous function, which is not differentiable at many points, and has large absolute values of derivatives wherever it is differentiable. Part of the attention chaos theory has received is because functions with highly bounded derivatives can generate complex behavior. We have nothing to offer on this hard conceptual problem.

We take the position in this book that, if a chaos is undetectable by a machine of finite resolution in a data set of the lengths that we can expect to obtain in economics where we can reasonably postulate stationarity, then that chaos is operationally random. Obviously it may be of little practical importance to be told that a time series of length 800 is from a 5,000-dimensional chaos or is from a stochastic process. We are saying that this may be interesting philosophically but not interesting from the empirical perspective taken in this book. We come to:

Question 3. How does one distinguish between (5.3.1) and (5.3.2) when the filter A(L) generates highly persistent series like those found in economics but the innovations are IID or a low-dimensional, reasonably "regular" chaos?

Conceptually one would measure the Grassberger and Procaccia 1983a,b correlation dimension at various scales and look for a knee in the plot. If the dimension of the knee kept increasing as the embedding dimension increases for the small scales then we would know that the innovations are a deterministic chaos. It is important to realize that high persistence, i.e., near unit roots, in A(L) creates a low measured dimension when one uses the Grassberger and Procaccia 1983a,b method. This problem was stressed by Brock 1986 and Brock and Sayers 1988 for economics. For meteorology a similar problem is discussed by Pierrehumbert 1989. Pierrehumbert's work stresses the

possible role of weather dynamics in taking medium- to high-
dimensional chaotic and transforming it into time series records that
look like low-dimensional chaos to dimension algorithms. This raises
a question of inference much like ours in economics. Theiler 1990a,
1990b raises related issues in the use of dimension estimates to infer
existence of chaos in physics.

While the methods propounded in this book stress estimation
of the structure that the scientist believes is generating the data under
scrutiny and then examine the standardized residuals (forecast errors)
for evidence of extra structure by use of the BDS test, we know that
the BDS test is triggered by nonforecastable nonstationarity as well as
extra forecastable nonlinear structure. This motivates:

Question 4. When BDS or some other general test for nonrandomness
that has power against nonforecastable nonstationarity rejects
randomness, how does one tell if this rejection is caused by
nonforecastable nonstationarity or extra structure that is potentially
forecastable, at least in the short term?

One possible line of attack that might be useful is to short term
forecast the series of length T under scrutiny by some nonlinear
method such as nearest neighbors, e.g., Farmer and Sidorowich 1987,
etc. Let $M(T,\{x_t\})$ be a measure, such as R^2, of the quality of the
forecast, where $\{x_t\}$ denotes the actual series being forecasted. Now
create B IID series of length T that have the same unconditional
moments as $\{x_t\}$ in the manner of Efron 1982. Forecast each of these
by the same nonlinear method and calculate the corresponding value
of M. Use the resulting B values of M to construct an empirical

histogram. Tick off a 5% rejection region of the null of independent and identical distribution from this histogram. Reject the null at the 5% level if the actual data $\{x_t\}$ yields a value of $M(T,\{x_t\})$ in this 5% rejection region.

5.4 Recent Work on Complex Dynamics Not Covered in Previous Chapters

There has been much recent work on complex dynamics in economics. We will use the term "complex" to refer to the case when the long-run behavior of the dynamics is more complicated that a rest point, limit cycle, or limit torus. A sample of some of the latest is in Barnett, Geweke, and Shell 1989. Work by Benhabib and Rustichini 1989 gets rich dynamics via time delays in construction of capital goods.

As the work of Mosekilde, Larson, and Sterman 1989 and Sterman 1989 points out, inventory dynamics are an important source of instability in experimental situations. Inventories look like a promising channel by which instability could enter actual economic dynamics. For example, imagine inventories being ordered with a lag at each stage of a chain of production structure. It seems plausible that a chain of lags could generate unstable dynamics through the chain of production. Furthermore, in aggregate data, this instability could get "washed out" by aggregating over different goods. Detection of such complex dynamics may require examination of a cross-section of disaggregated time series. Indeed we feel that analysis of disaggregated data is the way to go in complex systems research. Such analysis may give us an idea how the economy creates dynamics in general. Let us turn now to a closely related issue.

It is commonly acknowledged in aggregative economics that most economic time series, such as real GNP, unemployment, etc., exhibit what is called "Granger's typical spectral shape" (Sargent 1987a, p. 279). The spectrum is quite sharply downward sloping near the origin with most of the power in the low frequency—high periodicity bands. To put it another way, most economic time series are highly persistent. While asset returns like stock returns will not display much persistence, squared asset returns typically do display a lot of persistence. Processes that display downward sloping spectra are sometimes called "1/f" noises in natural science. This raises the following:

Question 5. What economic mechanisms are capable of converting random independent outside noise impacting on individual economic units into economic aggregates that display characteristics of 1/f noise?

A standard line of attack on this problem is recursive dynamic general equilibrium modeling (e.g., King, Plosser, and Rebelo 1988). But this relies on outside technological shocks that seem too large. Hall 1989 has recently been promoting temporal agglomeration theory as a device to turn small shocks into the strongly persistent processes seen in economic aggregates. Durlauf 1990a has put forth a microeconomic general equilibrium model that is stimulated by work on Ising models in physics. Firms in his model are located on a lattice. They are more likely to produce when "near neighbors" are successfully producing. Durlauf shows that, in equilibrium, this model generates nonergodic aggregative output time series provided the lattice is at least two-dimensional. In the case where it is two-dimensional, nonergodicity emerges if a "spillover parameter" is large enough. In the case of a one-dimensional lattice the aggregative time series of output are ergodic. The message is that initial conditions matter for long-run behavior of the aggregates provided the dimensionality of linkages or the strength of linkages is large enough. Also, the degree of persistence in the resulting time series is consistent with the degree of persistence documented by Nelson and Plosser 1982. Hence Durlauf's model could be thought of as at least a partial resolution of Question 5.

The idea of localized externalities of the Durlauf type either through consumption or production may be testable by the BDS statistic in the following way. Test the aggregative time series emerging from a Durlauf-type model calibrated to data in the manner of the Real Business Cycle school (cf. King, Plosser, and Rebelo 1988 and their references—especially to Kydland and Prescott) for linearity in the sense of Priestley 1981 as we outline in Section 5.6 below. The presence of agglomerative externalities in the sense of Hall 1989 and Durlauf 1990a should be revealed by extra nonlinear predictive potential above and beyond the best linear predictor. A natural way to test for this extra predictability is outlined in Section 5.6 below but that is surely not the most powerful test. The implementation of this idea must be deferred to future research. Let us turn now to a discussion of a closely related issue in stock returns.

There are differences in persistence in returns across firms sizes that cry out for explanation. A very preliminary attack on this persistence and firm size question is in Brock and LeBaron 1990, where the role of liquidity constraints in creating persistence was stressed. While that paper was not able to show creation of an amount of persistence from external IID shocks that appear in the real data, it did not take into account chains of interdependent firms that exist in the real economy as did Durlauf 1989a. Liquidity constraints propagating their effects through the chain of production and through their impacts on consumers as well as firms may well generate enough persistence to be consistent with real data. Coupling Brock and LeBaron's 1990 model with Hall's 1989 and Durlauf's 1989a seems a promising research route.

5.5 Nonlinear Time Series Work in Macroeconomics

Work on nonlinearity in macroeconomics has become voluminous in recent years. Indeed, even the more narrowly focused topic of chaos in macroeconomics is too large for us to cover in this book. We shall treat here what we think are key issues that are most closely related to the focus we wish to maintain. The issues are several.

First, in aggregative economics, datasets are small and of poor quality. Even datasets of monetary aggregates constructed by principles of aggregation theory such as Barnett's Divisia aggregates (Barnett and Singleton 1987, Barnett and Hinich 1990) require maintained hypotheses of formal aggregation theory to assert the superiority of their quality. Many writers in economics, such as Black 1987, will believe the world is too nonstationary for the maintained hypotheses of, for example, stationary preferences to be credible.

Second, many economic datasets such as stock returns have been studied by so many writers that one can imagine the following scenario happening accidentally. Let a scientist, investigating departures from the random walk hypothesis, notice an "interesting" but totally spurious pattern in stock returns. Imagine that he has subconsciously designed a "test" with maximal "power" against this particular pattern. Without being aware of the data snooping, he has created a "test" where the p-value of the alternative to the random walk null is meaningless.

What we are trying to dramatize here is Leamer's 1987 problem in the particular context of nonlinearity testing of a series like real GNP, industrial production, monetary aggregates, or any macroeconomic series that has been studied to death by perhaps hundreds of researchers.

Lo and MacKinlay 1990 have a precise formulation of this problem for financial asset pricing model testing. This problem is probably much worse for macroeconomics than it is for finance. It can be attenuated by careful investigation of other data coupled with specific theory development as in Potter 1990. Investment in building datasets in macroeconomics comparable to such investment in natural science as urged by Chen 1990b, for example, would help us make progress.

Third, there is the issue of who bears the burden of proof. Some set up the null hypothesis as deterministic chaos such as Chen 1990a, Barnett and Chen 1988, while others set up the null hypothesis as linearity of detrended data such as Brock and Sayers 1988 and Ramsey, Sayers, and Rothman 1988. Ramsey, Sayers, and Rothman 1988 are especially critical of claims to have found evidence of low-dimensional chaos in macroeconomic and financial data. Barnett and Hinich 1990 argue that the data on monetary aggregates are not informative enough to settle this debate.

At this point we feel that the evidence for low-dimensional deterministic chaos in macroeconomic aggregates is weak. We have learned much from the application of nonlinearity tests such as dimension estimation, bispectrum, and BDS. But, if low-dimensional deterministic chaos is truly present in the data, then there should be evidence of a pattern of short-term predictability that is a signature of chaos. Perhaps it would be fruitful to apply forecasting tests more along the lines of Sugihara and May 1990 and Sugihara, Grenfell, and May 1990. Let us explain what we have in mind here.

Sugihara, Grenfell, and May 1990 found evidence that "city-by-city scale measles data exhibits evidence of low-dimensional chaos (as has previously been found for measles in New York City), whereas on a larger country-wide scale the dynamics appears as a noisy 2-year cycle." Their paper reviews a debate between the biotic and climatic schools similar to the one we are having in economics. They dramatically show how aggregation of city-wide measles data to the country-wide level destroyed rather convincing evidence of chaos at the city-wide level. They examined the behavior of p-step-ahead predictability as a function of p. They showed that a measure (the correlation between predicted value and actual value) of p-step-ahead predictability fell off rapidly, then slowly to an asymptote for chaos, but fell off slowly (if at all) at a decreasing rate to an asymptote for linear autoregressions. This distinguishing signature of chaos was also stressed by Sugihara and May 1990.

Two issues for macroeconomics are raised by the Sugihara, Grenfell, and May 1990 research. The first is this: If chaos is generating the data, one should be able to do short-term prediction out of sample. They demonstrate existence of such predictability for measles data. The second issue they raise is that aggregation can easily destroy evidence of chaos. Indeed they discuss emergent linearity due to aggregation. This point is also stressed by Granger 1990.

We have not seen evidence of improved predictability with nonlinear predictors out of sample over best linear predictors for any aggregative macroeconomic time series. Until this is done, the case for low-dimensional chaos in macroeconomic data is not as well established as the case in measles data, for example.

The work of Potter 1990 represents the most recent line of attack that uses nonlinear time series methods applied to macroeconomic data. He shows some predictability improvement using nonlinear models. For example, Potter fitted the following to the logarithmic first difference of U.S. real GNP since World War II:

$$y_t = .75 + .31 y_{t-1} - .17 y_{t-5} + e_{1,t}, \qquad\qquad \text{for } y_{t-2} \geq .0$$

$$y_t = -.75 + .42 y_{t-1} - .86 y_{t-2} + .41 y_{t-5} + e_{2,t}, \qquad \text{for } y_{t-2} < .0, \qquad (5.5.1)$$

where $var(e_{1,t}) = .63$ and $var(e_{2,t}) = 1.35$. Note that Potter allows the autoregressive terms to vary across regimes. He does this to capture different dynamics in expansions versus contractions. The AIC (Akaike Information Criterion) value for Potter is -27.03 in contrast to -2.61 for the best fitting linear autoregressive model. Potter has shown that real business cycle models with asymmetric adjustment costs have a hard time accounting for the amount of asymmetry that seems present in the data. Potter's thesis not only develops a new class of parsimoniously parametrized nonlinear time series models for macroeconomics but also conducts an exhaustive survey of nonlinear econometrics.

Potter attempts to grapple with the problem of finding an "uncontaminated" holdout sample (for an "out" of sample forecast evaluation exercise) to test plausibility of nonlinear models over linear models for an over-researched series like U.S. real GNP. Several paths are taken: (i) adducing evidence that the dynamics are different in expansions versus contractions, (ii) examining the relative plausibility of estimated nonlinear impulse response functions versus estimated linear impulse response functions, (iii) attempting to measure statistically significant marginal predictive improvement of a nonlinear model over a linear model, and (iv) reviewing other work in macroeconomics to plausibly restrict nonlinearities and thereby increase precision of the resulting parameter estimates.

Economic theory suggests pathways for the emergence of endogenous dynamics for which stochastic linear approximations would be poor. We reviewed some of these in Chapter 1. A very recent pathway via emergent income and wealth inequality is in Das 1990. Pathways of emergence of endogenous dynamics at different frequencies are discussed by Brock 1990. Let us turn now to the general problem of testing for nonlinearity.

5.6 A General Test for Nonlinearity

It is worthwhile, at this point, to attempt to present a unified view of "testing for nonlinearity." This necessitates a precise definition of "nonlinearity." Here is our preferred approach. We know from Priestley 1981 (Section 10.1.1) that any stationary process $\{X_t\}$ with a purely continuous spectrum that satisfies the Paley-Wiener condition has a "Wold Representation,"

$$X_t = A(L)e_t, \qquad\qquad (5.6.1)$$

where $\{e_t\}$ is an uncorrelated process, $A(L) = \Sigma_{i=0}^{\infty} g_i L^i$, $\Sigma_{i=0}^{\infty} g_i^2 < \infty$, L is the lag operator, i.e., $L^k e_t = e_{t-k}$. Since we attempt to detrend and deseasonalize economic data before doing time series analysis, the regularity assumptions needed to get a one-sided Wold representation are not that strong. Therefore whatever our definition of "nonlinearity" is, it must be rejectable. We propose using Priestley's definition of nonlinearity.

Definition (Priestley 1981). A stationary process $\{X_t\}$ is a linear process if it has a Wold representation like (5.6.1) where the $\{e_t\}$ process is IID.

Note that Priestley's definition requires that $\{e_t\}$ is IID and this is what gives it empirical content. The definition seems natural. Our definition of linearity implies that the best mean squared error (MSE) predictor using the past is the linear predictor. However, only the martingale difference sequence property of the innovations, not the stronger IID property, is required to assure that the best MSE predictor is the linear predictor. See, for example, Kohn 1979. For ease of exposition, we shall refer to the definition of linearity given above as "P-linearity" for Priestley.

The BDS test seems a natural way to test for P-linearity. Estimate $A(L)$ and test the estimated residuals for independent and identical distribution. For a broad class of A(L) the methods of Appendix D can be used to prove that the first order asymptotic distribution of BDS is invariant whether the BDS statistic is evaluated at the estimated $\{e_t\}$ or the true ones. In addition, the invariance of the first order asymptotics can be shown to hold for any smooth function of BDS statistics provided that the components are invariant. Hence the functional central limit theorems of Denker and Keller 1983 may be used to build a class of potentially more powerful tests for P-nonlinearity, using estimated residuals from ARMA models, such as "Cramer and von Mises"-type tests based upon integral functionals of squares of difference of BDS-like correlation integral statistics across different values of ϵ. Cramer and von Mises-type statistics seem to perform well in other contexts (Durlauf 1990b). We see this line of research as a potentially fruitful avenue to building more powerful tests for linearity in Priestley's sense.

5.7   Relationship of This Book to the General Area of Nonlinear Time Series Analysis

We have said in Chapter 1 that the general area of nonlinear time series analysis is vast. Nevertheless we attempt here to give some perspective on how the methods propounded in this book fit into the general picture.

For our purposes nonlinear time series analysis can be divided into three broad components. We list them in order of relatedness to the nonlinear complex dynamics perspective taken in this book. First, there is much literature on construction of nonlinear predictors for time series emitted by dynamical systems that may be infected by measurement noise or noise in the system dynamics. The emphasis is on methods that work well for "reconstructing" chaotic dynamics. To put it another way the methods exploit the deterministic dynamical systems perspective on "randomness." The methods divide into the following broad classes.

5.7.1 Locally Linear Methods

The first approach takes very seriously the hypothesis that $\{X_t\}$, the time series sample under scrutiny, is generated by a process of the form

$$X_t = F(X_{t-1},...,X_{t-L}) + e_t, \tag{5.7.1}$$

where F is smooth (or piecewise smooth), F is chaotic, and $\{e_t\}$ is a strictly stationary noise process whose variance is small relative to the variance of the dynamics generated by F. Here L>0 denotes the number of lagged X's appearing in F. A generalization assumes $\{X_t\}$ is observed through a function $x_t = h(X_t)$ that may contain noise. We put h(x)=x here. The first kind of methods are those that attempt to fit locally linear regressions to obtain an estimate of F. A good example of this approach is the Farmer and Sidorowich work discussed in Eubank and Farmer 1989.

These methods do not impose maintained hypotheses of smoothness on F and exploit this to obtain, provided, of course, the data are actually generated by a smooth F in (5.7.1), faster rates of convergence as do the kernel methods.

Researchers in this component include H. Abarbanel, D. Broomhead, M. Casdagli, S. Eubank, D. Farmer, A. Fraser, G. King, J. Sidorowich, and others (cf. Eubank and Farmer 1989). Recent surveys and introductions that will ease the reader's pathway into this component are Eubank and Farmer 1989 and Casdagli and Eubank 1991.

We feel that the BDS test can be used to complement this first approach in the following way. The first type of approach must commit to the hypothesis of time stationarity of F as well as either estimate or commit to the number of lags, L. If one is willing to assume the noise process is IID then BDS can be used to do a portmanteau goodness-of-fit test by simply testing the estimated residuals for independent and identical distribution. To use the results in Appendix D, we must have $T^{\frac{1}{2}}$-consistency of the estimation process for F. Since such a result is absent, to our knowledge, BDS should only be used as a rough diagnostic test in this case. Such a result, however, may be available in cases where the investigator knows a priori that the map F is generated by a piecewise linear map or is approximated by such to a high order. Hence, it appears legitimate to use BDS as a rough diagnostic on the residuals. Even if the $\{e_t\}$ are not IID but are only a martingale difference sequence, say, then estimation of F may be improved by exploitation of predictability of higher order moments. So even though BDS may falsely reject (5.7.1) when F is correctly estimated because the noise was not IID but rather a martingale difference sequence (e.g., Kohn 1979, p. 1008), exploitation of the dependence in higher order moments, for example, the variance, can improve precision of estimation of F using much the same intuition as that used in generalized least squares in comparison to ordinary least squares.

Also it may be useful, as stressed to us by Simon Potter, to exploit extra structure in the innovations above and beyond the martingale difference property, in order to produce better MSE h-step-ahead forecasts for h>1, in cases where the chain rule of forecasting (Sargen 1987a, p. 305) does not hold. This will typically happen in the nonlinear case. The general point being made here is this. In many instances, it may be desirable to reduce estimated innovations as close as one can to pure randomness, i.e., the IID property. The BDS test is a useful tool in checking that such a reduction has approximately been achieved.

In this spirit, suppose one has estimated a nonchaotic parametric model with IID errors inadvertently upon chaotic data generated by (5.7.1). $T^{\frac{1}{2}}$-consistency under the null is typical under regularity conditions for estimation of parametric models. Hence the result in Appendix D justifies testing the estimated residuals of the parametric model for independent and identical distribution. The first order asymptotic distribution of the BDS statistic is the same under the null. As we have indicated in Section 5.1.3 of this chapter, rejection by BDS is suggestive that predictable structure exploitable by near neighbors is present. This suggests, perhaps, investing the effort to estimate a nonlinear predictor using local linear methods.

To summarize this part, we believe that BDS is a useful portmanteau goodness-of-fit diagnostic test for evaluation of models of type (5.7.1).

5.7.2 Neural Network Methods
The second approach uses neural network (NN) to obtain an estimate of F. NN methods posit that F can be well approximated by sums of composites of sigmoid-like functions accompanied by thresholds. Schematic diagrams that show the "network architecture" (i.e., number

of "hidden" layers, number of "connections" between each layer, and number of "input" units) typically accompany the parametric form of F to be estimated. These diagrams are suggestive of relationships between NNs and learning theories in psychology, neural science, and artificial intelligence. Perhaps this relationship, coupled with successful applications in these areas, is responsible for their overwhelming current popularity. It is, perhaps, wise to be cautious in application of NN methods to economic and financial time series forecasting. There is no reason, to our knowledge, to expect the particular parametric structure embodied in NN architecture to be parsimonious in economic and financial applications——especially in applications to aggregative time series.

Applications to disaggregative macroeconomic time series where a natural connection structure suggests itself may be more fruitful. In this case a plausible parsimonious parametrization may suggest itself when coupled with an exploration of connection structure between the various sectors where lags naturally emerge from adjustment costs, chain of production, and inventories. Thresholds might emerge from increasing returns phenomena like setup costs for organization and learning-by-doing associated with, for example, mass production technology.

From an abstract econometric point of view, NN methods can be viewed simply as a parametric nonlinear (least squares for example) estimation method. Taking this view White 1989 has developed conventional asymptotic estimation and inference theory for NNs.

Good examples of the NN approach include the Lapedes and Farber work discussed in Eubank and Farmer 1989, Weigend,

Huberman, and Rumelhart 1990, Hornik, Stinchcombe, and White 1989 and White 1988, 1989.

Unfortunately we have seen little evidence that asset returns can be predicted out of sample using NN methods or any other nonlinear predictor. To put it another way, available evidence suggests that nonlinear prediction techniques have not yet improved out-of-sample prediction over linear predictors. See Diebold and Nason 1990 and their references for the case of returns on foreign exchange and stocks, White 1988 for stock returns, and Prescott and Stengos 1988 for gold returns. Mizrach 1988 finds some evidence for predictability of returns on foreign exchange within the European Monetary System.

While most previous applications of nonlinear techniques have been unsuccessful in finding any out-of-sample predictability, some recent results suggest otherwise. Brock, Lakonishok, and LeBaron 1990 find evidence for some predictability in both first and second moments for Dow Jones stock returns applying some simple technical trading rules commonly used by investors. These rules are designed to detect changes in long run trends in the presence of large amounts of noise. It is possible that this noise may cause problems for the previously mentioned nonlinear techniques. LeBaron 1990a,b finds that conditional autocorrelations are larger for periods of lower volatility, and these larger correlations can be used to obtain small improvements in out-of-sample forecasts for stock returns and foreign exchange rates.

We expect that neural network or any other method will have to exploit structure in asset returns that helps isolate those conditions under which prediction is possible. We see nothing in the particular parametrizations of current neural network formulations that gives a comparative advantage in isolating such conditions. Be that as it may, for the same reasons outlined above, we feel that BDS is a useful goodness-of-fit test to evaluate a neural network estimate of F in (5.7.1) above. Under White's 1989 regularity conditions for $T^{\frac{1}{2}}$-consistent estimation of the parameters of the NN, under the assumption of IID errors, application of the BDS test to the estimated errors is asymptotically justified under the null model.

5.7.3 Kernel, Spline, and Semi-nonparametric Methods

There is a broad class of methods for estimating conditional densities of strictly stationary stochastic processes that may have generated a time series. Once one has estimated the one-step-ahead conditional density, then one can estimate conditional means, variances, etc. For a one-step-ahead forecast of the level of the series one can use the conditional mean; for a one-step-ahead predictor of the imprecision of the forecast one can use the conditional variance, and so on.

This class of methods divides into three subclasses: parametric methods, semi-nonparametric methods, and nonparametric methods. Parametric methods include linear methods, for example, Box and Jenkins 1976, ARCH models treated in Chapters 3 and 4, and general parametric models treated in the specification test of Chapter 2 and Appendix D, etc. Parametric methods require commitment to a particular parametric form of the conditional probability distribution of the stochastic process under scrutiny. Since Chapters 3 and 4, as well as the power studies in our Monte Carlo studies, treat a fairly broad class of parametric models, we say no more about them here.

Semi-nonparametric (SNP) methods (cf. Gallant and Tauchen 1989) view the conditional density as the fundamental statistical object of interest. The idea is to estimate the conditional density of a general nonlinear stationary process by a modified Hermite series expansion, but using an established parametric model for the leading term in the series expansion. The other terms are used to capture departures from that model. In this way the SNP approach deals with the curse of dimensionality that infects nonparametric methods such as kernels and splines at the expense of commitment to some parametric model for the leading term in the series. Recent work on semi-nonparametrics, as well as nonparametrics is discussed in Barnett, Powell, and Tauchen 1991.

We feel that BDS can be fruitfully used in application of SNP methods as a goodness-of-fit diagnostic by testing independence of the residuals in the same manner as the parametric case and the locally linear case discussed above. Caution must be applied however. For example, Gallant and Tauchen 1991 discuss papers that "recount experience with a number of alternative model selection procedures that did not work well, notably Akaike's (1969) criterion, the Brock, Dechert, and Scheinkman (1987) statistic, and upward likelihood ratio testing." They recommend using the Schwarz criterion "to move along an upward expansion path until an adequate model is determined. The Schwarz-preferred model is then subjected to a battery of specification tests to check for features of the data that the model fails to adequately approximate."

The skeptical reader conditioned by Lo and MacKinlay's 1990 work on data-snooping biases in tests of financial asset pricing models may worry about using an "established" model for the first term in the

SNP series expansion as well as the rest of this particular identification procedure unless this procedure is exercised on a new dataset. Unfortunately datasets in finance that have not played a role in "establishing" models are hard to find. We have not seen any evidence that SNP models can predict asset returns out of sample.

Nonparametric methods (cf. Barnett, Powell, and Tauchen 1990, Hardle 1990, Manski 1991, Silverman 1986, and Wahba 1990) involve estimation of densities, conditional densities, and nonlinear regression functions by methods that exploit maintained hypotheses (e.g., the regression function is continuously differentiable of order k for some positive integer k). Theorems in this area show that the speed of convergence of the estimator to the true regression function increases as k increases. Only in some special cases is the $T^{\frac{1}{2}}$ speed of convergence achieved that is typically available in the parametric case. This is the price one pays to avoid committing to a specific functional form as in the parametric case.

Model (5.7.1) is an example of a nonlinear regression function to which nonparametric methods could be applied to estimate. If the map F turned out to be chaotic and, hence, time series emitted by F are unpredictable in the long run, effective short-term prediction can still be done by estimating F by nonparametric regression. BDS could be used as a goodness-of-fit diagnostic test on the estimated errors. However, since convergence of the nonparametric estimate of F is typically less than rate $T^{\frac{1}{2}}$, application of BDS is not asymptotically justified by the result in Appendix D. Hence we recommend use of BDS only as a crude diagnostic in this case.

In view of this and other limitations, we recommend using BDS as a crude portmanteau goodness-of-fit diagnostic test on estimated residuals or estimated forecast errors in the manner of the Q statistic in Box and Jenkins 1976 (p. 291). These forecast errors must be extracted from a model of the form $X_t = G(I_t, u_t)$ where I_t is a general information set that can include past X's. As Appendix D shows, in general, even if the estimator converges with rate $T^{\frac{1}{2}}$, a correction will need to be made in the asymptotic distribution of the BDS statistic computed on the estimated $\{u_t\}$ even if the true u's are IID. However, if the errors are additive and IID and estimation is done $T^{\frac{1}{2}}$-consistently, then the correction will be zero as is shown in Appendix D.

In summary, this chapter has outlined related areas as well as a collection of future research projects that we believe show the potential use of the methods exposited in this book.

Appendix A. Size and Distribution of the BDS Statistic

Table A.1
Size of BDS Statistic
Standard Normal

| | ϵ/σ | | | | | |
	0.25	0.50	1.00	1.50	2.00	N(0,1)
m=2,T=100						
%< -2.33	28.28	13.06	3.90	3.94	5.62	1.00
%< -1.96	32.14	17.22	8.02	7.10	9.18	2.50
%< -1.64	35.60	21.86	12.30	12.04	13.82	5.00
%> 1.64	27.90	16.50	10.02	9.02	10.10	5.00
%> 1.96	25.22	13.38	6.44	5.66	7.12	2.50
%> 2.33	22.96	10.44	3.78	2.96	4.50	1.00
m=2,T=500						
%< -2.33	8.62	1.96	1.10	1.28	1.34	1.00
%< -1.96	12.96	4.44	3.04	3.26	3.52	2.50
%< -1.64	17.14	8.24	5.98	6.20	6.78	5.00
%> 1.64	16.94	9.32	6.92	6.04	6.58	5.00
%> 1.96	12.60	5.76	3.76	3.36	3.86	2.50
%> 2.33	8.98	3.42	1.80	1.68	1.88	1.00
m=2,T=1000						
%< -2.33	4.65	1.40	1.05	0.90	0.80	1.00
%< -1.96	8.95	3.25	2.90	2.45	2.65	2.50
%< -1.64	13.25	6.55	5.60	6.30	6.15	5.00
%> 1.64	9.50	6.20	4.70	4.20	5.50	5.00
%> 1.96	6.30	3.70	2.25	2.40	2.50	2.50
%> 2.33	3.60	1.55	0.90	0.70	0.90	1.00
m=5,T=500						
%< -2.33	12.80	0.84	0.94	1.16	1.12	1.00
%< -1.96	17.14	2.48	2.24	2.88	2.92	2.50
%< -1.64	21.76	5.58	5.52	5.62	5.86	5.00
%> 1.64	19.70	7.24	5.12	5.20	5.68	5.00
%> 1.96	16.10	4.56	3.10	2.96	3.16	2.50
%> 2.33	12.92	2.84	1.56	1.28	1.60	1.00
m=5,T=1000						
%< -2.33	6.05	0.70	0.70	0.85	0.60	1.00
%< -1.96	9.55	2.25	2.30	2.55	2.50	2.50
%< -1.64	13.70	4.60	5.35	5.50	5.40	5.00
%> 1.64	14.35	6.80	5.35	5.75	5.90	5.00
%> 1.96	11.00	4.20	3.10	3.50	3.55	2.50
%> 2.33	7.55	2.25	1.95	1.70	1.60	1.00
m=10,T=1000						
%< -2.33	95.00	5.45	0.40	0.85	0.90	1.00
%< -1.96	95.15	9.60	1.35	2.55	2.50	2.50
%< -1.64	95.40	14.75	3.85	4.60	5.55	5.00
%> 1.64	3.75	15.15	6.40	5.95	6.10	5.00
%> 1.96	3.70	12.60	3.90	3.05	3.15	2.50
%> 2.33	3.65	9.40	2.00	1.70	1.45	1.00

Table A.2
Size of BDS Statistic
Student-t with 3 Degrees of Freedom

			ϵ/σ			
	0.25	0.50	1.00	1.50	2.00	N(0,1)
m=2,T=100						
%< -2.33	11.36	3.10	2.18	2.40	3.00	1.00
%< -1.96	15.26	6.78	4.98	4.50	4.30	2.50
%< -1.64	20.28	11.32	8.66	8.28	6.02	5.00
%> 1.64	16.72	9.50	8.04	8.42	9.34	5.00
%> 1.96	13.42	6.84	5.16	5.88	6.94	2.50
%> 2.33	10.32	4.34	2.72	3.44	4.70	1.00
m=2,T=500						
%< -2.33	2.14	0.82	0.78	0.60	0.56	1.00
%< -1.96	4.62	2.48	2.38	2.32	1.72	2.50
%< -1.64	7.98	5.36	5.48	4.74	4.14	5.00
%> 1.64	7.80	5.72	5.38	5.82	6.58	5.00
%> 1.96	5.12	3.26	2.98	3.20	3.80	2.50
%> 2.33	2.80	1.48	1.34	1.48	2.08	1.00
m=2,T=1000						
%< -2.33	1.25	0.65	0.85	0.50	0.40	1.00
%< -1.96	3.25	2.50	2.20	2.05	1.20	2.50
%< -1.64	6.85	4.55	4.70	4.30	3.70	5.00
%> 1.64	6.70	5.65	5.65	5.70	6.95	5.00
%> 1.96	4.15	3.10	2.80	3.20	3.55	2.50
%> 2.33	1.90	1.50	1.10	1.45	1.80	1.00
m=5,T=500						
%< -2.33	12.80	0.84	0.94	1.16	1.12	1.00
%< -1.96	17.14	2.48	2.24	2.88	2.92	2.50
%< -1.64	21.76	5.58	5.52	5.62	5.86	5.00
%> 1.64	19.70	7.24	5.12	5.20	5.68	5.00
%> 1.96	16.10	4.56	3.10	2.96	3.16	2.50
%> 2.33	12.92	2.84	1.56	1.28	1.60	1.00
m=5,T=1000						
%< -2.33	6.05	0.70	0.70	0.85	0.60	1.00
%< -1.96	9.55	2.25	2.30	2.55	2.50	2.50
%< -1.64	13.70	4.60	5.35	5.50	5.40	5.00
%> 1.64	14.35	6.80	5.35	5.75	5.90	5.00
%> 1.96	11.00	4.20	3.10	3.50	3.55	2.50
%> 2.33	7.55	2.25	1.95	1.70	1.60	1.00
m=10,T=1000						
%< -2.33	95.00	5.45	0.40	0.85	0.90	1.00
%< -1.96	95.15	9.60	1.35	2.55	2.50	2.50
%< -1.64	95.40	14.75	3.85	4.60	5.55	5.00
%> 1.64	3.75	15.15	6.40	5.95	6.10	5.00
%> 1.96	3.70	12.60	3.90	3.05	3.15	2.50
%> 2.33	3.65	9.40	2.00	1.70	1.45	1.00

Table A.3
Size of BDS Statistic
Double Exponential

		ϵ/σ				
	0.25	0.50	1.00	1.50	2.00	N(0,1)
m=2,T=100						
%< -2.33	8.48	3.16	1.84	2.04	3.06	1.00
%< -1.96	13.22	6.32	5.02	4.82	4.58	2.50
%< -1.64	18.14	10.74	9.12	8.64	7.78	5.00
%> 1.64	15.70	8.78	7.58	8.44	10.34	5.00
%> 1.96	12.32	6.22	4.40	5.48	7.18	2.50
%> 2.33	9.00	3.68	2.36	2.88	4.12	1.00
m=2,T=500						
%< -2.33	1.28	0.96	0.76	0.70	0.52	1.00
%< -1.96	3.30	2.48	2.44	2.30	1.92	2.50
%< -1.64	6.80	5.56	5.36	5.06	4.68	5.00
%> 1.64	7.48	5.94	6.02	5.84	5.78	5.00
%> 1.96	4.50	3.48	3.06	3.24	3.62	2.50
%> 2.33	2.52	1.62	1.56	1.64	2.02	1.00
m=2,T=1000						
%< -2.33	1.25	0.95	0.75	0.70	0.60	1.00
%< -1.96	3.10	2.75	2.85	2.40	2.30	2.50
%< -1.64	6.00	5.30	5.60	5.25	5.25	5.00
%> 1.64	6.25	5.70	5.65	6.10	6.25	5.00
%> 1.96	3.30	3.00	3.20	3.30	3.10	2.50
%> 2.33	1.45	1.25	1.45	1.70	1.75	1.00
m=5,T=500						
%< -2.33	11.60	0.80	0.60	1.12	1.10	1.00
%< -1.96	16.04	2.62	2.14	2.54	2.84	2.50
%< -1.64	20.90	5.90	4.86	5.30	5.82	5.00
%> 1.64	19.38	7.08	5.10	4.62	4.80	5.00
%> 1.96	15.86	5.04	2.68	2.48	2.62	2.50
%> 2.33	12.66	3.26	1.32	1.24	1.24	1.00
m=5,T=1000						
%< -2.33	5.90	0.35	0.75	0.95	0.75	1.00
%< -1.96	9.65	2.10	2.40	2.60	2.75	2.50
%< -1.64	14.60	4.45	5.30	5.75	6.10	5.00
%> 1.64	14.00	6.40	4.50	4.45	4.60	5.00
%> 1.96	10.30	3.70	2.90	2.25	2.50	2.50
%> 2.33	7.00	1.75	1.25	0.95	1.30	1.00
m=10,T=1000						
%< -2.33	49.45	6.90	0.25	0.65	1.10	1.00
%< -1.96	95.90	12.50	1.00	2.00	2.80	2.50
%< -1.64	98.95	18.90	3.55	4.70	6.05	5.00
%> 1.64	1.00	16.65	6.15	4.60	4.25	5.00
%> 1.96	1.00	13.80	3.70	2.80	2.25	2.50
%> 2.33	1.00	11.15	2.15	1.25	1.30	1.00

Table A.4
Size of BDS Statistic
Chi-square with 4 Degrees of Freedom

		0.25	0.50	ϵ/σ 1.00	1.50	2.00	N(0,1)
m=2,T=100							
%<	-2.33	18.22	6.30	2.52	2.56	3.28	1.00
%<	-1.96	22.42	10.16	5.80	5.54	5.26	2.50
%<	-1.64	26.38	15.38	9.48	9.34	8.20	5.00
%>	1.64	23.22	12.82	8.34	8.30	8.72	5.00
%>	1.96	20.16	9.46	5.36	5.46	6.26	2.50
%>	2.33	16.76	6.66	3.16	3.18	4.04	1.00
m=2,T=500							
%<	-2.33	3.80	1.26	1.02	0.82	0.78	1.00
%<	-1.96	7.38	2.94	2.70	2.54	2.20	2.50
%<	-1.64	11.64	6.92	5.72	5.36	4.90	5.00
%>	1.64	10.88	6.68	5.88	6.18	6.26	5.00
%>	1.96	7.70	3.96	3.06	3.36	3.72	2.50
%>	2.33	4.88	2.10	1.40	1.50	1.90	1.00
m=2,T=1000							
%<	-2.33	1.65	0.90	1.10	1.20	1.10	1.00
%<	-1.96	5.00	3.05	3.00	3.35	2.45	2.50
%<	-1.64	8.05	6.15	6.10	6.10	4.95	5.00
%>	1.64	8.55	6.25	6.75	6.65	6.85	5.00
%>	1.96	5.05	3.80	3.85	3.90	3.70	2.50
%>	2.33	3.25	2.10	1.90	1.65	2.15	1.00
m=5,T=500							
%<	-2.33	24.06	1.88	0.50	0.80	0.82	1.00
%<	-1.96	27.76	4.58	2.02	2.52	2.62	2.50
%<	-1.64	31.56	8.22	5.20	5.50	5.76	5.00
%>	1.64	27.72	9.00	6.04	5.60	5.80	5.00
%>	1.96	24.44	6.16	3.66	3.10	3.14	2.50
%>	2.33	21.20	4.12	1.90	1.34	1.26	1.00
m=5,T=1000							
%<	-2.33	16.15	0.95	0.85	0.85	1.00	1.00
%<	-1.96	20.65	3.45	2.30	2.25	2.30	2.50
%<	-1.64	24.40	6.95	5.70	5.35	5.95	5.00
%>	1.64	22.60	8.55	6.20	5.30	5.70	5.00
%>	1.96	19.20	5.30	3.45	3.30	3.00	2.50
%>	2.33	15.40	2.95	1.75	1.25	1.50	1.00
m=10,T=1000							
%<	-2.33	98.95	19.10	0.30	0.50	0.55	1.00
%<	-1.96	98.95	24.35	1.55	1.85	2.15	2.50
%<	-1.64	98.95	30.25	3.95	4.30	5.95	5.00
%>	1.64	1.05	23.55	7.00	5.55	5.40	5.00
%>	1.96	1.05	20.90	4.60	3.65	2.85	2.50
%>	2.33	1.05	17.35	2.65	1.75	1.40	1.00

Table A.5
Size of BDS Statistic
Uniform Distribution

		ϵ/σ				
	0.25	0.50	1.00	1.50	2.00	N(0,1)
m=2,T=100						
%< -2.33	47.54	44.10	21.00	7.26	6.96	1.00
%< -1.96	48.30	45.48	25.52	11.98	10.70	2.50
%< -1.64	48.98	46.76	29.80	16.22	15.78	5.00
%> 1.64	44.60	40.32	23.10	13.54	12.72	5.00
%> 1.96	44.06	39.34	19.98	10.18	8.98	2.50
%> 2.33	43.42	38.44	17.44	6.76	5.38	1.00
m=2,T=500						
%< -2.33	46.54	31.66	3.94	1.68	2.02	1.00
%< -1.96	47.22	35.02	6.98	4.04	4.18	2.50
%< -1.64	47.94	37.66	11.74	7.34	7.12	5.00
%> 1.64	44.70	32.20	11.42	6.12	6.76	5.00
%> 1.96	44.00	29.80	7.96	3.76	3.44	2.50
%> 2.33	43.38	27.42	4.90	1.76	1.62	1.00
m=2,T=1000						
%< -2.33	44.95	21.75	1.45	1.40	1.40	1.00
%< -1.96	46.05	26.60	3.60	3.00	3.15	2.50
%< -1.64	47.25	31.15	7.65	6.05	6.15	5.00
%> 1.64	43.45	27.25	8.20	5.30	5.70	5.00
%> 1.96	42.45	24.30	5.05	2.85	2.85	2.50
%> 2.33	41.40	21.80	3.10	1.30	1.25	1.00
m=5,T=500						
%< -2.33	51.36	41.94	7.08	1.64	1.96	1.00
%< -1.96	51.56	43.62	11.52	3.84	4.20	2.50
%< -1.64	51.72	44.82	16.80	7.60	7.58	5.00
%> 1.64	46.76	41.42	14.74	6.46	6.24	5.00
%> 1.96	46.62	39.82	11.12	4.10	3.42	2.50
%> 2.33	46.50	38.52	7.88	2.36	1.98	1.00
m=5,T=1000						
%< -2.33	49.20	35.50	4.05	1.50	1.30	1.00
%< -1.96	49.60	37.40	7.55	3.00	2.95	2.50
%< -1.64	49.65	38.80	12.00	6.00	5.50	5.00
%> 1.64	48.15	40.95	9.85	6.65	5.70	5.00
%> 1.96	48.05	38.50	6.85	3.75	3.40	2.50
%> 2.33	47.90	36.85	4.30	1.55	1.25	1.00
m=10,T=1000						
%< -2.33	99.85	51.60	16.30	0.90	0.95	1.00
%< -1.96	99.85	51.95	20.85	3.40	2.50	2.50
%< -1.64	99.85	52.20	24.95	7.15	5.60	5.00
%> 1.64	0.15	42.75	22.55	6.85	5.70	5.00
%> 1.96	0.15	42.30	18.70	4.40	3.55	2.50
%> 2.33	0.15	41.20	15.50	2.50	1.70	1.00

Table A.6
Size of BDS Statistic
Bimodal Distribution

		ϵ/σ				
	0.25	0.50	1.00	1.50	2.00	N(0,1)
m=2,T=100						
%< -2.33	21.62	21.86	49.80	15.72	6.10	1.00
%< -1.96	25.86	26.40	52.12	20.48	10.14	2.50
%< -1.64	29.32	30.58	53.98	25.38	15.18	5.00
%> 1.64	24.86	23.12	29.46	19.54	11.32	5.00
%> 1.96	21.54	20.40	28.44	16.40	7.72	2.50
%> 2.33	18.18	17.24	27.50	13.14	4.80	1.00
m=2,T=500						
%< -2.33	5.48	4.64	55.58	3.40	2.00	1.00
%< -1.96	9.24	8.30	56.94	6.48	4.50	2.50
%< -1.64	14.02	13.22	58.32	10.50	7.20	5.00
%> 1.64	11.78	11.32	30.78	8.88	5.38	5.00
%> 1.96	8.60	8.24	30.08	6.06	3.24	2.50
%> 2.33	5.56	5.56	29.30	3.94	1.70	1.00
m=2,T=1000						
%< -2.33	2.30	2.55	52.70	1.40	1.10	1.00
%< -1.96	5.45	5.00	54.70	3.85	3.10	2.50
%< -1.64	9.40	8.85	55.85	6.90	5.85	5.00
%> 1.64	9.45	8.55	29.85	6.85	5.55	5.00
%> 1.96	6.45	5.75	29.20	3.85	3.05	2.50
%> 2.33	3.45	3.05	28.10	2.05	1.40	1.00
m=5,T=500						
%< -2.33	24.26	12.70	50.50	3.70	1.50	1.00
%< -1.96	28.08	17.78	51.30	7.48	3.88	2.50
%< -1.64	31.76	22.76	52.02	12.62	7.60	5.00
%> 1.64	26.66	18.84	41.28	10.30	5.46	5.00
%> 1.96	23.58	15.24	40.62	7.36	3.12	2.50
%> 2.33	20.50	11.84	39.74	4.96	1.44	1.00
m=5,T=1000						
%< -2.33	15.45	7.25	46.00	2.50	1.45	1.00
%< -1.96	20.00	10.80	47.20	5.70	3.30	2.50
%< -1.64	23.70	14.50	48.15	9.05	6.45	5.00
%> 1.64	21.30	13.60	41.70	7.80	5.40	5.00
%> 1.96	17.85	10.25	41.05	5.30	2.70	2.50
%> 2.33	13.65	6.85	39.95	2.80	1.40	1.00
m=10,T=1000						
%< -2.33	93.10	35.50	47.95	5.80	0.90	1.00
%< -1.96	93.10	39.15	48.40	9.75	2.90	2.50
%< -1.64	93.10	41.50	48.60	14.30	6.55	5.00
%> 1.64	6.90	34.55	47.50	11.55	5.85	5.00
%> 1.96	6.90	32.55	47.00	8.85	3.10	2.50
%> 2.33	6.90	30.45	46.55	5.30	1.40	1.00

Table A.7
Distribution of BDS Statistic
Standard Normal

	\multicolumn{5}{c}{ϵ/σ}	
	0.25	0.50	1.00	1.50	2.00	N(0,1)
m=2,T=100						
Median	-0.46	-0.29	-0.20	-0.19	-0.23	0.00
Mean	-0.18	-0.17	-0.13	-0.14	-0.16	0.00
Std dev	5.63	2.12	1.36	1.30	1.43	1.00
Skewness	10.68	0.48	0.28	0.16	0.10	0.00
Kurtosis	403.08	5.19	3.33	3.05	3.37	3.00
m=2,T=500						
Median	-0.09	-0.09	-0.05	-0.06	-0.08	0.00
Mean	-0.03	-0.02	-0.02	-0.03	-0.03	0.00
Std dev	1.73	1.22	1.08	1.07	1.10	1.00
Skewness	0.23	0.29	0.19	0.12	0.13	0.00
Kurtosis	3.17	3.14	2.98	2.90	2.99	3.00
m=2,T=1000						
Median	-0.11	-0.11	-0.10	-0.10	-0.10	0.00
Mean	-0.11	-0.08	-0.08	-0.08	-0.07	0.00
Std dev	1.34	1.07	1.00	1.00	1.02	1.00
Skewness	0.04	0.19	0.08	0.04	0.07	0.00
Kurtosis	2.90	3.03	2.93	2.84	2.82	3.00
m=5,T=500						
Median	-0.43	-0.11	-0.12	-0.12	-0.11	0.00
Mean	0.17	0.00	-0.04	-0.06	-0.07	0.00
Std dev	6.13	1.71	1.12	1.09	1.11	1.00
Skewness	0.63	0.39	0.43	0.24	0.18	0.00
Kurtosis	3.87	3.49	3.34	2.99	2.98	3.00
m=5,T=1000						
Median	-0.20	-0.13	-0.13	-0.11	-0.09	0.00
Mean	-0.08	-0.06	-0.07	-0.07	-0.07	0.00
Std dev	4.18	1.38	1.03	1.02	1.02	1.00
Skewness	0.20	0.27	0.30	0.23	0.19	0.00
Kurtosis	3.42	3.06	3.04	3.02	3.00	3.00
m=10,T=1000						
Median	-5.43	-1.21	-0.12	-0.14	-0.12	0.00
Mean	-0.09	0.19	-0.04	-0.08	-0.08	0.00
Std dev	140.03	7.16	1.16	1.03	1.03	1.00
Skewness	26.50	1.50	0.55	0.35	0.23	0.00
Kurtosis	714.71	5.83	3.50	3.22	3.16	3.00

Table A.8
Distribution of BDS Statistic
Student-t with 3 Degrees of Freedom

	ϵ/σ					
	0.25	0.50	1.00	1.50	2.00	N(0,1)
m=2,T=100						
Median	-0.22	-0.18	-0.17	-0.20	-0.31	0.00
Mean	-0.12	-0.10	-0.11	-0.11	-0.11	0.00
Std dev	2.03	1.32	1.18	1.22	1.30	1.00
Skewness	0.41	0.41	0.32	0.39	0.45	0.00
Kurtosis	4.72	3.39	3.19	3.54	5.88	3.00
m=2,T=500						
Median	-0.11	-0.09	-0.09	-0.13	-0.19	0.00
Mean	-0.05	-0.05	-0.05	-0.06	-0.06	0.00
Std dev	1.18	1.04	1.02	1.04	1.06	1.00
Skewness	0.21	0.20	0.18	0.32	0.57	0.00
Kurtosis	3.05	2.95	2.90	3.04	3.60	3.00
m=2,T=1000						
Median	-0.01	-0.01	-0.06	-0.06	-0.08	0.00
Mean	-0.01	-0.01	-0.01	0.00	-0.01	0.00
Std dev	1.10	1.03	1.00	1.00	1.02	1.00
Skewness	0.17	0.16	0.14	0.24	0.40	0.00
Kurtosis	3.13	3.07	3.10	3.13	3.14	3.00
m=5,T=500						
Median	-0.20	-0.13	-0.09	-0.11	-0.17	0.00
Mean	-0.03	-0.04	-0.06	-0.08	-0.10	0.00
Std dev	2.13	1.11	1.03	1.03	1.05	1.00
Skewness	0.50	0.49	0.22	0.17	0.28	0.00
Kurtosis	3.95	3.53	3.06	3.02	3.20	3.00
m=5,T=1000						
Median	-0.13	-0.09	-0.06	-0.06	-0.09	0.00
Mean	-0.01	-0.02	-0.02	-0.03	-0.04	0.00
Std dev	1.60	1.06	1.02	1.03	1.04	1.00
Skewness	0.49	0.41	0.27	0.21	0.20	0.00
Kurtosis	3.72	3.41	3.30	3.01	2.92	3.00
m=10,T=1000						
Median	-3.00	-0.27	-0.10	-0.10	-0.12	0.00
Mean	-0.16	-0.02	-0.03	-0.05	-0.07	0.00
Std dev	26.05	1.73	1.03	1.03	1.04	1.00
Skewness	20.80	1.15	0.49	0.29	0.23	0.00
Kurtosis	603.80	5.95	3.40	3.03	3.02	3.00

Table A.9
Distribution of BDS Statistic
Double Exponential

	0.25	0.50	1.00	1.50	2.00	N(0,1)
			ϵ/σ			
m=2,T=100						
Median	-0.21	-0.16	-0.17	-0.17	-0.26	0.00
Mean	-0.09	-0.10	-0.09	-0.08	-0.10	0.00
Std dev	1.83	1.29	1.18	1.20	1.28	1.00
Skewness	0.50	0.34	0.25	0.25	0.32	0.00
Kurtosis	4.57	3.33	2.94	3.01	3.57	3.00
m=2,T=500						
Median	-0.04	-0.06	-0.07	-0.09	-0.14	0.00
Mean	-0.02	-0.04	-0.04	-0.05	-0.05	0.00
Std dev	1.13	1.04	1.03	1.04	1.04	1.00
Skewness	0.24	0.20	0.20	0.28	0.46	0.00
Kurtosis	3.11	2.96	2.87	3.04	3.45	3.00
m=2,T=1000						
Median	-0.03	-0.05	-0.04	-0.06	-0.10	0.00
Mean	-0.03	-0.03	-0.03	-0.03	-0.05	0.00
Std dev	1.04	1.02	1.03	1.03	1.04	1.00
Skewness	0.12	0.12	0.17	0.21	0.32	0.00
Kurtosis	2.93	2.97	3.01	3.02	3.19	3.00
m=5,T=500						
Median	-0.19	-0.16	-0.14	-0.13	-0.14	0.00
Mean	0.01	-0.05	-0.08	-0.09	-0.10	0.00
Std dev	2.06	1.12	1.01	1.01	1.03	1.00
Skewness	0.60	0.57	0.31	0.21	0.24	0.00
Kurtosis	3.86	3.72	3.07	3.07	3.17	3.00
m=5,T=1000						
Median	-0.06	-0.12	-0.12	-0.09	-0.11	0.00
Mean	-0.01	-0.04	-0.08	-0.09	-0.09	0.00
Std dev	1.54	1.03	1.00	1.00	1.02	1.00
Skewness	0.30	0.39	0.21	0.13	0.18	0.00
Kurtosis	3.11	3.08	3.04	2.91	2.94	3.00
m=10,T=1000						
Median	-2.32	-0.29	-0.16	-0.18	-0.15	0.00
Mean	-0.12	0.00	-0.06	-0.11	-0.12	0.00
Std dev	25.96	1.95	1.01	0.99	1.02	1.00
Skewness	15.60	1.28	0.59	0.27	0.17	0.00
Kurtosis	301.76	5.93	3.45	3.02	2.94	3.00

Table A.10
Distribution of BDS Statistic
Chi-square with 4 Degrees of Freedom

	0.25	0.50	1.00	1.50	2.00	N(0,1)
			ϵ/σ			
m=2,T=100						
Median	-0.22	-0.19	-0.15	-0.16	-0.24	0.00
Mean	-0.06	-0.09	-0.09	-0.10	-0.11	0.00
Std dev	2.95	1.58	1.24	1.22	1.28	1.00
Skewness	0.57	0.39	0.28	0.30	0.37	0.00
Kurtosis	7.89	3.94	3.23	3.26	3.91	3.00
m=2,T=500						
Median	-0.06	-0.09	-0.04	-0.07	-0.09	0.00
Mean	-0.03	-0.03	-0.03	-0.02	-0.03	0.00
Std dev	1.36	1.10	1.04	1.04	1.05	1.00
Skewness	0.26	0.25	0.15	0.17	0.28	0.00
Kurtosis	3.11	3.07	3.03	2.95	3.01	3.00
m=2,T=1000						
Median	-0.06	-0.07	-0.07	-0.05	-0.10	0.00
Mean	-0.02	-0.03	-0.03	-0.03	-0.02	0.00
Std dev	1.20	1.08	1.07	1.08	1.07	1.00
Skewness	0.27	0.30	0.24	0.19	0.32	0.00
Kurtosis	3.15	3.31	3.22	3.11	3.20	3.00
m=5,T=500						
Median	-0.25	-0.13	-0.13	-0.09	-0.12	0.00
Mean	-0.06	-0.05	-0.06	-0.06	-0.07	0.00
Std dev	3.22	1.25	1.04	1.02	1.04	1.00
Skewness	0.43	0.50	0.43	0.23	0.24	0.00
Kurtosis	3.72	3.59	3.42	3.06	3.01	3.00
m=5,T=1000						
Median	-0.11	-0.12	-0.06	-0.06	-0.12	0.00
Mean	-0.01	-0.03	-0.03	-0.05	-0.06	0.00
Std dev	2.30	1.15	1.04	1.03	1.04	1.00
Skewness	0.23	0.39	0.27	0.15	0.19	0.00
Kurtosis	3.05	3.18	3.06	2.88	3.05	3.00
m=10,T=1000						
Median	-4.38	-0.38	-0.12	-0.12	-0.13	0.00
Mean	0.20	0.01	-0.02	-0.05	-0.09	0.00
Std dev	47.88	2.77	1.05	1.01	1.02	1.00
Skewness	11.53	1.03	0.58	0.33	0.27	0.00
Kurtosis	146.16	5.15	3.61	3.06	3.06	3.00

Table A.11
Distribution of BDS Statistic
Uniform Distribution

| | ϵ/σ | | | | | |
	0.25	0.50	1.00	1.50	2.00	N(0,1)
m=2,T=100						
Median	-1.18	-0.81	-0.31	-0.14	-0.11	0.00
Mean	-48.21	9.28	0.05	-0.10	-0.10	0.00
Std dev	1739.32	555.49	13.98	1.57	1.51	1.00
Skewness	-35.73	38.45	55.87	0.20	0.07	0.00
Kurtosis	1422.75	1821.99	3741.01	3.02	2.85	3.00
m=2,T=500						
Median	-0.72	-0.35	-0.11	-0.05	-0.03	0.00
Mean	-2.77	-0.07	-0.04	-0.04	-0.03	0.00
Std dev	168.91	4.67	1.39	1.11	1.11	1.00
Skewness	-6.95	0.45	0.35	0.05	0.00	0.00
Kurtosis	242.77	4.65	3.31	3.01	3.00	3.00
m=2,T=1000						
Median	-0.77	-0.22	-0.13	-0.07	-0.06	0.00
Mean	0.14	0.07	-0.05	-0.05	-0.04	0.00
Std dev	14.78	3.17	1.18	1.05	1.04	1.00
Skewness	0.37	0.56	0.32	0.06	0.06	0.00
Kurtosis	5.46	3.67	3.19	2.95	2.89	3.00
m=5,T=500						
Median	-4.65	-0.38	-0.20	-0.11	-0.11	0.00
Mean	5.57	-0.13	-0.09	-0.08	-0.09	0.00
Std dev	564.48	10.36	1.64	1.12	1.10	1.00
Skewness	7.74	0.13	0.32	0.24	0.15	0.00
Kurtosis	379.05	3.94	3.34	3.22	3.10	3.00
m=5,T=1000						
Median	-1.18	0.01	-0.19	-0.17	-0.17	0.00
Mean	1.02	0.17	-0.10	-0.09	-0.09	0.00
Std dev	67.15	6.87	1.34	1.07	1.05	1.00
Skewness	0.09	0.13	0.38	0.31	0.27	0.00
Kurtosis	4.38	3.34	3.61	3.18	3.18	3.00
m=10,T=1000						
Median	-84.50	-25.66	-0.23	-0.19	-0.17	0.00
Mean	11.14	-0.36	-0.08	-0.10	-0.10	0.00
Std dev	2978.33	60.13	2.32	1.12	1.06	1.00
Skewness	32.85	2.13	0.27	0.58	0.46	0.00
Kurtosis	1144.67	10.18	3.16	4.07	3.71	3.00

Table A.12
Distribution of BDS Statistic
Bimodal Distribution

	ϵ/σ					
	0.25	0.50	1.00	1.50	2.00	N(0,1)
m=2,T=100						
Median	-0.25	-0.38	-2.30	-0.35	-0.12	0.00
Mean	-0.09	-0.14	-2.03	-0.12	-0.13	0.00
Std dev	3.17	3.03	1291.09	2.42	1.45	1.00
Skewness	0.53	0.72	16.05	0.94	0.08	0.00
Kurtosis	6.06	5.13	2178.03	6.97	2.99	3.00
m=2,T=500						
Median	-0.16	-0.16	-3.86	-0.13	-0.04	0.00
Mean	-0.10	-0.08	-7.04	-0.07	-0.06	0.00
Std dev	1.46	1.45	647.97	1.28	1.09	1.00
Skewness	0.30	0.42	2.32	0.28	-0.02	0.00
Kurtosis	3.29	3.64	702.13	3.40	3.12	3.00
m=2,T=1000						
Median	-0.10	-0.07	-2.64	-0.02	-0.04	0.00
Mean	-0.03	-0.02	0.10	-0.01	-0.02	0.00
Std dev	1.25	1.23	18.91	1.12	1.04	1.00
Skewness	0.20	0.22	9.42	0.18	0.06	0.00
Kurtosis	3.03	3.22	181.50	3.16	3.14	3.00
m=5,T=500						
Median	-0.27	-0.22	-2.61	-0.19	-0.11	0.00
Mean	-0.14	-0.10	-34.02	-0.10	-0.09	0.00
Std dev	3.06	2.03	1051.81	1.36	1.09	1.00
Skewness	0.30	0.32	-12.20	0.36	0.15	0.00
Kurtosis	3.27	3.17	573.42	3.19	3.09	3.00
m=5,T=1000						
Median	-0.09	-0.09	-1.03	-0.13	-0.08	0.00
Mean	-0.06	-0.05	0.00	-0.09	-0.06	0.00
Std dev	2.20	1.58	21.91	1.20	1.06	1.00
Skewness	0.27	0.26	0.83	0.24	0.11	0.00
Kurtosis	3.20	3.21	9.08	3.22	3.03	3.00
m=10,T=1000						
Median	-7.01	-0.56	-0.15	-0.23	-0.15	0.00
Mean	-0.13	-0.07	-0.55	-0.13	-0.10	0.00
Std dev	28.81	5.10	57.17	1.47	1.05	1.00
Skewness	5.09	0.38	-2.50	0.35	0.24	0.00
Kurtosis	33.04	3.27	54.07	3.21	2.99	3.00

Appendix B. Power and Distribution of the BDS Statistic

Table B.1
Power of BDS Statistic: Tent Map

		ϵ/σ					N(0,1)
		0.25	0.50	1.00	1.50	2.00	
m=2,T=100							
%<	-2.33	0.00	0.00	0.00	0.65	71.55	1.00
%<	-1.96	0.00	0.00	0.00	0.75	75.35	2.50
%<	-1.64	0.00	0.00	0.00	1.00	77.95	5.00
%>	1.64	100.00	100.00	100.00	85.90	4.45	5.00
%>	1.96	100.00	100.00	100.00	83.75	3.60	2.50
%>	2.33	100.00	100.00	100.00	81.45	3.25	1.00
m=2,T=500							
%<	-2.33	0.00	0.00	0.00	0.00	97.20	1.00
%<	-1.96	0.00	0.00	0.00	0.00	98.10	2.50
%<	-1.64	0.00	0.00	0.00	0.00	98.45	5.00
%>	1.64	100.00	100.00	100.00	100.00	0.10	5.00
%>	1.96	100.00	100.00	100.00	99.95	0.05	2.50
%>	2.33	100.00	100.00	100.00	99.90	0.00	1.00
m=2,T=1000							
%<	-2.33	0.00	0.00	0.00	0.00	99.70	1.00
%<	-1.96	0.00	0.00	0.00	0.00	99.80	2.50
%<	-1.64	0.00	0.00	0.00	0.00	99.85	5.00
%>	1.64	100.00	100.00	100.00	100.00	0.00	5.00
%>	1.96	100.00	100.00	100.00	100.00	0.00	2.50
%>	2.33	100.00	100.00	100.00	100.00	0.00	1.00
m=5,T=500							
%<	-2.33	0.00	0.00	0.00	2.25	26.50	1.00
%<	-1.96	0.00	0.00	0.00	3.20	32.25	2.50
%<	-1.64	0.00	0.00	0.00	4.55	37.95	5.00
%>	1.64	100.00	100.00	100.00	56.05	14.40	5.00
%>	1.96	100.00	100.00	100.00	50.65	11.15	2.50
%>	2.33	100.00	100.00	100.00	44.90	8.90	1.00
m=5,T=1000							
%<	-2.33	0.00	0.00	0.00	0.95	29.15	1.00
%<	-1.96	0.00	0.00	0.00	1.40	34.35	2.50
%<	-1.64	0.00	0.00	0.00	2.10	39.30	5.00
%>	1.64	100.00	100.00	100.00	70.55	14.65	5.00
%>	1.96	100.00	100.00	100.00	66.00	11.60	2.50
%>	2.33	100.00	100.00	100.00	60.20	9.00	1.00
m=10,T=1000							
%<	-2.33	0.00	0.00	0.00	15.70	8.30	1.00
%<	-1.96	0.00	0.00	0.00	21.35	11.45	2.50
%<	-1.64	0.00	0.00	0.00	26.75	14.10	5.00
%>	1.64	100.00	100.00	100.00	20.05	32.05	5.00
%>	1.96	100.00	100.00	100.00	16.85	27.70	2.50
%>	2.33	100.00	100.00	100.00	14.15	22.05	1.00

Table B.2
Power of BDS Statistic
AR1 ($\rho=.5$)

		0.25	0.50	ϵ/σ 1.00	1.50	2.00	N(0,1)
m=2,T=100							
%<	-2.33	3.60	0.30	0.00	0.05	0.05	1.00
%<	-1.96	4.20	0.35	0.10	0.10	0.10	2.50
%<	-1.64	5.15	0.60	0.10	0.10	0.15	5.00
%>	1.64	78.50	87.70	92.50	93.30	91.40	5.00
%>	1.96	76.20	84.40	89.70	90.75	89.05	2.50
%>	2.33	73.25	80.55	85.85	87.50	85.15	1.00
m=2,T=500							
%<	-2.33	0.00	0.00	0.00	0.00	0.00	1.00
%<	-1.96	0.00	0.00	0.00	0.00	0.00	2.50
%<	-1.64	0.00	0.00	0.00	0.00	0.00	5.00
%>	1.64	100.00	100.00	100.00	100.00	100.00	5.00
%>	1.96	100.00	100.00	100.00	100.00	100.00	2.50
%>	2.33	100.00	100.00	100.00	100.00	100.00	1.00
m=2,T=1000							
%<	-2.33	0.00	0.00	0.00	0.00	0.00	1.00
%<	-1.96	0.00	0.00	0.00	0.00	0.00	2.50
%<	-1.64	0.00	0.00	0.00	0.00	0.00	5.00
%>	1.64	100.00	100.00	100.00	100.00	100.00	5.00
%>	1.96	100.00	100.00	100.00	100.00	100.00	2.50
%>	2.33	100.00	100.00	100.00	100.00	100.00	1.00
m=5,T=500							
%<	-2.33	6.35	0.00	0.00	0.00	0.00	1.00
%<	-1.96	6.80	0.00	0.00	0.00	0.00	2.50
%<	-1.64	7.65	0.00	0.00	0.00	0.00	5.00
%>	1.64	83.60	99.85	100.00	100.00	100.00	5.00
%>	1.96	82.15	99.80	100.00	100.00	100.00	2.50
%>	2.33	80.75	99.55	100.00	100.00	100.00	1.00
m=5,T=1000							
%<	-2.33	0.20	0.00	0.00	0.00	0.00	1.00
%<	-1.96	0.35	0.00	0.00	0.00	0.00	2.50
%<	-1.64	0.45	0.00	0.00	0.00	0.00	5.00
%>	1.64	97.85	100.00	100.00	100.00	100.00	5.00
%>	1.96	97.65	100.00	100.00	100.00	100.00	2.50
%>	2.33	97.35	100.00	100.00	100.00	100.00	1.00
m=10,T=1000							
%<	-2.33	99.55	6.85	0.00	0.00	0.00	1.00
%<	-1.96	99.55	6.90	0.00	0.00	0.00	2.50
%<	-1.64	99.55	7.50	0.00	0.00	0.00	5.00
%>	1.64	0.45	82.00	100.00	100.00	100.00	5.00
%>	1.96	0.45	81.85	100.00	100.00	100.00	2.50
%>	2.33	0.45	80.80	100.00	100.00	100.00	1.00

Table B.3
Power of BDS Statistic
MA1 (θ=.5)

		0.25	0.50	ϵ/σ 1.00	1.50	2.00	N(0,1)
m=2,T=100							
%<	-2.33	9.85	0.45	0.00	0.10	0.20	1.00
%<	-1.96	11.95	0.90	0.05	0.10	0.25	2.50
%<	-1.64	13.20	1.80	0.15	0.15	0.55	5.00
%>	1.64	59.10	66.30	71.55	74.90	74.30	5.00
%>	1.96	55.50	60.95	65.55	68.70	67.15	2.50
%>	2.33	51.60	54.95	58.50	60.50	59.95	1.00
m=2,T=500							
%<	-2.33	0.00	0.00	0.00	0.00	0.00	1.00
%<	-1.96	0.00	0.00	0.00	0.00	0.00	2.50
%<	-1.64	0.00	0.00	0.00	0.00	0.00	5.00
%>	1.64	99.05	99.85	100.00	100.00	100.00	5.00
%>	1.96	98.45	99.65	100.00	100.00	100.00	2.50
%>	2.33	97.60	99.30	99.75	99.95	99.90	1.00
m=2,T=1000							
%<	-2.33	0.00	0.00	0.00	0.00	0.00	1.00
%<	-1.96	0.00	0.00	0.00	0.00	0.00	2.50
%<	-1.64	0.00	0.00	0.00	0.00	0.00	5.00
%>	1.64	100.00	100.00	100.00	100.00	100.00	5.00
%>	1.96	100.00	100.00	100.00	100.00	100.00	2.50
%>	2.33	100.00	100.00	100.00	100.00	100.00	1.00
m=5,T=500							
%<	-2.33	10.45	0.00	0.00	0.00	0.00	1.00
%<	-1.96	11.40	0.00	0.00	0.00	0.00	2.50
%<	-1.64	12.45	0.00	0.00	0.00	0.00	5.00
%>	1.64	72.75	97.75	99.65	99.80	99.70	5.00
%>	1.96	71.30	96.80	99.25	99.60	99.50	2.50
%>	2.33	69.25	95.45	98.50	99.10	98.55	1.00
m=5,T=1000							
%<	-2.33	1.00	0.00	0.00	0.00	0.00	1.00
%<	-1.96	1.30	0.00	0.00	0.00	0.00	2.50
%<	-1.64	1.75	0.00	0.00	0.00	0.00	5.00
%>	1.64	93.15	99.95	100.00	100.00	100.00	5.00
%>	1.96	92.30	99.95	100.00	100.00	100.00	2.50
%>	2.33	91.05	99.95	100.00	100.00	100.00	1.00
m=10,T=1000							
%<	-2.33	99.70	12.10	0.00	0.00	0.00	1.00
%<	-1.96	99.70	12.25	0.00	0.00	0.00	2.50
%<	-1.64	99.70	13.90	0.00	0.00	0.00	5.00
%>	1.64	0.30	70.15	99.90	99.95	100.00	5.00
%>	1.96	0.30	69.40	99.90	99.95	99.90	2.50
%>	2.33	0.30	68.20	99.70	99.75	99.60	1.00

Table B.4
Power of BDS Statistic
Threshold AR

	ϵ/σ					
	0.25	0.50	1.00	1.50	2.00	N(0,1)
m=2,T=100						
%< -2.33	10.10	1.70	0.30	0.95	3.65	1.00
%< -1.96	11.60	2.05	0.85	2.00	5.30	2.50
%< -1.64	13.70	2.95	1.60	3.45	8.70	5.00
%> 1.64	58.40	61.65	50.00	35.80	24.60	5.00
%> 1.96	55.75	56.80	43.05	29.20	19.50	2.50
%> 2.33	51.75	50.80	35.35	21.00	14.30	1.00
m=2,T=500						
%< -2.33	0.00	0.00	0.00	0.00	0.00	1.00
%< -1.96	0.00	0.00	0.00	0.00	0.10	2.50
%< -1.64	0.00	0.00	0.00	0.00	0.55	5.00
%> 1.64	97.75	98.45	95.85	83.10	55.95	5.00
%> 1.96	96.85	97.55	93.20	75.60	47.10	2.50
%> 2.33	95.35	95.75	89.65	66.10	38.05	1.00
m=2,T=1000						
%< -2.33	0.00	0.00	0.00	0.00	0.00	1.00
%< -1.96	0.00	0.00	0.00	0.00	0.00	2.50
%< -1.64	0.00	0.00	0.00	0.00	0.05	5.00
%> 1.64	99.95	100.00	99.95	97.45	79.30	5.00
%> 1.96	99.95	100.00	99.75	94.90	72.10	2.50
%> 2.33	99.90	99.95	99.40	91.20	62.85	1.00
m=5,T=500						
%< -2.33	16.85	0.00	0.00	0.00	0.15	1.00
%< -1.96	17.65	0.00	0.00	0.05	0.25	2.50
%< -1.64	18.70	0.05	0.00	0.10	0.50	5.00
%> 1.64	64.95	88.20	86.50	67.95	45.35	5.00
%> 1.96	63.95	84.10	80.05	59.30	36.30	2.50
%> 2.33	61.15	79.70	71.25	48.35	27.45	1.00
m=5,T=1000						
%< -2.33	3.40	0.00	0.00	0.00	0.00	1.00
%< -1.96	4.15	0.00	0.00	0.00	0.00	2.50
%< -1.64	4.85	0.00	0.00	0.00	0.00	5.00
%> 1.64	83.65	99.20	98.75	90.85	70.60	5.00
%> 1.96	81.80	98.60	97.20	85.70	60.50	2.50
%> 2.33	80.20	97.30	94.50	78.00	49.10	1.00
m=10,T=1000						
%< -2.33	100.00	20.35	0.00	0.00	0.00	1.00
%< -1.96	100.00	20.40	0.00	0.00	0.05	2.50
%< -1.64	100.00	22.30	0.00	0.00	0.10	5.00
%> 1.64	0.00	54.60	87.70	72.10	49.20	5.00
%> 1.96	0.00	54.05	82.35	62.75	39.55	2.50
%> 2.33	0.00	53.20	75.40	51.95	28.70	1.00

Table B.5
Power of BDS Statistic
Nonlinear MA ($\gamma=.8$)

		0.25	0.50	ϵ/σ 1.00	1.50	2.00	N(0,1)
m=2,T=100							
%<	-2.33	11.50	1.60	0.40	0.40	0.45	1.00
%<	-1.96	13.50	2.95	0.70	0.80	0.95	2.50
%<	-1.64	15.20	4.25	1.35	1.20	1.75	5.00
%>	1.64	51.75	53.20	57.35	59.15	60.35	5.00
%>	1.96	48.30	47.85	51.00	53.15	54.90	2.50
%>	2.33	44.10	40.50	42.15	45.40	46.60	1.00
m=2,T=500							
%<	-2.33	0.00	0.00	0.00	0.00	0.00	1.00
%<	-1.96	0.00	0.00	0.00	0.00	0.00	2.50
%<	-1.64	0.05	0.00	0.00	0.00	0.00	5.00
%>	1.64	92.60	96.25	98.05	98.85	99.10	5.00
%>	1.96	90.20	94.65	97.00	97.90	98.05	2.50
%>	2.33	86.20	91.20	94.95	96.60	96.95	1.00
m=2,T=1000							
%<	-2.33	0.00	0.00	0.00	0.00	0.00	1.00
%<	-1.96	0.00	0.00	0.00	0.00	0.00	2.50
%<	-1.64	0.00	0.00	0.00	0.00	0.00	5.00
%>	1.64	99.65	100.00	100.00	100.00	100.00	5.00
%>	1.96	99.55	99.95	100.00	100.00	100.00	2.50
%>	2.33	98.90	99.95	100.00	100.00	100.00	1.00
m=5,T=500							
%<	-2.33	5.35	0.00	0.00	0.00	0.00	1.00
%<	-1.96	6.40	0.00	0.00	0.00	0.00	2.50
%<	-1.64	6.90	0.00	0.00	0.00	0.00	5.00
%>	1.64	82.25	99.70	100.00	99.95	99.95	5.00
%>	1.96	80.60	99.45	99.95	99.85	99.85	2.50
%>	2.33	78.90	99.00	99.60	99.65	99.75	1.00
m=5,T=1000							
%<	-2.33	0.15	0.00	0.00	0.00	0.00	1.00
%<	-1.96	0.20	0.00	0.00	0.00	0.00	2.50
%<	-1.64	0.25	0.00	0.00	0.00	0.00	5.00
%>	1.64	98.05	100.00	100.00	100.00	100.00	5.00
%>	1.96	97.40	100.00	100.00	100.00	100.00	2.50
%>	2.33	96.55	100.00	100.00	100.00	100.00	1.00
m=10,T=1000							
%<	-2.33	99.20	3.30	0.00	0.00	0.00	1.00
%<	-1.96	99.20	5.55	0.00	0.00	0.00	2.50
%<	-1.64	99.20	6.35	0.00	0.00	0.00	5.00
%>	1.64	0.80	86.55	100.00	100.00	100.00	5.00
%>	1.96	0.80	85.85	100.00	100.00	100.00	2.50
%>	2.33	0.80	84.70	100.00	100.00	100.00	1.00

Table B.6
Power of BDS Statistic
ARCH ($\phi=.5$)

		0.25	0.50	ϵ/σ 1.00	1.50	2.00	N(0,1)
m=2,T=100							
%<	-2.33	4.20	0.65	0.05	0.00	0.10	1.00
%<	-1.96	4.75	0.85	0.10	0.05	0.25	2.50
%<	-1.64	5.65	1.10	0.15	0.15	0.35	5.00
%>	1.64	74.10	83.40	87.55	88.30	86.10	5.00
%>	1.96	71.25	79.70	84.10	84.80	81.55	2.50
%>	2.33	68.20	74.90	78.55	79.65	77.20	1.00
m=2,T=500							
%<	-2.33	0.00	0.00	0.00	0.00	0.00	1.00
%<	-1.96	0.00	0.00	0.00	0.00	0.00	2.50
%<	-1.64	0.00	0.00	0.00	0.00	0.00	5.00
%>	1.64	100.00	100.00	100.00	100.00	100.00	5.00
%>	1.96	100.00	100.00	100.00	100.00	100.00	2.50
%>	2.33	99.95	100.00	100.00	100.00	100.00	1.00
m=2,T=1000							
%<	-2.33	0.00	0.00	0.00	0.00	0.00	1.00
%<	-1.96	0.00	0.00	0.00	0.00	0.00	2.50
%<	-1.64	0.00	0.00	0.00	0.00	0.00	5.00
%>	1.64	100.00	100.00	100.00	100.00	100.00	5.00
%>	1.96	100.00	100.00	100.00	100.00	100.00	2.50
%>	2.33	100.00	100.00	100.00	100.00	100.00	1.00
m=5,T=500							
%<	-2.33	3.25	0.00	0.00	0.00	0.00	1.00
%<	-1.96	3.80	0.00	0.00	0.00	0.00	2.50
%<	-1.64	4.40	0.00	0.00	0.00	0.00	5.00
%>	1.64	85.85	99.55	99.95	100.00	100.00	5.00
%>	1.96	84.40	99.25	99.95	99.95	99.90	2.50
%>	2.33	82.70	98.75	99.85	99.95	99.85	1.00
m=5,T=1000							
%<	-2.33	0.00	0.00	0.00	0.00	0.00	1.00
%<	-1.96	0.00	0.00	0.00	0.00	0.00	2.50
%<	-1.64	0.05	0.00	0.00	0.00	0.00	5.00
%>	1.64	98.90	100.00	100.00	100.00	100.00	5.00
%>	1.96	98.50	100.00	100.00	100.00	100.00	2.50
%>	2.33	97.55	100.00	100.00	100.00	100.00	1.00
m=10,T=1000							
%<	-2.33	99.15	3.05	0.00	0.00	0.00	1.00
%<	-1.96	99.15	3.90	0.00	0.00	0.00	2.50
%<	-1.64	99.15	4.30	0.00	0.00	0.00	5.00
%>	1.64	0.85	87.75	100.00	100.00	100.00	5.00
%>	1.96	0.85	86.65	100.00	100.00	100.00	2.50
%>	2.33	0.85	85.25	99.95	100.00	99.95	1.00

Table B.7
Power of BDS Statistic
GARCH ($\phi=.1, \psi=.8$)

		0.25	0.50	1.00	1.50	2.00	N(0,1)
				ϵ/σ			
m=2,T=100							
%<	-2.33	19.30	5.95	1.65	1.85	2.95	1.00
%<	-1.96	22.20	8.25	3.15	2.95	5.10	2.50
%<	-1.64	24.65	11.35	5.25	4.85	7.60	5.00
%>	1.64	36.65	30.80	25.60	25.00	22.20	5.00
%>	1.96	33.00	25.85	20.20	18.70	17.40	2.50
%>	2.33	29.40	21.35	14.40	13.40	13.55	1.00
m=2,T=500							
%<	-2.33	0.75	0.05	0.00	0.00	0.00	1.00
%<	-1.96	1.05	0.15	0.00	0.10	0.20	2.50
%<	-1.64	1.50	0.30	0.10	0.20	0.25	5.00
%>	1.64	61.00	64.10	67.75	69.95	69.50	5.00
%>	1.96	53.40	55.65	58.85	61.90	61.90	2.50
%>	2.33	46.05	45.55	48.25	50.90	52.60	1.00
m=2,T=1000							
%<	-2.33	0.00	0.00	0.00	0.00	0.00	1.00
%<	-1.96	0.00	0.00	0.00	0.00	0.00	2.50
%<	-1.64	0.05	0.00	0.00	0.00	0.00	5.00
%>	1.64	84.75	88.70	90.35	91.95	93.00	5.00
%>	1.96	79.60	83.10	85.90	88.50	88.60	2.50
%>	2.33	72.25	75.20	80.30	83.40	84.00	1.00
m=5,T=500							
%<	-2.33	16.70	0.20	0.00	0.00	0.00	1.00
%<	-1.96	18.45	0.50	0.00	0.00	0.00	2.50
%<	-1.64	19.50	0.60	0.00	0.00	0.00	5.00
%>	1.64	60.15	81.05	87.40	89.55	89.00	5.00
%>	1.96	58.75	77.30	83.00	84.60	84.85	2.50
%>	2.33	56.25	71.75	76.60	79.25	78.80	1.00
m=5,T=1000							
%<	-2.33	3.65	0.00	0.00	0.00	0.00	1.00
%<	-1.96	4.40	0.00	0.00	0.00	0.00	2.50
%<	-1.64	5.40	0.00	0.00	0.00	0.00	5.00
%>	1.64	78.75	97.90	98.90	99.35	99.35	5.00
%>	1.96	76.85	96.65	98.35	98.85	99.10	2.50
%>	2.33	74.65	94.45	97.20	98.35	98.40	1.00
m=10,T=1000							
%<	-2.33	100.00	100.00	100.00	100.00	100.00	1.00
%<	-1.96	100.00	100.00	100.00	100.00	100.00	2.50
%<	-1.64	100.00	100.00	100.00	100.00	100.00	5.00
%>	1.64	0.00	0.00	0.00	0.00	0.00	5.00
%>	1.96	0.00	0.00	0.00	0.00	0.00	2.50
%>	2.33	0.00	0.00	0.00	0.00	0.00	1.00

Table B.8
Distribution of BDS Statistic
Tent Map

	ϵ/σ					
	0.25	0.50	1.00	1.50	2.00	N(0,1)
m=2,T=100						
Median	576.28	933.27	43.40	5.34	-4.35	0.00
Mean	2845.14	3785.76	42.37	5.11	-4.01	0.00
Std dev	36729.57	35393.96	8.86	2.96	3.01	1.00
Skewness	39.20	38.24	-0.18	-0.30	0.45	0.00
Kurtosis	1645.78	1594.11	4.20	2.83	2.75	3.00
m=2,T=500						
Median	4653.93	663.90	83.06	11.62	-8.73	0.00
Mean	16820.76	635.76	82.23	11.47	-8.52	0.00
Std dev	69217.05	131.67	4.01	2.78	3.04	1.00
Skewness	14.43	-0.76	-1.29	-0.28	0.31	0.00
Kurtosis	292.52	2.88	6.62	2.90	2.94	3.00
m=2,T=1000						
Median	4829.52	862.18	115.60	16.33	-12.19	0.00
Mean	4986.94	833.74	114.90	16.22	-12.02	0.00
Std dev	1786.98	117.72	3.25	2.77	3.09	1.00
Skewness	0.23	-0.97	-1.65	-0.17	0.29	0.00
Kurtosis	2.39	3.53	8.23	2.89	3.00	3.00
m=5,T=500						
Median	64201.33	2014.91	86.91	1.99	-0.91	0.00
Mean	232540.12	1932.15	86.65	2.19	-0.82	0.00
Std dev	959657.06	430.32	6.21	2.49	2.31	1.00
Skewness	14.74	-0.66	-0.29	0.34	0.25	0.00
Kurtosis	308.79	2.78	4.44	2.90	3.03	3.00
m=5,T=1000						
Median	66433.75	2614.57	121.25	3.05	-1.00	0.00
Mean	68503.09	2524.70	121.02	3.10	-0.92	0.00
Std dev	24900.69	387.80	5.49	2.53	2.37	1.00
Skewness	0.23	-0.85	-0.40	0.24	0.14	0.00
Kurtosis	2.38	3.33	4.37	2.96	2.82	3.00
m=10,T=1000						
Median	17493800.	35142.01	184.06	-0.30	0.66	0.00
Mean	18175300.	34589.29	185.24	-0.11	0.69	0.00
Std dev	7147600.	6748.46	14.73	2.25	2.16	1.00
Skewness	0.38	-0.29	0.48	0.66	0.15	0.00
Kurtosis	2.60	3.01	3.92	3.66	3.01	3.00

Table B.9
Distribution of BDS Statistic
AR1 ($\rho=.5$)

	ϵ/σ					
	0.25	0.50	1.00	1.50	2.00	N(0,1)
m=2,T=100						
Median	5.05	4.99	4.78	4.75	4.73	0.00
Mean	6.46	5.72	5.21	4.93	4.79	0.00
Std dev	8.94	4.47	3.02	2.38	2.32	1.00
Skewness	6.93	2.23	1.32	0.48	0.20	0.00
Kurtosis	103.83	14.55	7.60	3.57	2.95	3.00
m=2,T=500						
Median	11.24	11.22	11.20	11.19	11.13	0.00
Mean	11.50	11.41	11.27	11.16	11.10	0.00
Std dev	3.44	2.95	2.42	2.06	2.00	1.00
Skewness	0.48	0.41	0.24	0.03	-0.04	0.00
Kurtosis	3.35	3.25	3.09	2.91	2.94	3.00
m=2,T=1000						
Median	15.83	15.87	15.85	15.86	15.85	0.00
Mean	16.09	16.09	15.98	15.90	15.85	0.00
Std dev	3.21	2.91	2.46	2.13	2.07	1.00
Skewness	0.37	0.37	0.24	0.13	0.07	0.00
Kurtosis	3.30	3.32	3.34	3.39	3.28	3.00
m=5,T=500						
Median	9.09	9.67	9.23	8.87	8.63	0.00
Mean	10.17	9.95	9.33	8.86	8.63	0.00
Std dev	9.23	3.69	2.52	1.98	1.83	1.00
Skewness	0.72	0.57	0.33	0.11	0.05	0.00
Kurtosis	3.90	3.43	3.21	3.02	3.04	3.00
m=5,T=1000						
Median	13.91	13.65	13.15	12.62	12.36	0.00
Mean	14.24	13.91	13.25	12.68	12.37	0.00
Std dev	6.66	3.36	2.51	2.02	1.86	1.00
Skewness	0.44	0.40	0.28	0.15	0.07	0.00
Kurtosis	3.61	3.22	3.35	3.31	3.23	3.00
m=10,T=1000						
Median	-5.42	11.52	11.76	10.46	9.64	0.00
Mean	10.94	14.47	12.08	10.57	9.68	0.00
Std dev	248.42	15.22	3.38	2.20	1.78	1.00
Skewness	15.64	1.34	0.61	0.31	0.17	0.00
Kurtosis	254.45	6.02	3.86	3.37	3.17	3.00

Table B.10
Distribution of BDS Statistic
MA1 ($\theta=.5$)

	0.25	0.50	1.00	1.50	2.00	N(0,1)
			ϵ/σ			
m=2,T=100						
Median	2.49	2.65	2.75	2.76	2.77	0.00
Mean	3.38	3.15	3.00	2.89	2.83	0.00
Std dev	5.75	3.20	2.13	1.80	1.83	1.00
Skewness	1.69	2.00	0.84	0.38	0.16	0.00
Kurtosis	10.47	14.86	4.54	3.22	2.95	3.00
m=2,T=500						
Median	6.58	6.59	6.74	6.90	6.98	0.00
Mean	6.73	6.72	6.78	6.90	6.99	0.00
Std dev	2.50	2.04	1.72	1.55	1.57	1.00
Skewness	0.43	0.47	0.24	0.10	0.04	0.00
Kurtosis	3.33	3.50	3.15	2.99	2.89	3.00
m=2,T=1000						
Median	9.32	9.40	9.66	9.85	10.03	0.00
Mean	9.46	9.51	9.68	9.88	10.03	0.00
Std dev	2.25	2.01	1.76	1.60	1.61	1.00
Skewness	0.27	0.31	0.19	0.09	0.06	0.00
Kurtosis	3.21	3.30	3.37	3.30	3.14	3.00
m=5,T=500						
Median	5.96	6.21	5.84	5.51	5.20	0.00
Mean	6.80	6.48	5.92	5.53	5.24	0.00
Std dev	7.97	2.74	1.74	1.42	1.38	1.00
Skewness	0.72	0.57	0.28	0.15	0.10	0.00
Kurtosis	4.13	3.69	3.31	3.18	3.06	3.00
m=5,T=1000						
Median	9.05	8.86	8.40	7.89	7.54	0.00
Mean	9.27	9.00	8.46	7.93	7.57	0.00
Std dev	5.47	2.36	1.69	1.39	1.33	1.00
Skewness	0.33	0.40	0.27	0.15	0.10	0.00
Kurtosis	3.47	3.68	3.60	3.37	3.13	3.00
m=10,T=1000						
Median	-5.43	6.03	7.04	6.19	5.64	0.00
Mean	4.77	8.78	7.20	6.26	5.69	0.00
Std dev	190.04	12.07	2.19	1.51	1.30	1.00
Skewness	19.35	1.29	0.66	0.35	0.23	0.00
Kurtosis	393.26	5.45	4.41	3.58	3.27	3.00

Table B.11
Distribution of BDS Statistic
Threshold AR

| | ϵ/σ | | | | | |
	0.25	0.50	1.00	1.50	2.00	N(0,1)
m=2,T=100						
Median	2.57	2.39	1.65	1.06	0.58	0.00
Mean	3.54	2.75	1.75	1.09	0.59	0.00
Std dev	10.41	3.44	1.79	1.55	1.64	1.00
Skewness	24.12	4.79	0.44	0.05	0.10	0.00
Kurtosis	855.56	67.06	3.46	2.94	3.26	3.00
m=2,T=500						
Median	5.99	5.40	4.09	2.90	1.86	0.00
Mean	6.25	5.52	4.14	2.92	1.90	0.00
Std dev	2.58	2.01	1.50	1.34	1.41	1.00
Skewness	0.55	0.53	0.22	0.01	0.08	0.00
Kurtosis	3.52	3.68	3.08	2.77	2.84	3.00
m=2,T=1000						
Median	8.53	7.59	5.80	4.18	2.81	0.00
Mean	8.65	7.69	5.84	4.19	2.82	0.00
Std dev	2.32	1.93	1.51	1.37	1.41	1.00
Skewness	0.31	0.28	0.14	0.09	0.15	0.00
Kurtosis	3.19	3.06	2.99	2.90	2.93	3.00
m=5,T=500						
Median	4.21	4.24	3.17	2.26	1.49	0.00
Mean	4.98	4.45	3.25	2.31	1.54	0.00
Std dev	7.60	2.50	1.51	1.31	1.33	1.00
Skewness	0.68	0.58	0.38	0.13	0.12	0.00
Kurtosis	4.23	3.72	3.26	2.92	2.92	3.00
m=5,T=1000						
Median	6.53	5.97	4.55	3.34	2.30	0.00
Mean	6.85	6.10	4.60	3.34	2.32	0.00
Std dev	5.45	2.14	1.46	1.29	1.30	1.00
Skewness	0.42	0.40	0.26	0.21	0.17	0.00
Kurtosis	3.55	3.35	3.18	3.07	3.12	3.00
m=10,T=1000						
Median	-5.44	2.99	3.40	2.40	1.61	0.00
Mean	-5.48	4.89	3.51	2.46	1.68	0.00
Std dev	0.59	10.18	1.71	1.32	1.25	1.00
Skewness	-0.43	1.53	0.62	0.41	0.26	0.00
Kurtosis	3.47	7.82	4.06	3.33	3.21	3.00

Table B.12
Distribution of BDS Statistic
Nonlinear MA (γ=.8)

	ϵ/σ					
	0.25	0.50	1.00	1.50	2.00	N(0,1)
m=2,T=100						
Median	1.81	1.83	2.00	2.09	2.17	0.00
Mean	1.70	1.95	2.02	2.12	2.17	0.00
Std dev	16.05	2.23	1.74	1.75	1.90	1.00
Skewness	-40.11	0.40	0.16	0.10	0.12	0.00
Kurtosis	1730.51	3.76	2.96	2.87	2.92	3.00
m=2,T=500						
Median	4.41	4.50	4.86	5.25	5.65	0.00
Mean	4.44	4.53	4.84	5.26	5.63	0.00
Std dev	1.91	1.63	1.54	1.60	1.77	1.00
Skewness	0.14	0.14	0.02	0.00	0.03	0.00
Kurtosis	3.11	3.10	2.92	2.92	2.90	3.00
m=2,T=1000						
Median	6.34	6.39	6.90	7.55	8.13	0.00
Mean	6.35	6.46	6.90	7.51	8.06	0.00
Std dev	1.80	1.61	1.55	1.60	1.74	1.00
Skewness	0.06	0.12	0.07	0.02	0.02	0.00
Kurtosis	2.77	2.81	2.76	2.75	2.74	3.00
m=5,T=500						
Median	7.40	7.18	6.72	6.34	6.19	0.00
Mean	7.77	7.41	6.80	6.43	6.21	0.00
Std dev	6.74	2.57	1.75	1.51	1.48	1.00
Skewness	0.46	0.45	0.26	0.10	0.08	0.00
Kurtosis	3.48	3.17	3.03	3.00	2.88	3.00
m=5,T=1000						
Median	10.74	10.45	9.60	9.14	8.89	0.00
Mean	10.91	10.54	9.68	9.17	8.88	0.00
Std dev	5.10	2.36	1.77	1.52	1.44	1.00
Skewness	0.37	0.39	0.22	0.10	-0.01	0.00
Kurtosis	3.40	3.47	3.14	3.00	2.84	3.00
m=10,T=1000						
Median	-4.62	11.28	9.33	7.84	7.13	0.00
Mean	15.63	12.98	9.63	7.97	7.18	0.00
Std dev	262.18	11.16	2.72	1.84	1.49	1.00
Skewness	17.53	1.25	0.58	0.33	0.12	0.00
Kurtosis	382.99	6.56	3.33	2.96	2.81	3.00

Table B.13
Distribution of BDS Statistic
ARCH ($\phi=.5$)

	0.25	0.50	ϵ/σ 1.00	1.50	2.00	N(0,1)
m=2,T=100						
Median	3.88	3.83	3.89	3.88	3.87	0.00
Mean	4.01	3.85	3.84	3.92	3.92	0.00
Std dev	4.06	2.36	1.91	1.94	2.12	1.00
Skewness	0.85	-0.07	-0.03	0.00	0.03	0.00
Kurtosis	10.04	3.65	3.03	2.94	2.88	3.00
m=2,T=500						
Median	8.30	8.36	8.60	8.93	9.22	0.00
Mean	8.34	8.41	8.64	9.05	9.42	0.00
Std dev	2.01	1.74	1.67	1.85	2.18	1.00
Skewness	0.16	0.15	0.14	0.27	0.36	0.00
Kurtosis	3.06	3.03	3.18	3.45	3.52	3.00
m=2,T=1000						
Median	11.80	11.89	12.28	12.87	13.36	0.00
Mean	11.86	11.92	12.26	12.85	13.45	0.00
Std dev	1.91	1.74	1.70	1.88	2.25	1.00
Skewness	0.03	-0.03	-0.03	0.11	0.24	0.00
Kurtosis	2.84	2.91	3.05	3.14	3.28	3.00
m=5,T=500						
Median	7.21	7.57	7.60	7.75	7.89	0.00
Mean	7.67	7.74	7.65	7.78	7.97	0.00
Std dev	5.96	2.75	2.11	2.00	2.11	1.00
Skewness	0.51	0.38	0.20	0.13	0.17	0.00
Kurtosis	3.80	3.19	3.02	2.96	2.96	3.00
m=5,T=1000						
Median	10.74	10.79	10.83	11.07	11.39	0.00
Mean	10.92	10.91	10.88	11.09	11.42	0.00
Std dev	4.43	2.52	2.09	1.98	2.12	1.00
Skewness	0.29	0.27	0.11	0.11	0.11	0.00
Kurtosis	3.31	3.00	3.00	3.12	3.08	3.00
m=10,T=1000						
Median	-4.26	9.71	9.49	9.10	9.06	0.00
Mean	7.15	10.84	9.78	9.26	9.09	0.00
Std dev	160.78	9.04	3.10	2.28	2.06	1.00
Skewness	18.20	1.38	0.58	0.28	0.12	0.00
Kurtosis	394.99	8.01	3.55	3.25	3.06	3.00

Table B.14
Distribution of BDS Statistic
GARCH ($\phi=.1, \psi=.8$)

	\multicolumn{5}{c}{ϵ/σ}	
	0.25	0.50	1.00	1.50	2.00	N(0,1)
m=2,T=100						
Median	0.57	0.63	0.64	0.62	0.45	0.00
Mean	0.73	0.75	0.69	0.65	0.52	0.00
Std dev	4.35	2.16	1.54	1.50	1.59	1.00
Skewness	-0.03	0.49	0.22	0.21	0.11	0.00
Kurtosis	8.98	4.30	3.11	3.12	3.29	3.00
m=2,T=500						
Median	2.11	2.18	2.28	2.36	2.42	0.00
Mean	2.23	2.25	2.36	2.47	2.54	0.00
Std dev	1.91	1.53	1.45	1.49	1.61	1.00
Skewness	0.22	0.22	0.21	0.24	0.37	0.00
Kurtosis	3.02	3.02	2.92	3.07	3.33	3.00
m=2,T=1000						
Median	3.28	3.32	3.51	3.67	3.85	0.00
Mean	3.33	3.38	3.55	3.77	3.96	0.00
Std dev	1.64	1.47	1.45	1.53	1.70	1.00
Skewness	0.09	0.16	0.15	0.26	0.42	0.00
Kurtosis	2.93	2.86	2.98	3.12	3.38	3.00
m=5,T=500						
Median	3.38	3.57	3.64	3.70	3.78	0.00
Mean	3.93	3.82	3.81	3.86	3.89	0.00
Std dev	6.76	2.55	1.97	1.86	1.89	1.00
Skewness	0.69	0.59	0.50	0.41	0.41	0.00
Kurtosis	4.35	3.75	3.30	3.22	3.20	3.00
m=10,T=1000						
Median	5.27	5.36	5.52	5.76	5.92	0.00
Mean	5.57	5.54	5.66	5.85	6.03	0.00
Std dev	4.77	2.22	1.90	1.84	1.93	1.00
Skewness	0.30	0.44	0.34	0.34	0.40	0.00
Kurtosis	3.04	3.21	3.14	3.25	3.39	3.00
m=10,T=1000						
Median	-4.97	-5.45	-7.85	-13.77	-28.24	0.00
Mean	-5.01	-5.49	-7.88	-13.78	-28.21	0.00
Std dev	0.55	0.52	0.46	0.49	1.04	1.00
Skewness	-0.37	-0.41	-0.41	-0.18	0.16	0.00
Kurtosis	3.27	3.30	3.28	3.04	3.05	3.00

Appendix C. Quantiles of the BDS Statistic

Table C.1
Quantiles of BDS Statistic
Normal Random Variables
100 Observations

	m					
	2	3	4	5	10	N(0,1)
$\epsilon=.5\sigma$						
1.0%	-4.87	-5.59	-7.04	-8.86		-2.33
2.5%	-3.87	-4.54	-5.50	-7.11		-1.96
5.0%	-3.24	-3.64	-4.55	-5.79		-1.64
10.0%	-2.56	-2.86	-3.43	-4.47		-1.28
90.0%	2.40	2.82	3.57	4.64		1.28
95.0%	3.36	3.80	4.99	6.75		1.64
97.5%	4.33	5.05	6.48	8.98		1.96
99.0%	5.60	6.65	8.69	11.63		2.33
$\epsilon=\sigma$						
1.0%	-2.92	-2.92	-3.05	-3.09		-2.33
2.5%	-2.58	-2.55	-2.63	-2.63		-1.96
5.0%	-2.20	-2.23	-2.25	-2.28		-1.64
10.0%	-1.79	-1.80	-1.80	-1.88		-1.28
90.0%	1.65	1.67	1.74	1.79		1.28
95.0%	2.22	2.28	2.39	2.62		1.64
97.5%	2.70	2.84	3.07	3.31		1.96
99.0%	3.40	3.60	3.85	4.07		2.33

Based on 5000 replications.

Table C.2
Quantiles of BDS Statistic
Normal Random Variables
250 Observations

| | \multicolumn{5}{c}{m} | |
	2	3	4	5	10	N(0,1)
$\epsilon=.5\sigma$						
1.0%	-3.05	-3.38	-4.06	-4.86	-4.96	-2.33
2.5%	-2.64	-2.92	-3.37	-4.11	-4.58	-1.96
5.0%	-2.24	-2.47	-2.87	-3.49	-4.23	-1.64
10.0%	-1.82	-1.99	-2.32	-2.80	-3.89	-1.28
90.0%	1.74	1.94	2.24	2.85	-2.23	1.28
95.0%	2.35	2.59	3.02	3.88	18.48	1.64
97.5%	2.98	3.23	3.84	4.98	46.15	1.96
99.0%	3.71	4.04	4.85	6.44	78.67	2.33
$\epsilon=\sigma$						
1.0%	-2.52	-2.47	-2.50	-2.52	-5.80	-2.33
2.5%	-2.15	-2.17	-2.17	-2.18	-5.49	-1.96
5.0%	-1.88	-1.87	-1.89	-1.89	-5.22	-1.64
10.0%	-1.52	-1.54	-1.55	-1.57	-4.94	-1.28
90.0%	1.44	1.43	1.44	1.49	-3.63	1.28
95.0%	1.86	1.91	1.98	2.10	-3.50	1.64
97.5%	2.27	2.37	2.39	2.56	-3.39	1.96
99.0%	2.79	2.92	2.96	3.06	-3.28	2.33

Based on 5000 replications.

Table C.3
Quantiles of BDS Statistic
Normal Random Variables
500 Observations

	2	3	m 4	5	10	N(0,1)
$\epsilon=.5\sigma$						
1.0%	-2.62	-2.81	-3.08	-3.67	-5.76	-2.33
2.5%	-2.25	-2.38	-2.62	-3.16	-5.43	-1.96
5.0%	-1.93	-2.02	-2.22	-2.66	-5.21	-1.64
10.0%	-1.56	-1.62	-1.81	-2.15	-4.94	-1.28
90.0%	1.54	1.62	1.85	2.16	11.14	1.28
95.0%	1.98	2.25	2.42	2.98	20.55	1.64
97.5%	2.46	2.74	3.01	3.67	29.52	1.96
99.0%	3.00	3.30	3.64	4.45	42.61	2.33
$\epsilon=\sigma$						
1.0%	-2.37	-2.30	-2.33	-2.29	-2.43	-2.33
2.5%	-2.02	-2.02	-2.00	-2.02	-2.09	-1.96
5.0%	-1.74	-1.73	-1.71	-1.71	-1.84	-1.64
10.0%	-1.40	-1.41	-1.39	-1.38	-1.53	-1.28
90.0%	1.34	1.38	1.40	1.43	1.71	1.28
95.0%	1.81	1.83	1.87	1.94	2.39	1.64
97.5%	2.18	2.26	2.26	2.32	2.95	1.96
99.0%	2.61	2.73	2.87	2.99	3.99	2.33

Based on 5000 replications.

Appendix D. The Nuisance Parameter Property of the BDS Statistic

This appendix provides two statements of the "nuisance parameter" free property of the BDS statistic. The first part follows Brock and Dechert 1988b.

First, consider the data generator

$$y_t = f(I_t, \beta) + \sigma u_t, \tag{D.1}$$

where I_t is an information set available at time t and $\{u_t\}$ is IID with mean zero and finite variance. Here I_t can contain past y's but no current and futures y's. Furthermore, u_t is independent of I_t for all t.

We assume that β and σ can be estimated $T^{\frac{1}{2}}$-consistently by β_T and σ_T, respectively. Denote $f_T = f(I_t, \beta_T)$. We apply the BDS test to the "standardized" residuals

$$u_{t,T} = (y_t - f_T)/\sigma_T. \tag{D.2}$$

Under the null model, $u_{t,T} \xrightarrow{d} u_t$. Note that

$$u_{t,T}$$

$$= (f + \sigma u_t - f_T)/\sigma_T,$$

$$= (f - f_T)/\sigma_T + (\sigma - \sigma_T)u_t/\sigma_T + u_t$$

We thank Pedro de Lima for correcting some of the mistakes in Appendix D.

$\equiv d_{t,T} + u_t.$ (D.3)

Theorem D.1. Under smoothness conditions on the kernel, moment conditions on the interaction of the kernel with the data generation process, and regularity conditions on the strength of temporal dependence to be detailed below, the first order asymptotic distribution of the BDS statistic is the same whether one calculates the statistic at the estimated standardized residuals, $\{u_{t,T}\}$, or at the true ones, $\{u_t\}$.

We will prove this theorem in two stages: first we derive a similar result for the case of a smooth symmetric kernel, and then we prove an approximation theorem for the (nonsmooth) kernel used in the BDS statistic.

Theorem D.2, to be stated and proved below, applies to the model (D.1) under the regularity conditions (A1–A5) stated below. In the case where the standard deviation, σ, is known, sufficient conditions on (D.1) for such regularity may easily be found by expanding (D.2) in a Taylor series about the true value of σ. The theorem does not apply in the case where σ must be estimated because (A4) fails. However, for the BDS statistic itself, Theorem D.5 below does apply because the moment condition (A2) holds. This can be verified under the regularity hypotheses of Theorem D.5 by expanding (D.2) in a Taylor series about the true value of σ and computing out the expression for the moment in (A2) and verifying directly that this moment is zero for the BDS statistic itself. Note that this moment is not zero for the correlation integral. Turn now to the statement and proof of Theorem D.2.

Theorem D.2. Let $\{u_t\}$ be IID with a symmetric distribution function F, and let $\{u_{t,T}\}$, $\{\xi_t\}$, and $\{\psi_T\}$ satisfy the following:

(A1) $u_{t,T} - u_t = \psi_T \, \xi_t + o(\psi_T)$,

(A2) $\psi_T \xrightarrow{P} 0$,

(A3) $T^{\frac{1}{2}}\psi_T \xrightarrow{d} Z$, with $E[Z^2] < \infty$,

(A4) ξ_t is F_{t-1} measurable,

(A5) $\sup_T T^{-1} \Sigma_{t=1}^T E[\xi_t^2] < \infty$,

where F_t is the σ-algebra generated by u_t, u_{t-1},.... Let ϕ be an even C^1 function which also satisfies

(A6) $0 \le \phi \le 1$, $\sup_u \{|\phi'(u)|, |\phi''(u)|\} < \infty$,

and let

(A7) $U_T = T^{-2} \Sigma_{s=1}^T \Sigma_{t=1}^T \phi(u_t - u_s)$,

(A8) $\hat{U}_T = T^{-2} \Sigma_{s=1}^T \Sigma_{t=1}^T \phi(u_{t,T} - u_{s,T})$,

and define $\Delta_T = \hat{U}_T - U_T$. Then

$T^{\frac{1}{2}} \Delta_T \xrightarrow{P} 0$.

Proof. To save notation, the summation sign "Σ_s" shall denote "$\Sigma_{s=1}^T$" unless otherwise specified. From the definition of Δ_T,

$$\Delta_T \quad = T^{-2} \; \Sigma_s \; \Sigma_t \; \phi(u_{t,T}-u_{s,T}) - \phi(u_t-u_s),$$

$$\overset{L}{=} T^{-2} \; \Sigma_s \; \Sigma_t \; \phi'(u_t-u_s)[(u_{t,T}-u_t) - (u_{s,T}-u_s)],$$

$$= 2T^{-2} \; \Sigma_s \; \Sigma_t \; \phi'(u_t-u_s)(u_{t,T}-u_t),$$

$$= 2\psi_T T^{-2} \; \Sigma_s \; \Sigma_t \; \phi'(u_t-u_s)\xi_t + o(\psi_T),$$

$$= 2\psi_T \; \{T^{-1} \; \Sigma_t \; [T^{-1} \; \Sigma_s \; \phi'(u_t-u_s)-\phi_1'(u_t)]\xi_t$$
$$+ T^{-1} \; \Sigma_t \; \phi_1'(u_t)\xi_t\} + o(\psi_T), \tag{D.4}$$

where the third equality follows from the even property of ϕ, and function ϕ_1 is given by

$$\phi_1 = \int \phi(u-v) \; dF(v), \tag{D.5}$$

and "$\overset{L}{=}$" means that only the first order terms have been retained. It is straightforward to use (A6) to show that the higher order terms converge in distribution to zero when multiplied by $T^{\frac{1}{2}}$. Thus, up to the linear terms, $T^{\frac{1}{2}} \Delta_T$ is of the form $Z_T W_T + o(\psi_T)$, where $Z_T \overset{P}{\to} 0$ and $T^{\frac{1}{2}} o(\psi_T) \overset{P}{\to} 0$. Now if $W_T \overset{P}{\to} 0$, then $Z_T W_T \overset{d}{\to} 0$, so $Z_T W_T \overset{P}{\to} 0$. Thus, to show that $T^{\frac{1}{2}} \Delta_T \overset{P}{\to} 0$, it is sufficient to show that

$$T^{-1} \; \Sigma_t \; [T^{-1} \; \Sigma_s \; \phi'(u_t-u_s)-\phi_1'(u_t)]\xi_t + T^{-1} \; \Sigma_t \; \phi_1'(u_t)\xi_t \tag{D.6}$$

converges to zero in probability.

Consider the L^1-norm of the first term in equation (D.6),

$$E \mid T^{-1} \Sigma_t [T^{-1} \Sigma_s \phi'(u_t-u_s)-\phi_1'(u_t)]\xi_t \mid$$

$$\leq T^{-1} \Sigma_t E \mid T^{-1} \Sigma_s \phi'(u_t-u_s)-\phi_1'(u_t) \mid |\xi_t|$$

$$\leq \{T^{-1} \Sigma_t E [T^{-1} \Sigma_s \phi'(u_t-u_s)-\phi_1'(u_t)]]^2 \}^{\frac{1}{2}}$$
$$\times \{T^{-1} \Sigma_t E \xi_t^2\}^{\frac{1}{2}}, \qquad (D.7)$$

where the latter inequality follows from Hölder's inequality. By assumption, $\sup_T T^{-1} \Sigma_t E[\xi_t^2] < \infty$, so we need only show that the first term converges to zero:

$$T^{-1} \Sigma_t E [T^{-1} \Sigma_s \phi'(u_t-u_s)-\phi_1'(u_t)] \cdot [T^{-1} \Sigma_r \phi'(u_t-u_r)-\phi_1'(u_t)]$$

$$= T^{-1} \Sigma_{t=1}^{T} E [T^{-2} \Sigma_r \Sigma_s \phi'(u_t-u_s)\phi'(u_t-u_r)$$

$$- 2\phi_1'(u_t) T^{-1} \Sigma_s \phi'(u_t-u_s) + \phi_1'(u_t)^2]. \qquad (D.8)$$

The expected value of these terms can be evaluated with the help of the following:

Lemma D.3. If F is symmetric, then

$$\int \phi_1'(u)dF(u) = \int\int \phi'(u-v)dF(v)dF(u) = 0.$$

Proof.

$\iint \phi'(u-v)dF(v)dF(u)$

$= \int_{-\infty}^{\infty} \int_{-\infty}^{u} \phi'(u-v)dF(v)dF(u)$

$\quad + \int_{-\infty}^{\infty} \int_{u}^{\infty} \phi'(u-v)dF(v)dF(u).$ \hfill (D.9)

Symmetry of F implies that $\int_{a}^{b} g(u)dF(u) = \int_{-b}^{-a} g(-u)dF(u)$. Apply this to the second integral in (D.9)

$\int_{-\infty}^{\infty} \int_{u}^{\infty} \phi'(u-v)dF(v)dF(u)$

$= \int_{-\infty}^{\infty} \int_{-\infty}^{-u} \phi'(-u-v)dF(v)dF(u)$

$= \int_{-\infty}^{\infty} \int_{-\infty}^{-u} \phi'(-u+v)dF(v)dF(u)$

$= - \int_{-\infty}^{\infty} \int_{u}^{\infty} \phi'(-u+v)dF(v)dF(u)$

$= \int_{-\infty}^{\infty} \int_{u}^{\infty} \phi'(u-v)dF(v)dF(u),$ \hfill (D.10)

where the last equality follows from the fact that ϕ' is an odd function, $\phi'(-x)=-\phi'(x)$. Thus we have that

$\iint \phi'(u-v)dF(v)dF(u)$

$= \int_{-\infty}^{\infty} \int_{u}^{\infty} \phi'(u-v)dF(v)dF(u) - \int_{-\infty}^{\infty} \int_{u}^{\infty} \phi'(u-v)dF(v)dF(u)$

$= 0.$ \hfill (D.11)

\hfill Q.E.D.

Apply this lemma to the terms in the summation in equation (D.8), we get:

$E[\phi'(u_t-u_r)\phi'(u_t-u_s)] =$

$\phi'(0)^2,$ $\qquad\qquad\qquad\qquad\qquad\qquad$ r = s = t

$\phi'(0)E[\phi'(u_t-u_s)] = 0,$ $\qquad\qquad\qquad\qquad$ s ≠ r = t

$\phi'(0)E[\phi'(u_t-u_r)] = 0,$ $\qquad\qquad\qquad\qquad$ r ≠ s = t

$\int\int \phi'(u-v)^2 \, dF(u) \, dF(v),$ $\qquad\qquad\qquad$ r = s ≠ t

$\int\int\int\phi'(u-v)\phi'(u-w)dF(v)dF(u)dF(w) = \int\phi_1'(u)^2 \, dF(u)$ $\quad$ r ≠ s ≠ t

and

$E[\phi_1'(u_t)\phi'(u_t-u_s)] =$

$\phi'(0)E[\phi_1'(u_t)] = 0,$ $\qquad\qquad\qquad\qquad\qquad$ s = t

$\int\int\phi_1'(u)\phi'(u-v)dF(v)dF(u) = \int\phi_1'(u)^2 \, dF(u)$ $\qquad$ s ≠ t

and

$E[\phi_1'(u_t)^2] = \int\phi_1'(u)^2 \, dF(u).$

Putting these terms together,

$$T^{-1} \Sigma_t E [T^{-1} \Sigma_s \phi'(u_t - u_s) - \phi'_1(u_t)]^2$$

$$= T^{-1} [\Sigma_t T^{-2} \{\phi'(0)^2 + (T-1)\int\int\phi'(u-v)dF(v)dF(u)$$
$$+ T(T-1)\int\phi'_1(u)dF(u) - 2(1-T^{-1})\int\phi'_1(u)^2dF(u)$$
$$+ \int\phi'_1(u)^2dF(u)]$$

$$= T^{-2}\phi'(0)^2 + (T-1)/T^2 \int\int\phi'(u-v)^2dF(v)dF(u)$$
$$+ ([T^2-T]/T^2 - 2[T^2-T]/T + 1) \int\phi'_1(u)^2dF(u)$$

$$= T^{-2}\phi'(0)^2 + (T-1)/T^2 \int\int\phi'(u-v)^2dF(v)dF(u)$$
$$+ T^{-1} \int\phi'_1(u)^2dF(u) \qquad\qquad\qquad (D.12)$$

$$\rightarrow 0 \quad \text{as } T\rightarrow\infty.$$

Therefore, the first term in the expression for $T^{\frac{1}{2}} \Delta_T$ in equation (D.6) converges to zero in L_1-norm, and hence in probability. Now consider the L_2-norm of the second term in (D.6),

$$E[\{T^{-1} \Sigma_t \phi'_1(u_t)\xi_t \}^2]$$

$$= T^{-2} \Sigma_s \Sigma_t E[\phi'_1(u_t)\phi'_1(u_s)\xi_t\xi_s]. \qquad\qquad (D.13)$$

Denote by E_t the conditional expectation given F_t. Then for $s=t$,

$$E[\phi'_1(u_t)^2\xi_t^2] = E[\xi_t^2 E_{t-1}[\phi'_1(u_t)^2]] = E[\xi_t^2] \int\phi'_1(u)^2dF(u), \qquad (D.14)$$

where the first equality follows from the fact that ξ_t is F_{t-1} measurable and the second equality follows from the fact that u_t is independent of F_{t-1}. For s<t,

$$E[\phi_1^{\prime}(u_t)\phi_1^{\prime}(u_s)\xi_t\xi_s] = E[\xi_s\phi_1^{\prime}(u_s)E_s\xi_tE_{t-1}[\phi_1^{\prime}(u_t)]] = 0.$$

Similarly, for s>t, $E[\phi_1^{\prime}(u_t)\phi_1^{\prime}(u_s)\xi_t\xi_s] = 0$. Thus,

$$E[\,\{T^{-1}\,\Sigma_t\,\phi_1^{\prime}(u_t)\xi_t\,\}^2\,]$$

$$= T^{-2}\,\Sigma_t\,E[\xi_t^2]\,\int\phi_1^{\prime}(u)^2dF(u)$$

$$= T^{-1}\int\phi_1^{\prime}(u)^2dF(u)\,T^{-1}\,\Sigma_t\,E[\xi_t^2] \qquad (D.15)$$

$\to 0$, and $T\to\infty$.

Since convergence in L_2-norm implies convergence in probability,

$$T^{-1}\,\Sigma_t\,\phi_1^{\prime}(u_t)\xi_t\xrightarrow{P}0$$

and the conclusion that $T^{\frac{1}{2}}\,\Delta_T\xrightarrow{P}0$ follows.   Q.E.D.

We cannot directly apply Theorem D.2 to the BDS statistic because the indicator kernel is not smooth. A promising approach would be to extend the results of Randles (1982) following a suggestion of Professor Edward Frees of the Department of Statistics at the University of Wisconsin at Madison. More will be said about this later. The Monte Carlo work reported in this book suggests that Theorem D.2 is approximately true for the BDS statistic. Two "plausibility" arguments will be outlined below that suggests that Theorem D.2 may apply.

To plausibly apply Theorem D.2 to the BDS statistic, we need to do two things. First, we need to prove an approximation result for the nonsmooth kernel, $I_\epsilon(x,y)=\chi(\epsilon-|u-v|)$, which is the basis for the BDS statistic. Let $\epsilon>0$ be given and for all $\delta<\epsilon$ let ϕ_δ be an even C^1 function that also satisfies:

$\phi_\delta(x) = 0$, if $|x|\geq\epsilon$; $\phi_\delta(x) = 1$, if $|x|\leq\epsilon-\delta$,

as well as

$0 \leq \phi_\delta(x) \leq 1$,

$|\phi_\delta'| \leq 2\delta^{-1}$.

Let $A = \{(u,v): \epsilon-\delta < |u-v| < \epsilon\}$. Then for any ϕ_δ,

$\int\int[\phi_\delta(u-v) - \chi(\epsilon-|u-v|)]^p \, dF(u) \, dF(v)$

$\leq \int\int_A \, dF(u) \, dF(v)$

$= P(\epsilon-\delta<|u-v|<\epsilon)$ (D.16)

$\rightarrow 0$ as $\delta\rightarrow0$.

Therefore, $\phi_\delta \overset{L_p}{\rightarrow} \chi$, and the kernel for the BDS statistic can be approximated arbitrarily well in the L_p sense by ϕ_δ. Since the asymptotic variance of the BDS statistic is a smooth function of C and K that, in turn are L_p continuous at $\delta = 0$, therefore we can approximate the asymptotic variance in the L_p sense as close as we like.

Here are the details. As for the estimate of the variance using ϕ_δ, define

$$C_\delta = \iint \phi_\delta(u-v) \, dF(u) \, dF(v) \tag{D.16.1}$$

and

$$K_\delta = \int [\phi_{1,\delta}(u) - C_\delta]^2 \, df(u), \tag{D.16.2}$$

where $\phi_{1,\delta}(u) = \int \phi_\delta'(u-v) \, dF(v)$. Then

$$|C_\delta - C|$$

$$= |\iint [\phi_\delta'(u-v) - \chi(\epsilon - |u-v|)] \, dF(u) \, dF(v)|$$

$$\leq \iint |\phi_\delta'(u-v) - \chi(\epsilon - |u-v|)| \, dF(u) \, dF(v)$$

$$\leq \iint_A \, dF(u) \, dF(v)$$

and therefore $\lim_{\delta \to 0} C_\delta = C$. It can be similarly shown that $\lim_{\delta \to 0} K_\delta = K$. Since the denominator of the BDS statistic involves terms in C and K, it can also be approximated arbitrarily close by using the kernel ϕ_δ. It is also easy to see that asymptotic moment expressions that appear in the correction terms for nuisance parameters (cf. D.36

below) are L_p-continuous in δ at $\delta=0$.

Second, we must show that Theorem D.2 can be extended to $\Phi(x_t^m, y_t^m)$, $\Psi(x_t^m, y_t^m)$ of the form: $\Phi(x_t^m, y_t^m) \equiv \Pi_{i=0}^m \phi(x_i - y_i)$, and $\Psi(x_t^m, y_t^m) \equiv \Phi(x_t^m, y_t^m) - c_1^m - m\, c_1^{m-1}(\phi(x_t - y_t) - c_1)$, where $c_1 = \int\int \phi(u-v) dF(v) dF(u)$. This chore may be accomplished by tedious computations along the lines of the above steps.

Let us say a few words about how to do this chore. Note that Ψ is the kernel of the BDS statistic after the delta method has been applied. In the case of model (D.1), for the case where σ is known, one can extend Theorem D.2 to cover the BDS statistic itself by expanding (D.2) in a Taylor series around σ to locate conditions on (D.1) sufficient for the regularity (A1—A5) that is needed. Sufficient conditions for such regularity is almost sure bounded first and second derivatives of f with respect to σ. But this is more than what is needed. One can do a separate computation using the fact that ϕ appears in two places in Ψ to establish Theorem D.2 for the case of model (D.1) when σ must be estimated. The rather different approach leading to Theorem D.5 seems simpler. All one must do is compute the moment (A2) for the BDS kernel for the model (D.2) and check that the moment is zero even though σ must both be estimated. However, this moment is not zero for general ARCH models as will be seen in example 2, (D.45) below.

It is worth pointing out the role of the symmetry assumption on F in the proof of Theorem D.2. The crucial step is that

$$\int \phi_1^*(u)\, dF(u) = 0$$

is used to show that certain terms in equation (D.8) are zero. For a general function, ϕ, we need the symmetry of F in order to draw this conclusion. However, for the approximating functions ϕ_δ we need only assume that F is twice differentiable. In that case,

$$\iint \phi'(u-v)f(u)f(v) \, dudv = \iint \phi(u-v)f'(u)f(v) \, dudv \qquad (D.17)$$

and

$$\lim_{\delta \to 0} \iint \phi_\delta(u-v)f'(u)f(v) \, dudv$$

$$= \iint \chi(\epsilon-|u-v|)f'(u)f(v) \, dudv$$

$$= \iint_{v-\epsilon}^{v+\epsilon} f'(u)f(v) \, dudv$$

$$= \int [f(v+\epsilon)-f(v-\epsilon)]f(v) \, dv. \qquad (D.18)$$

Hence, for the kernel in the BDS statistic, the hypothesis of Theorem D.2. can be changed to require that the distribution function, F, of the u_t be twice differentiable.

So far, we have shown, for the case m=1, that the asymptotic distribution of the correlation integral, $C_m(\epsilon)$, is the same whether it is calculated using true residuals or estimated residuals, as T→∞. In the remainder of this appendix, we discuss the impact upon the first order asymptotic distribution of the BDS test when evaluated at residuals of estimated models. We show that, for a class of null models with IID innovations, the first order asymptotic distribution for the test statistic is the same whether it is computed on the original IID residuals of the null model or on the estimated residuals of the null model. We state and prove a theorem on the invariance of the first order asymptotics to the estimation process provided that the estimation process is $T^{\frac{1}{2}}$-consistent and provided that some regularity conditions are satisfied. Before we do this, it is helpful to first, set up notation and second, restate the BDS theorem using the new notation. The following is based on Brock 1987.

Notation.

$h(u,v){:}R^2{\rightarrow}R$: C^2 symmetric function (called a kernel function).

$\{u_t\}$: IID scalar-valued stochastic process defined on a common probability triple of elementary events, set of measurable subsets, and probability measure P. We will use the same symbol for a random variable (a function from a probability triple to the real line equipped with the sigma algebra generated by the open intervals) and for its value, except where confusion may result.

$$u_t^m{=}(u_t,...,u_{t+m-1}){=}x_t,$$

$h_m(u_t^m,u_s^m){=}h(u_t,u_s)...h(u_{t+m-1},u_{s+m-1}){=}$product of m subsequently valued kernels.

$C(m)$: $C(m){=}\Sigma_{t=1}^{T}\Sigma_{s=1}^{T}h_m(u_t^m,u_s^m)/T^2$.

For ease of notation, Σ_t shall always denote $\Sigma_{t=1}^{T}$, unless otherwise stated.

$c_m = EC(m) = \{E[h(u_t,u_s)]\}^m = [c_1]^m$ for $\{u_t\}$ IID (Brock and Dechert 1988a).

$Y_t = (y_t, y_{t-1}, \dots) =$ the t-past of stochastic process $\{y_s\}$.

$y_t = F(Y_{t-1}, b, u_t) =$ Data Generating Process (DGP). F is C^2, b is a finite dimensional vector of parameters to be estimated. The innovation process $\{u_t\}$ is scalar valued IID with zero mean and finite variance.

b_T: $T^{\frac{1}{2}}$-consistent estimator of the $k \times 1$ parameter vector b on sample of length T.

$u_t = G(Y_t, b)$, $u_{tT} = G(Y_t, b_T)$: Actual innovations and estimated innovations obtained from solving the DGP for u_t. The DGP function F is assumed globally invertible in the u argument with C^2 inverse.

$W(C(m), C(1)) = C(m) - [C(1)]^m$: A measure of difference between non-IID and IID computed from the $\{u_t\}$ process. In population W will be zero if $\{u_t\}$ is IID. Brock and Dechert 1988a showed that $W \to 0$, a.s. P, as $T \to \infty$, if $\{u_t\}$ is IID. This is the numerator of the BDS statistic when multiplied by $T^{1/2}$.

$a(x_t, x_s, m) = [h_m(x_t, x_s)] - c_m - m[c_1]^{m-1}[h(u_t, u_s) - c_1]$: This is a symmetric kernel on $R^m \times R^m$. It will play a key role. We will suppress the "m" in the notation when no confusion will result.

$a_m(u_t^m) = E\{a(u_t^m, u_s^m) | u_t^m\}$. The conditional expectation of a on u_t^m. This is called the projection of the kernel (Serfling 1980, p. 187). Denote by $h_{mm}(u_t^m)$, $h_{11}(u_t)$ the projections of h_m, $h_1 = h$ respectively.

a', a_m' denote gradients.

$J(Y_{t+m-1}, Y_{s+m-1}, b)$: The kernel a with all u_{t+i} and u_{s+i} replaced by $G(Y_{t+i}, b)$, $G(Y_{s+i}, b)$.

Note that J and all its partial derivatives with respect to b are symmetric in Y. We denote the partial derivatives of J with respect to b_i, b_j by J_i', J_{ij}''.

$\hat{k}$: $\hat{k}(u_i, u_j, u_k) = (1/3!) \ \Sigma_i \Sigma_j \Sigma_k \ h(u_i, u_j) h(u_j, u_k)$.

H: $H(Y_r, Y_s, Y_t, b) = \hat{k}(G(Y_r, b), G(Y_s, b), G(Y_t, b))$.

L: $L(Y_s, Y_t, b) = h(G(Y_s, b), G(Y_t, b))$.

Starred quantities: Any quantity evaluated at the estimated innovations u_{tT} instead of the true innovations u_t will be starred.

The Assumptions listed below will be used in what follows.

Catalogue of Assumptions.

A1 (DGP). The DGP generates a stochastic process $\{y_t\}$ that satisfies one of the three "mixing" assumptions of Denker and Keller 1983 (Theorem 1, p. 507). This amounts to assuming that dependence falls off fast enough to get a central limit theorem.

<u>A2</u>. $\mu = Ea'.G' = 0$.

Remark. Sufficient for A2 is the condition

$Eh_{11}'(u_t) = 0$

provided that G' is measurable $\{u_{t-1}, u_{t-2}, \ldots\}$, i.e., G' depends only on past u's. For the kernel $h_1(u,v) = I_\epsilon(u,v)$ which is one if $|u-v| < \epsilon$, we have $h_{11}(u) = F(u+\epsilon) - F(u-\epsilon)$, $h_{11}'(u) = f(u+\epsilon) - f(u-\epsilon)$, where F,f denote the distribution function and density function of u_t. Hence, $Eh_{11}'(u) = 0$ for this kernel. But this kernel does not satisfy the smoothness conditions we require. It appears that we can approximate it close enough, as in the discussion following Theorem D.2 above, by smooth kernels to be usable in practice. This is the approach taken in this book.

We will sometimes call A2 the "moment condition." The term μ appears in the first order asymptotic distribution of the test statistic of Theorem D.4 below. Assumption A2 is shown to hold for Example 1 below.

<u>A3</u>. $T^{1/2}(b_T - b) \rightarrow N(0, v_b)$, $v_b > 0$.

Here convergence is in distribution, and b_T is an estimator on a sample of length n of the parameter vector b. A3 says that the estimation sequence $\{b_T\}$ is $T^{\frac{1}{2}}$-consistent. When b is a vector the symbol v_b stands for the variance covariance matrix and $v_b > 0$ means positive definite.

<u>A4</u>. There is a compact set K such that the range of the random variable b_T is contained in K for all n.

<u>A5</u>.   All kernels are nondegenerate, i.e., the variance of each projection is positive. As in Denker and Keller 1983 (p. 507) all kernels of V-statistics appearing below have bounded "2+d" moments: Sup E{$|H|^{2+d}$}<∞, for some d>0. Here "Sup" is shorthand notation for "supremum of the expectation over all permutations of temporal arguments."

<u>A6</u>. All kernels appearing below are at least C^2.

<u>A7</u>. For X=any element of {H', L", J"}, Sup{E|X(.,.,z)|}<∞. Recall the Sup is taken over all temporal permutations and z. From this point on, convergence of random variables is in distribution unless otherwise noted.

We restate the BDS theorem here for convenience.

Theorem D.4. Assume {u_t} is IID and A5 holds for the kernels in the C(m) statistic, and in the $\hat{K}$ statistic in (D.25). Then,

$$T^{1/2}[W(C(m),C(1)]\to N(0,V(m)), \quad T\to\infty, \tag{D.19}$$

$$V(m)/4=2\Sigma_{j=1}^{m-1}k^{m-j}c^{2j}+k^m+(m-1)^2c^{2m}-m^2kc^{2(m-1)}, \tag{D.20}$$

$$c=Eh(u_t,u_s), \quad k=E[h(u_r,u_s)h(u_s,u_t)], \tag{D.21}$$

where convergence is in distribution and $N(0,V)$ denotes the normal distribution with mean zero and variance V.

Proof. This follows from use of the delta method (Serfling 1980, p. 118) and Denker and Keller's 1983 (Theorem 1). Denker and Keller's mixing conditions are trivially satisfied for the stochastic process $\{u_t^m\}$ since it is m-dependent. Assumption A5 allows application of Denker and Keller 1983 (Equation 1 and Theorem 1) to each $C(m)$:

$$C(m)=c_m+(2/T)\Sigma_t[h_m(u_t^m)-c_m]+R_{mT}, \quad T^{1/2}R_{mT}\rightarrow 0, \ T\rightarrow\infty. \tag{D.22}$$

As in applying the delta method, expand (D.19) in an exact second order Taylor series about c_m, c_1. Use (D.22) to represent $C(m)$, $C(1)$. Doing this and collecting all first order terms, one will get the kernel $a(x_t,x_s,m)$ for the first order part. Now show the second order terms go to zero in distribution. The formula (D.20) for the variance follows from taking the limit of $E\{(2/T^{1/2})\Sigma a\}^2$ as $T\rightarrow\infty$. Q.E.D.

Remark. The variance V can be consistently estimated by

$$C(1)=\Sigma_t\Sigma_s h(u_t,u_s)/T^2, \tag{D.23}$$

$$K(1)=\Sigma_t\Sigma_s\Sigma_r[h(u_r,u_s)h(u_s,u_t)]/T^3, \tag{D.24}$$

$$\hat{K}=\Sigma_t\Sigma_s\Sigma_r\hat{k}(u_r,u_s,u_t)/T^3, \tag{D.25}$$

$$\hat{k}=(1/3!)\Sigma_i\Sigma_j\Sigma_k\Sigma h(u_i,u_j)h(u_j,u_k), \tag{D.26}$$

$\hat{V}=V[C(1),\hat{K}]$,   (D.27)

where $V[.,.]$ is given by (D.20). As Serfling 1980 (p. 172) points out the nonsymmetric kernel in (D.24) can be symmetrized without loss of generality via (D.25) and (D.26). Assumption A5 on the kernel $\hat{k}$ and application of Denker and Keller 1983 (Theorem 1) implies the estimate $\hat{K}$ converges in distribution to k. Application of Serfling 1980 (p. 24) proves that the estimate (D.27) converges in distribution to $V[c_1,k]$ since (D.23) and (D.25) converge in distribution to c_1, k.

Hence, if we compute $T^{1/2}W/V^{1/2}$ by replacing V with any consistent estimator $\hat{V}$, we have a statistic that converges in distribution to $N(0,1)$ under the null of IID. The first draft of Brock, Dechert, and Scheinkman 1987 (hereafter BDS) proved Theorem D.4. The Denker and Keller results allow Theorem D.4 to be proved immediately. Brock, Dechert, Scheinkman, and LeBaron 1989 (hereafter BDSL) contain a similar proof.

Distribution theory can be worked out for any vector valued function of "C-statistics" by using the delta method and the Cramer-Wold device (Serfling 1980). This may be of use in some applications. This was done in BDS 1987.

Recall that convergence is always in distribution unless otherwise stated.

Theorem D.5. Assume the hypotheses of Theorem D.4. Also assume the "moment condition" A2, and assume A5 on the "kernels" $J'(Y_{t+m}, Y_{s+m},b)$, $L'(Y_t,Y_s,b)$, assume A4, and A7 with $X=J''$. Then,

$T^{1/2}[W(C^*(m),C^*(1))-W(C(m),C(1))]\to 0$, $T\to\infty$.   (D.28)

Proof. Write an exact Taylor expansion for each W, around c_m, c_1.

$$W(C^*(m),C^*(1))=T^{-2}\Sigma\Sigma a^*-m(m-1)[c_1^{**}]^{m-2}(C^*(1)-c_1)^2/2, \qquad (D.29)$$

$$W(C(m),C(1))=T^{-2}\Sigma\Sigma a-m(m-1)[c_1^{**}]^{m-2}(C(1)-c_1)^2/2. \qquad (D.30)$$

Here the superscript "*" denotes evaluation at estimated residuals and the double superscripts "**" denote evaluation at an intermediate point so that the expansion is exact. The second order terms in (D.29), (D.30) will be disposed of in Lemma D.6 below where the condition A5 on L' will be used. We must show

$$A(n)=T^{1/2}[\Sigma\Sigma(a^*-a)/T^2]\to 0, \ T\to\infty. \qquad (D.31)$$

Insert the formula

$$u_{tT}=G(Y_t,b_T), \ u_t=G(Y_t,b), \qquad (D.32)$$

into (D.31), then expand in a Taylor series about b with exact second order remainder, to obtain, noting that J'=a'.G', and putting M=J",

$$A(T)=B_T\Sigma\Sigma[a_m'.G']/T^2+(1/2)\Sigma\Sigma[B_T.M.B_T]/T^{5/2}, \qquad (D.33)$$

where

$$B_T=T^{1/2}(b_T-b), \qquad (D.34)$$

and M is a k×k matrix of second order partial derivatives where k is the number of parameters to be estimated. Here "." denotes matrix or vector multiplication. It will be used only when emphasis is needed. In order to save notation we forgo separate notation for transposes. For convenience we record,

$$M_{ij}=J''_{ij}. \tag{D.35}$$

Now $B_T=O_p(1)$. Therefore it is sufficient to show

$$\Sigma\Sigma[a'.G']/T^2\to\mu=E[a'.G']=0, \tag{D.36}$$

and the second order terms in (D.33) converge in probability to zero. Observe $a'.G'=J'$ is the derivative of a symmetric (in Y_t and Y_s) kernel $J(Y_t,Y_s,b)$ with respect to the kx1 vector b, hence $\Sigma\Sigma J'/T^2$ is a V-statistic. Under the mixing condition A1 and the nondegeneracy, and bounded 2+d moment condition A5 on the kernel $H=J'$, Denker and Keller 1983 (Theorem 1) asserts

$$\Sigma\Sigma J'(Y_t,Y_s,b)/T^2\to EJ', \quad T\to\infty. \tag{D.37}$$

But $EJ'=\mu=0$ by A2. Turn now to the second order terms in (D.33). Since each component of B_T converges in distribution to $O_p(1)$, it is enough to show (Serfling 1980, Theorem and Corollary B, p. 19, Theorem, p. 24), for each element i,j

$$\Sigma\Sigma J''_{ij}(Y_t,Y_s,\hat{b}_T)/T^{5/2}\to0, \quad T\to\infty. \tag{D.38}$$

Here the extra superscript ^ on b_T denotes values of components of b in between b and b_T. To show (D.38) it is sufficient to show convergence in L_1. Thus it is sufficient to show that there is a bound $B<\infty$ such that for all elements i,j:

$$Sup\{E|J_{ij}''(Y_t,Y_s,z)|, \text{ all nonnegative t,s}\}<B, \qquad (D.39)$$

where the sup is taken over z in some compact set K. But (D.39) follows from Assumption A4 which, to recall, states that the values of b_T lie in a compact set K, which is independent of T, and from A7 which states that $Sup\{E|J_{ij}''|$, all nonnegative t,s\} is finite. Q.E.D.

Remark. When the moment condition $\mu=0$ does not hold the asymptotic variance of the first order limit distribution of the BDS statistic must be corrected by using the formula

$$T^{1/2}W(C^*(m),C^*(1))=T^{1/2}W(C(m),C(1))+B_T\cdot\mu_T, \qquad (D.40)$$

where μ_T converges in distribution to the constant vector μ and B_T converges in distribution to $N(0,v_b)$ as $T\rightarrow\infty$. Note that the first term of the RHS is just the BDS statistic evaluated at the true residuals, so its limiting mean and variance is known. But in general, when the moment term μ is not zero the limiting variance will not be the same and must be estimated and computed using the above formula for each different model one estimates.

Lemma D.6. Consider the second order terms S_1, S_2 in (D.29), (D.30). Assume the kernel h(u,v) is bounded between zero and $B<\infty$, and assume A4, A5, A6, A7. Then

$T^{1/2}S_i \rightarrow 0$, $i=1,2$.

Proof. Since m is not less than 2 the terms involving c_1^{**} are bounded above and below. Hence upon division by $T^{1/2}$ and using Serfling 1980 (p. 19) it is sufficient to show

$$T^{1/2}(C^*(1)-c_1)=O_p(1), \quad T^{1/2}(C(1)-c_1)=O_p(1).$$

Convergence of the last term follows from the same type of argument as that used in Theorem D.4. The first term requires attention. We have via expansion in an exact Taylor series

$$C^*(1)=\Sigma_t\Sigma_s h(G(Y_t,b_T,G(Y_s,b_T)))/T^2 \equiv \Sigma_t\Sigma_s L(Y_t,Y_s,b_T)/T^2$$

$$=C(1)+\Sigma_t\Sigma_s L'(Y_t,Y_s,b)(b_T-b)/T^2$$

$$+(1/2)\Sigma_t\Sigma_s(b_T-b)'L''(Y_t,Y_s,\hat{b}_T)(b_T-b)/T^2$$

$$\equiv C(1)+A+B.$$

Here $\hat{b}_T$ denotes a value between b, b_T. Now

$$T^{1/2}(b_T-b)\rightarrow N(0,v_b), \quad T\rightarrow\infty,$$

so $T^{1/2}A=O_p(1)$ since A5 allows application of Denker and Keller 1983 (Theorem 1) to $\Sigma\Sigma L'/T^2$ so that $\Sigma\Sigma L'/T^2\rightarrow EL'$. Furthermore $T^{1/2}B\rightarrow 0$ by using A4, A6, and A7 with X=L''.   Q.E.D.

Remark. Note that we have shown in the proof of the lemma that

$$T^{1/2}(C^*(1)-c_1) \to N(\mu^*, v^*), \quad T \to \infty,$$

where the mean and variance are easily computed from the above proofs.

While Theorem D.5 shows that, under the moment condition, A2, the first order asymptotic distribution of W is invariant to evaluation at u_{tT} or u_t we still need a practical estimator of the variance $V(m)$ for the statistic to be of practical use. Theorem D.7 takes care of this problem.

Theorem D.7. The estimator $\hat{V}$ in (D.27) evaluated at u_{tT}, call it V^*, is a consistent estimator of $V(m)$.

Proof. We must show

$$V^* \to V(m), \quad T \to \infty. \tag{D.41}$$

The estimate V^* can be written

$$V^* = \Sigma_t \Sigma_s \Sigma_r H(Y_r, Y_t, Y_s, b_T)/T^3. \tag{D.42}$$

Expand (D.42) in an exact first order Taylor series about b. One gets V plus first order terms in $(b_T - b)$. V is a consistent estimator of $V(m)$ since it is a function of V-statistics that converge in distribution individually to each argument of $V(m)$ (Serfling 1980, p. 24). We have

$T^{1/2}(b_T-b) \rightarrow O_p(1)$, $T \rightarrow \infty$. By A7 there is a bound $B<\infty$ such that

$$SupE\{|H'(Y_r,Y_s,Y_t,z)|, \text{ all nonnegative } r,s,t\}<B<\infty. \qquad (D.43)$$

Hence we may show, as we did for the second order terms in Theorem D.6, that the first order terms go to zero in distribution.   Q.E.D.

Remark. The role played by the restrictive assumptions A4 and A7 in the proofs of the theorems could be played by the less restrictive but less "primitive":

<u>A7'</u>. For all i,j, limSup $\{E|X_{ij}(.,\hat{b}_T)|\}=B<\infty$, for $\hat{b}_T \rightarrow b$, $T \rightarrow \infty$. Here the lim is taken as $T \rightarrow \infty$, the Sup is taken as in A7.

Acknowledgement. Brock would like to thank J. Stock for his help in correcting and organizing on the first order asymptotic invariance Theorem D.5. Brock's original proof, given at the Econometric Society in 1987, was cumbersome and incomplete because he did not expand around b. Stock suggested that the expansion be conducted around b as in the above proof. Brock expanded around u_t, which caused errors. Stock also suggested reorganizing the original attempt at proof around an assumption like A2 above and a style of argument like that used above.

Remark. Applications of the W statistic of BDS 1987 have all used the kernel function $h(u,v)=I_\epsilon(u,v)$ where the indicator $I_\epsilon(u,v)$ is one if $|u-v|<\epsilon$ and is zero otherwise. This kernel is not smooth. Hence it does not satisfy the smoothness assumptions that we impose in the theorems above. However, note the formula $V(m)$ for the variance is continuous in its arguments c_1, k_1.

Conjecture D.8. For every $q>0$ we can find a kernel $h_1(u,v)$ that satisfies A5, A6, A7 such that the absolute value of the difference between the variance computed at the indicator kernel I_ϵ and the variance computed at the kernel h_1 is less than q. Furthermore the absolute value of the "distortion" constant is also less than q.

"Proof." As in (D.16), construct a symmetric about zero, C^∞ "bump" function that is one on $\{|z=u-v|<\epsilon\}$ and is zero off of $\{|z|>d+\epsilon\}$ for d sufficiently small and positive. Inspection of the formula for $V(m)$ and the formula for the distortion constant in A2 finishes the argument.

Remark. It would be nice to have a proof of Theorem D.5 without the awkward and inelegant approximations in Conjecture D.8. We have not been able to obtain such a proof. However, as we pointed out before, a generalization of the approach of Randles 1982 to our time series case seems promising. Randles shows in the case of "illegal" indicator kernels that distribution theory for U-statistics in the presence of estimated parameters may be treated by expansion in a first order Taylor series around the true parameter value and an interchange of expectation and derivative operators even though the statistic is not differentiably smooth at the true value of the estimated parameter. See Randles 1982 (p. 463, equation 1.3). While we have been able to show that Randles' regularity conditions (1982, p. 465, Conditions 2.2 and 2.3) are satisfied for certain special cases, we have not been able to finish the generalization of Randles in time for this book to go to press. The generalization would not only streamline the proof of the nuisance parameter theorem, but also close the gap in the asymptotic normality proof for the case of the non-differentiable indicator kernel that is actually used in all empirical work that we are aware of that uses the BDS statistic.

Remark. The compact range assumption on the random variables b_T is awkward and restrictive. While we think an approach will work where this assumption is replaced by dominating functions with assumptions on the rate of growth in the "b" arguments together with assumptions on the rate of decay of probability mass on large values of b_T uniformly in T, we have not done this.

Examples. Here are some applications of the above theorems.

Example 1. AR(1)

Let $\{y_t\}$ be generated by

$$y_t = by_{t-1} + u_t, \tag{D.44}$$

where $|b| < 1$, $\{u_t\}$ is IID with zero mean, finite variance, and compact range. Then $G(Y_t, b) = y_t - by_{t-1}$. It is easy to verify that $E\{a'.G'\}$ is near 0 for a C^∞ bump function kernel that approximates the indicator kernel. Actually for C^2 kernels of the form $h_1(u,v) = h(u-v)$ where $h(z)$ is an even function about 0, A2 holds exactly. Since $|b| < 1$ the strong mixing, i.e., alpha mixing, condition A1 holds for a class of $\{u_t\}$

including Gaussian and $\{u_t\}$ that satisfies Doeblin's condition (White and Domowitz 1984, p. 146). All the other assumptions hold as well provided that the $T^{\frac{1}{2}}$-consistent estimation sequence $\{b_T\}$ has uniformly compact range. Hence Theorems D.4, D.5, and D.6 hold and our test can be used to asymptotically test the null hypothesis (D.44) on estimated innovations u_{tT} without having to make a correction for the variance of the limiting normal distribution.

The above type of example can be generalized to ARMA(p,q) models under invertibility and stability assumptions.

Example 2. ARCH(1)

Consider the DGP

$$y_t = u_t h_t, \tag{D.45}$$

where $\{u_t\}$ is normal IID with mean zero and variance one, and,

$$h_t = a_o + a_1 [y_{t-1}]^2. \tag{D.46}$$

Let a_{oT}, a_{1T} $T^{\frac{1}{2}}$-consistently estimate a_o, a_1 and suppose that a_1 is small enough so that y_t satisfies the strong mixing condition A1. Then $G(Y_t, b) = y_t / (h_t)^{1/2}$, $b = (a_o, a_1)$. There are two terms in A2 that must be evaluated to check whether the "moment" condition holds. Since the derivative of G with respect to a_o contains y_t and, hence, is not measurable with respect to the past, one would expect the moment condition A2 not to hold in general. Therefore the limiting variance must be corrected. This is consistent with computer results of Hsieh

1989, and in Section 2.5 of this book where the limiting variance is shown to be distorted in large samples.

It appears that some other tests based on moments have the same first order asymptotics on ARCH standardized estimated residuals as on the true IID residuals. This is still under investigation.

Truth in Advertising

1. We have provided no theory for the choice of m and ϵ. Hsieh and LeBaron's 1988 work discussed in this book contain Monte Carlo work that suggests that a choice of e between one-half and three halves of the standard deviation of the $\{u_t\}$ gives good results on size and power against five non-IID alternatives for m between two and five for samples sizes 500 and above. As Robinson 1990 and others point out, one should expect statistics of the form treated here to be sensitive to choices of "bandwidth" parameters such as ϵ. The approach of this book has been to do Monte Carlo simulations, to choose "bandwidth" ϵ in a range of values to optimize performance on size and power.

Another method to improve small sample performance may be to use the bootstrap (Efron 1982) to estimate the distribution of the BDS statistic on estimated residuals of the null model. The discussion in Efron and Tibshirani 1986 suggests that bootstrapping may pick up some of the effects of higher order terms in the Edgeworth expansion. Hence we may hope that bootstrapping will improve the performance of BDS. This issue is under investigation.

2. The spirit of the methods propounded here is to encapsulate one's prior beliefs in a null model $y_t = F(Y_{t-1}, I_t, u_t, b)$, where I_t are other observed information variables, invert to put $u_t = G(Y_t, I_t, b)$, $T^{\frac{1}{2}}$-

consistently estimate b to get b_T, and then test $\{u_{tT}\}$ for IID using Theorem D.2 to test the null. While we think the property that the distortion parameter $\mu=0$ is an attractive property, we warn the user that outside of the work of Hsieh and LeBaron 1988 and the Monte Carlo simulations reported here, little is known about the performance of this procedure for sample sizes that arise in practice. We know that performance is not good for sample sizes less than 200 in many cases. It is tolerably good for sample sizes 500 and greater in some cases. The cautionary posture taken in Robinson 1990 is appropriate here.

3.   The formulation $u_t=G(Y_t,I_t,b)$ allows a larger collection of null models to be "specification tested" using BDS than the collection treated by Brock and Dechert 1988. The invariance property of the first order asymptotics established here is a nice property of BDS–type statistics.   However, there are other tests of IID that have this property. A way of generating such tests seems to be this. Take any function $T(u_t, u_{t-1},..., u_{t-q})$ whose expectation is zero under the null of independence and identical distribution. Look at test statistics of the form

$$T^{1/2}Z, \; Z=(T^{-1})\Sigma_s T_s.$$

Fix up the function Z so that when ones expands the argument in a second order Taylor series around b as in Theorem D.2 above and take limits, the "orthogonality condition" A2 is satisfied. For example, the autocorrelation function of squared residuals is a good candidate.

Future work intends to explore and compare to BDS a general class of alternative methods of testing IID that have invariant first order asymptotics to a broad class of estimation processes. BDS may be working fairly well because the double summation character explores regions of the whole space for dependence rather than a subset of the space.

Remark. It is worthwhile to speculate on how to find tests for independence that have first order asymptotics invariant on residuals from a $T^{\frac{1}{2}}$-consistent estimation process. A mechanical way to generate them works as follows. Write down any test for independence: $F[EH_1(U(t), EH_2(U(t)),...])=0$ where $U(t)=\{u(t),u(t-1),...\}$. Now replace "E" by an estimator "Est" evaluated at the true residuals $\{u\}$ on a sample of length T. Denote by "Est*" the same estimator evaluated at estimated residuals $\{u*\}$ on a sample of length T. Look at $T^{1/2}[F[Est(H_1(U(t)),...]-F[Est*(H_1(U*(t)),...]]$. This will typically, under regularity conditions, converge to a normally distributed random variable times a moment expression. This moment expression is basically the gradient of H in the direction of the data generating process solved for u. Note that BDS is a function of estimators (U or V statistics) that is zero, in population, under the null. It has invariant first order asymptotics for data generating processes $u(t)=G(.,.,b)$ such that the gradient G_b is measurable with respect to $U(t-1)$. Work under investigation is classifying independence tests where this moment condition is zero for a broad class of data generating processes.

We hasten to add that there are many tests for independence available in the literature. A particularly interesting one based upon the Kullback-Leibler information is Robinson 1990. This book has focused on the BDS test because it fits naturally into the general approach to testing for nonlinearity in the sense of Priestley 1981 that we are developing here. The reader is advised that many other independence tests may well turn in a better performance than does the BDS test.

Appendix E. Size of the BDS Statistic on Residuals

Table E.1
Size of BDS Statistic
AR1 Residuals ($\rho=.5$)

	ϵ/σ				N(0,1)
	0.50	1.00	1.50	2.00	
m=2,T=100					
%< -2.33	12.75	4.85	4.10	6.20	1.00
%< -1.96	18.15	9.20	8.55	10.35	2.50
%< -1.64	23.30	14.15	13.35	15.10	5.00
%> 1.64	15.95	7.65	6.95	8.55	5.00
%> 1.96	12.95	5.20	3.80	6.30	2.50
%> 2.33	10.15	2.70	2.55	3.80	1.00
m=2,T=500					
%< -2.33	2.10	1.45	1.70	2.25	1.00
%< -1.96	4.80	3.75	4.05	4.40	2.50
%< -1.64	8.75	7.20	7.45	7.80	5.00
%> 1.64	7.65	5.55	5.15	6.00	5.00
%> 1.96	4.95	3.15	2.85	3.30	2.50
%> 2.33	3.00	1.25	1.35	1.55	1.00
m=2,T=1000					
%< -2.33	1.20	1.10	1.15	1.20	1.00
%< -1.96	3.25	2.90	2.60	2.65	2.50
%< -1.64	6.40	4.70	5.95	5.50	5.00
%> 1.64	7.85	6.05	6.25	7.15	5.00
%> 1.96	4.50	3.25	3.25	3.70	2.50
%> 2.33	1.90	1.65	1.20	1.50	1.00
m=5,T=500					
%< -2.33	7.55	1.45	1.60	1.85	1.00
%< -1.96	12.30	3.70	3.85	3.95	2.50
%< -1.64	16.85	6.70	7.25	8.10	5.00
%> 1.64	16.05	6.55	5.70	6.00	5.00
%> 1.96	12.55	4.25	3.80	3.60	2.50
%> 2.33	8.65	2.50	1.75	1.40	1.00
m=5,T=1000					
%< -2.33	3.55	0.90	0.90	1.10	1.00
%< -1.96	5.75	2.45	2.75	2.85	2.50
%< -1.64	10.05	5.15	5.45	5.35	5.00
%> 1.64	10.35	6.35	5.65	6.50	5.00
%> 1.96	6.90	3.45	2.90	3.30	2.50
%> 2.33	4.60	1.35	1.40	1.25	1.00
m=10,T=1000					
%< -2.33	39.85	1.00	0.45	1.00	1.00
%< -1.96	40.15	2.40	1.70	2.45	2.50
%< -1.64	42.25	6.10	4.95	5.90	5.00
%> 1.64	33.90	7.70	6.35	6.55	5.00
%> 1.96	33.05	5.60	3.90	3.55	2.50
%> 2.33	31.80	3.70	1.85	1.65	1.00

Table E.2
Size of BDS Statistic
AR1 Residuals ($\rho=.95$)

	ϵ/σ				
	0.50	1.00	1.50	2.00	N(0,1)
m=2,T=100					
%< -2.33	11.55	3.45	3.20	5.15	1.00
%< -1.96	16.50	7.90	6.70	8.85	2.50
%< -1.64	21.55	12.70	11.65	13.20	5.00
%> 1.64	18.80	11.35	9.35	10.90	5.00
%> 1.96	14.80	8.00	6.10	8.10	2.50
%> 2.33	11.45	5.10	3.90	5.65	1.00
m=2,T=500					
%< -2.33	2.60	1.45	1.25	1.35	1.00
%< -1.96	5.55	3.00	3.35	3.85	2.50
%< -1.64	8.95	6.40	6.65	6.45	5.00
%> 1.64	7.70	6.15	5.80	6.45	5.00
%> 1.96	4.65	3.45	3.10	3.55	2.50
%> 2.33	2.30	1.50	1.60	2.05	1.00
m=2,T=1000					
%< -2.33	1.40	1.20	1.25	1.10	1.00
%< -1.96	3.75	2.65	2.95	3.00	2.50
%< -1.64	7.40	6.40	6.55	6.15	5.00
%> 1.64	7.10	5.45	5.15	5.50	5.00
%> 1.96	4.20	3.25	3.20	3.20	2.50
%> 2.33	1.80	1.25	1.25	1.40	1.00
m=5,T=500					
%< -2.33	7.30	0.90	0.95	1.25	1.00
%< -1.96	11.65	2.65	2.95	3.40	2.50
%< -1.64	15.60	5.55	5.70	6.90	5.00
%> 1.64	16.75	6.90	6.70	6.50	5.00
%> 1.96	12.65	4.55	3.95	4.05	2.50
%> 2.33	10.00	2.35	2.20	2.40	1.00
m=5,T=1000					
%< -2.33	3.90	1.15	1.15	1.35	1.00
%< -1.96	6.95	3.00	3.35	3.65	2.50
%< -1.64	11.55	6.05	6.05	6.80	5.00
%> 1.64	10.85	6.20	5.65	5.15	5.00
%> 1.96	7.50	3.70	2.45	3.15	2.50
%> 2.33	4.25	1.45	1.35	1.25	1.00
m=10,T=1000					
%< -2.33	41.70	1.00	0.65	1.25	1.00
%< -1.96	41.85	3.30	2.80	3.50	2.50
%< -1.64	44.50	6.15	5.75	6.40	5.00
%> 1.64	32.10	8.05	5.25	4.30	5.00
%> 1.96	31.20	5.10	3.30	2.40	2.50
%> 2.33	30.10	3.35	1.80	1.25	1.00

Table E.3
Size of BDS Statistic
MA1 Residuals ($\theta=.5$)

		0.50	1.00	1.50	2.00	N(0,1)
				ϵ/σ		

m=2,T=100						
%<	-2.33	13.10	4.65	4.90	6.65	1.00
%<	-1.96	17.80	8.70	8.20	10.65	2.50
%<	-1.64	24.00	13.90	13.75	15.20	5.00
%>	1.64	15.30	7.00	6.95	8.05	5.00
%>	1.96	12.20	4.60	3.85	5.40	2.50
%>	2.33	9.05	2.80	1.90	3.30	1.00
m=2,T=500						
%<	-2.33	1.90	1.30	2.05	2.00	1.00
%<	-1.96	4.85	3.55	4.00	4.65	2.50
%<	-1.64	8.95	6.65	7.50	7.60	5.00
%>	1.64	7.00	5.45	5.00	5.45	5.00
%>	1.96	4.80	3.10	2.60	3.05	2.50
%>	2.33	2.75	1.30	1.30	1.40	1.00
m=2,T=1000						
%<	-2.33	1.30	1.00	1.25	1.20	1.00
%<	-1.96	3.10	2.65	2.60	3.05	2.50
%<	-1.64	6.85	5.05	5.75	5.70	5.00
%>	1.64	7.90	6.10	6.20	7.25	5.00
%>	1.96	4.40	3.20	3.30	3.75	2.50
%>	2.33	1.90	1.70	1.30	1.50	1.00
m=5,T=500						
%<	-2.33	7.05	1.30	1.85	1.95	1.00
%<	-1.96	11.55	3.75	3.60	3.90	2.50
%<	-1.64	16.80	6.85	6.75	8.15	5.00
%>	1.64	15.60	6.45	5.90	5.60	5.00
%>	1.96	11.75	4.15	3.25	3.20	2.50
%>	2.33	8.00	2.65	1.50	1.40	1.00
m=5,T=1000						
%<	-2.33	3.40	0.85	1.00	1.05	1.00
%<	-1.96	6.75	2.40	2.60	3.05	2.50
%<	-1.64	11.05	5.15	5.15	5.10	5.00
%>	1.64	10.25	6.20	5.65	6.10	5.00
%>	1.96	6.85	3.70	3.10	3.20	2.50
%>	2.33	4.30	1.55	1.35	1.25	1.00
m=10,T=1000						
%<	-2.33	40.90	1.00	0.50	1.00	1.00
%<	-1.96	41.10	2.70	1.75	2.45	2.50
%<	-1.64	43.15	6.20	4.85	5.65	5.00
%>	1.64	33.80	8.35	6.35	6.20	5.00
%>	1.96	33.00	5.50	4.05	3.65	2.50
%>	2.33	31.55	3.80	1.95	1.65	1.00

Table E.4
Size of BDS Statistic
MA1 Residuals ($\theta=.95$)

		ϵ/σ			
	0.50	1.00	1.50	2.00	N(0,1)
m=2,T=100					
%< -2.33	12.30	3.95	3.55	5.45	1.00
%< -1.96	17.10	7.80	7.00	8.70	2.50
%< -1.64	22.80	11.95	11.15	12.80	5.00
%> 1.64	17.35	10.60	9.85	11.40	5.00
%> 1.96	14.05	7.45	5.80	7.90	2.50
%> 2.33	10.65	4.95	3.50	4.95	1.00
%< -2.33	2.55	1.15	1.40	1.45	1.00
%< -1.96	5.35	3.00	3.55	3.40	2.50
%< -1.64	9.20	6.15	6.15	6.35	5.00
%> 1.64	7.75	6.10	5.85	6.25	5.00
%> 1.96	4.25	3.25	3.25	3.50	2.50
%> 2.33	2.60	1.45	1.65	2.10	1.00
%< -2.33	1.55	1.20	1.20	1.15	1.00
%< -1.96	3.85	2.90	3.10	2.95	2.50
%< -1.64	7.70	6.15	6.85	6.05	5.00
%> 1.64	6.90	5.75	5.55	5.45	5.00
%> 1.96	4.00	2.90	2.85	3.20	2.50
%> 2.33	1.90	1.25	1.25	1.20	1.00
%< -2.33	7.50	0.60	0.95	1.05	1.00
%< -1.96	10.85	2.45	2.95	3.70	2.50
%< -1.64	15.50	5.70	5.50	6.45	5.00
%> 1.64	14.90	7.10	6.95	6.50	5.00
%> 1.96	11.20	4.70	4.00	3.80	2.50
%> 2.33	8.95	2.25	1.90	2.15	1.00
%< -2.33	4.05	1.05	1.10	1.40	1.00
%< -1.96	7.60	2.90	3.25	3.40	2.50
%< -1.64	11.75	6.10	5.90	6.65	5.00
%> 1.64	11.20	6.25	5.55	5.60	5.00
%> 1.96	7.60	3.80	2.65	3.10	2.50
%> 2.33	4.55	1.30	1.30	1.25	1.00
%< -2.33	39.50	0.95	0.70	1.30	1.00
%< -1.96	39.85	2.95	2.85	3.40	2.50
%< -1.64	42.30	6.45	5.35	6.30	5.00
%> 1.64	32.25	7.60	5.20	4.60	5.00
%> 1.96	31.65	4.55	3.25	2.50	2.50
%> 2.33	30.25	2.80	1.70	1.45	1.00

Table E.5
Size of BDS Statistic
ARCH Residuals ($\phi = .5$)

		ϵ/σ			
	0.50	1.00	1.50	2.00	N(0,1)
m=2,T=100					
%< -2.33	8.95	1.20	0.75	2.30	1.00
%< -1.96	12.10	3.25	2.00	4.20	2.50
%< -1.64	15.90	5.25	4.00	6.30	5.00
%> 1.64	15.35	6.65	6.15	9.35	5.00
%> 1.96	11.70	4.25	4.30	6.00	2.50
%> 2.33	8.75	2.00	2.25	4.15	1.00
m=2,T=500					
%< -2.33	0.20	0.00	0.00	0.05	1.00
%< -1.96	0.70	0.00	0.05	0.25	2.50
%< -1.64	1.85	0.20	0.40	1.05	5.00
%> 1.64	2.60	0.65	0.60	2.00	5.00
%> 1.96	1.20	0.25	0.25	0.50	2.50
%> 2.33	0.40	0.00	0.00	0.15	1.00
m=2,T=1000					
%< -2.33	0.05	0.00	0.00	0.00	1.00
%< -1.96	0.15	0.10	0.05	0.05	2.50
%< -1.64	0.40	0.25	0.15	0.70	5.00
%> 1.64	1.25	0.45	0.60	1.35	5.00
%> 1.96	0.35	0.05	0.10	0.35	2.50
%> 2.33	0.00	0.00	0.00	0.05	1.00
m=5,T=500					
%< -2.33	5.80	0.15	0.05	0.10	1.00
%< -1.96	9.40	0.45	0.40	0.70	2.50
%< -1.64	13.30	1.55	1.40	1.75	5.00
%> 1.64	13.20	2.00	1.55	1.65	5.00
%> 1.96	9.30	1.05	0.55	0.40	2.50
%> 2.33	6.40	0.35	0.00	0.00	1.00
m=5,T=1000					
%< -2.33	1.75	0.00	0.00	0.05	1.00
%< -1.96	3.85	0.20	0.05	0.10	2.50
%< -1.64	7.35	0.85	0.50	1.00	5.00
%> 1.64	6.05	0.75	0.55	0.80	5.00
%> 1.96	4.05	0.35	0.20	0.45	2.50
%> 2.33	2.25	0.20	0.10	0.10	1.00
m=10,T=1000					
%< -2.33	40.50	0.30	0.00	0.25	1.00
%< -1.96	40.65	1.10	0.40	1.15	2.50
%< -1.64	42.65	3.65	2.15	3.25	5.00
%> 1.64	33.35	5.80	2.65	2.15	5.00
%> 1.96	32.50	3.55	1.10	0.95	2.50
%> 2.33	31.30	2.00	0.50	0.20	1.00

Table E.6
Size of BDS Statistic
ARCH Residuals ($\phi=.95$)

	ϵ/σ				
	0.50	1.00	1.50	2.00	N(0,1)
m=2,T=100					
%< -2.33	8.50	1.70	1.05	2.95	1.00
%< -1.96	12.50	3.65	2.65	4.65	2.50
%< -1.64	16.35	6.65	5.05	7.45	5.00
%> 1.64	20.70	12.25	11.25	13.05	5.00
%> 1.96	16.60	9.00	7.65	9.85	2.50
%> 2.33	13.65	6.45	5.40	6.95	1.00
m=2,T=500					
%< -2.33	0.75	0.75	0.85	0.75	1.00
%< -1.96	2.25	1.25	1.40	1.75	2.50
%< -1.64	4.65	2.70	2.60	3.20	5.00
%> 1.64	6.95	4.80	5.00	6.20	5.00
%> 1.96	4.95	3.35	3.35	4.10	2.50
%> 2.33	3.10	2.20	2.40	2.65	1.00
m=2,T=1000					
%< -2.33	1.95	2.15	2.30	2.15	1.00
%< -1.96	3.20	3.00	3.05	3.10	2.50
%< -1.64	5.25	4.65	4.60	4.95	5.00
%> 1.64	4.80	4.10	4.50	4.85	5.00
%> 1.96	3.60	3.00	2.80	3.00	2.50
%> 2.33	2.55	2.05	2.10	2.05	1.00
m=5,T=500					
%< -2.33	5.75	0.90	0.90	0.95	1.00
%< -1.96	9.20	1.85	2.00	2.10	2.50
%< -1.64	13.25	3.10	3.40	3.35	5.00
%> 1.64	17.00	5.85	5.45	5.70	5.00
%> 1.96	13.15	4.30	3.50	4.15	2.50
%> 2.33	9.85	2.90	2.65	2.95	1.00
m=5,T=1000					
%< -2.33	3.50	2.35	2.60	2.55	1.00
%< -1.96	5.85	3.30	3.55	3.75	2.50
%< -1.64	9.95	5.35	5.20	5.30	5.00
%> 1.64	9.05	4.00	3.55	4.20	5.00
%> 1.96	6.35	2.85	2.65	3.15	2.50
%> 2.33	4.20	2.30	2.10	2.00	1.00
m=10,T=1000					
%< -2.33	41.20	1.55	1.60	1.80	1.00
%< -1.96	41.35	3.45	3.30	3.85	2.50
%< -1.64	44.05	6.50	5.75	6.25	5.00
%> 1.64	32.05	7.90	4.85	4.35	5.00
%> 1.96	31.35	5.65	3.70	3.00	2.50
%> 2.33	30.20	3.90	2.40	2.25	1.00

Table E.7
Size of BDS Statistic
GARCH Residuals ($\phi=.1, \psi=.8$)

	ϵ/σ				
	0.50	1.00	1.50	2.00	N(0,1)
m=2,T=100					
%< -2.33	11.35	2.55	2.00	4.75	1.00
%< -1.96	16.20	5.80	5.05	7.90	2.50
%< -1.64	21.05	9.55	8.15	11.65	5.00
%> 1.64	15.50	6.90	5.80	8.75	5.00
%> 1.96	12.50	4.20	3.30	6.00	2.50
%> 2.33	9.45	2.65	1.60	3.50	1.00
m=2,T=500					
%< -2.33	12.50	3.65	2.90	4.75	1.00
%< -1.96	17.70	6.35	5.40	7.90	2.50
%< -1.64	22.90	11.00	9.60	11.65	5.00
%> 1.64	16.15	8.00	6.65	8.75	5.00
%> 1.96	13.40	5.65	4.05	6.00	2.50
%> 2.33	10.60	3.35	2.10	3.50	1.00
m=2,T=1000					
%< -2.33	1.15	0.50	0.35	0.45	1.00
%< -1.96	2.85	1.45	1.30	1.55	2.50
%< -1.64	5.75	3.15	3.10	3.35	5.00
%> 1.64	4.50	2.00	1.45	1.65	5.00
%> 1.96	2.45	0.85	0.45	0.45	2.50
%> 2.33	1.30	0.40	0.20	0.20	1.00
m=5,T=500					
%< -2.33	0.40	0.30	0.20	0.25	1.00
%< -1.96	1.55	0.95	0.80	0.95	2.50
%< -1.64	4.40	2.90	2.55	2.25	5.00
%> 1.64	3.55	2.40	1.90	1.60	5.00
%> 1.96	1.80	1.15	0.80	0.45	2.50
%> 2.33	0.90	0.20	0.10	0.05	1.00
m=5,T=1000					
%< -2.33	1.25	0.00	0.00	0.00	1.00
%< -1.96	3.30	0.05	0.00	0.00	2.50
%< -1.64	6.00	0.20	0.20	0.15	5.00
%> 1.64	6.05	0.65	0.20	0.15	5.00
%> 1.96	3.55	0.30	0.05	0.05	2.50
%> 2.33	2.00	0.10	0.00	0.00	1.00
m=10,T=1000					
%< -2.33	40.45	0.00	0.00	0.00	1.00
%< -1.96	40.60	0.05	0.00	0.00	2.50
%< -1.64	43.00	1.10	0.00	0.00	5.00
%> 1.64	31.10	2.75	0.45	0.20	5.00
%> 1.96	30.55	1.70	0.10	0.05	2.50
%> 2.33	29.70	1.00	0.00	0.00	1.00

Table E.8
Size of BDS Statistic
NMA Residuals ($\gamma=.5$)

	ϵ/σ				
	0.50	1.00	1.50	2.00	N(0,1)
m=2,T=100					
% <-2.33	12.80	4.15	3.85	5.70	1.00
% <-1.96	17.00	7.85	7.00	9.10	2.50
% <-1.64	21.10	13.20	11.70	13.30	5.00
% > 1.64	17.20	10.70	8.90	10.80	5.00
% > 1.96	14.35	7.50	5.95	7.90	2.50
% > 2.33	12.15	4.50	3.70	4.90	1.00
m=2,T=500					
% <-2.33	2.40	1.20	1.20	1.55	1.00
% <-1.96	5.10	3.05	3.30	3.60	2.50
% <-1.64	8.90	6.50	6.55	6.55	5.00
% > 1.64	7.90	6.35	5.95	6.85	5.00
% > 1.96	4.60	3.50	3.55	4.30	2.50
% > 2.33	2.65	1.60	1.80	2.35	1.00
m=2,T=1000					
% <-2.33	1.60	1.10	1.25	1.00	1.00
% <-1.96	3.75	2.70	2.90	3.00	2.50
% <-1.64	7.45	6.50	7.05	6.35	5.00
% > 1.64	6.70	5.65	5.70	6.25	5.00
% > 1.96	4.40	3.25	3.50	3.75	2.50
% > 2.33	2.05	1.70	1.65	1.95	1.00
m=5,T=500					
% <-2.33	7.85	0.65	0.95	1.35	1.00
% <-1.96	12.50	2.50	3.05	3.70	2.50
% <-1.64	16.50	5.70	6.45	7.15	5.00
% > 1.64	15.60	7.00	6.50	6.65	5.00
% > 1.96	12.40	4.55	3.85	4.50	2.50
% > 2.33	8.70	2.60	2.50	2.75	1.00
m=5,T=1000					
% <-2.33	3.95	0.90	1.10	1.25	1.00
% <-1.96	7.25	2.80	3.30	3.65	2.50
% <-1.64	12.40	6.25	6.25	6.85	5.00
% > 1.64	11.25	6.70	6.35	6.25	5.00
% > 1.96	7.95	4.15	3.30	3.80	2.50
% > 2.33	4.65	1.55	1.80	2.10	1.00
m=10,T=1000					
% <-2.33	12.80	4.15	3.85	5.70	1.00
% <-1.96	17.00	7.85	7.00	9.10	2.50
% <-1.64	21.10	13.20	11.70	13.30	5.00
% > 1.64	17.20	10.70	8.90	10.80	5.00
% > 1.96	14.35	7.50	5.95	7.90	2.50
% > 2.33	12.15	4.50	3.70	4.90	1.00

Appendix F. Distribution and Quantiles of the BDS Statistic on GARCH Residuals

Table F.1
Distribution and Quantiles of BDS Statistic
Garch(1,1) Standardized Residuals
100 Observations

| | m | | | | N(0,1) |
	2	3	4	5	
$\epsilon=.5\sigma$					
Median	-0.27	-0.27	-0.34	-0.63	0.00
Mean	-0.16	-0.17	-0.17	-0.17	0.00
Std dev	2.01	2.29	2.93	4.09	1.00
Skewness	0.72	0.41	0.36	0.78	0.00
Kurtosis	6.35	6.12	4.79	5.47	3.00
Quantile					
1.0%	-4.76	-5.78	-7.32	-9.45	-2.33
2.5%	-3.82	-4.44	-5.73	-7.25	-1.96
5.0%	-3.06	-3.56	-4.59	-5.97	-1.64
10.0%	-2.39	-2.74	1.40	-4.59	-1.28
90.0%	2.23	2.64	3.41	4.81	1.28
95.0%	3.04	3.64	4.77	7.12	1.64
97.5%	4.17	4.44	6.31	9.41	1.96
99.0%	5.63	6.15	8.01	12.03	2.33
$\epsilon=\sigma$					
Median	-0.14	-0.17	-0.21	-0.21	0.00
Mean	-0.13	-0.14	-0.15	-0.15	0.00
Std dev	1.19	1.15	1.19	1.29	1.00
Skewness	0.19	0.19	0.20	0.38	0.00
Kurtosis	3.24	3.30	3.66	4.17	3.00
Quantile					
1.0%	-2.81	-2.62	-2.93	-3.20	-2.33
2.5%	-2.35	-2.29	-2.36	-2.51	-1.96
5.0%	-2.04	-1.98	-2.01	-2.11	-1.64
10.0%	-1.62	-1.57	-1.63	-1.71	-1.28
90.0%	1.36	1.34	1.41	1.45	1.28
95.0%	1.83	1.79	1.90	2.11	1.64
97.5%	2.35	2.24	2.34	2.54	1.96
99.0%	3.01	2.88	2.94	3.42	2.33

Based on 2000 replications.

Table F.2
Distribution and Quantiles of BDS Statistic
Garch(1,1) Standardized Residuals
500 Observations

	m					
	2	3	4	5	10	N(0,1)
$\epsilon=.5\sigma$						
Median	-0.16	-0.10	-0.07	-0.13	-4.06	0.00
Mean	-0.13	-0.07	-0.03	-0.01	-0.23	0.00
Std dev	0.99	1.04	1.19	1.52	9.96	1.00
Skewness	0.17	0.22	0.25	0.30	3.55	0.00
Kurtosis	3.19	3.15	3.21	3.28	21.88	3.00
Quantile						
1.0%	-2.43	-2.49	-2.59	-3.30	-5.81	-2.33
2.5%	-2.00	-1.95	-2.19	-2.74	-5.46	-1.96
5.0%	-1.71	-1.69	-1.92	-2.34	-5.26	-1.64
10.0%	-1.34	-1.37	-1.53	-1.85	-4.96	-1.28
90.0%	1.15	1.28	1.53	1.99	11.34	1.28
95.0%	1.56	1.68	2.00	2.65	20.42	1.64
97.5%	1.95	2.08	2.46	3.25	28.86	1.96
99.0%	2.45	2.65	2.95	3.73	40.47	2.33
$\epsilon=\sigma$						
Median	-0.13	-0.09	-0.08	-0.07	-0.01	0.00
Mean	-0.11	-0.07	-0.04	-0.01	0.10	0.00
Std dev	0.84	0.74	0.70	0.70	1.07	1.00
Skewness	0.06	0.17	0.29	0.37	0.90	0.00
Kurtosis	3.23	3.50	3.59	3.50	5.91	3.00
Quantile						
1.0%	-2.07	-1.82	-1.61	-1.49	-1.98	-2.33
2.5%	-1.75	-1.52	-1.35	-1.29	-1.64	-1.96
5.0%	-1.45	-1.24	-1.17	-1.10	-1.45	-1.64
10.0%	-1.14	-1.01	-0.91	-0.86	-1.12	-1.28
90.0%	0.97	0.88	0.85	0.86	1.43	1.28
95.0%	1.23	1.15	1.10	1.18	1.96	1.64
97.5%	1.51	1.39	1.33	1.46	2.32	1.96
99.0%	1.84	1.82	1.83	1.86	3.02	2.33

Based on 2000 replications.

Table F.3
Distribution and Quantiles of BDS Statistic
Garch(1,1) Standardized Residuals
1000 Observations

	2	3	m 4	5	10	N(0,1)
$\epsilon=.5\sigma$						
Median	-0.08	-0.10	-0.05	-0.04	-1.32	0.00
Mean	-0.07	-0.07	-0.03	-0.02	-0.28	0.00
Std dev	0.92	0.88	0.92	1.08	6.81	1.00
Skewness	0.16	0.27	0.27	0.18	1.82	0.00
Kurtosis	3.15	3.38	3.29	3.10	8.80	3.00
Quantile						
1.0%	-2.11	-1.96	-2.09	-2.45	-7.31	-2.33
2.5%	-1.84	-1.72	-1.80	-2.05	-6.93	-1.96
5.0%	-1.59	-1.50	-1.49	-1.77	-6.63	-1.64
10.0%	-1.27	-1.19	-1.19	-1.35	-6.33	-1.28
90.0%	1.08	1.05	1.14	1.38	8.65	1.28
95.0%	1.44	1.47	1.55	1.74	11.76	1.64
97.5%	1.80	1.79	1.92	2.19	16.83	1.96
99.0%	2.29	2.18	2.25	2.69	23.48	2.33
$\epsilon=\sigma$						
Median	-0.07	-0.07	-0.06	-0.06	-0.01	0.00
Mean	-0.07	-0.07	-0.05	-0.03	0.03	0.00
Std dev	0.84	0.72	0.65	0.62	0.79	1.00
Skewness	0.06	0.19	0.22	0.23	0.44	0.00
Kurtosis	2.97	3.13	3.09	3.27	3.79	3.00
Quantile						
1.0%	-1.97	-1.64	-1.42	-1.45	-1.66	-2.33
2.5%	-1.69	-1.41	-1.26	-1.20	-1.46	-1.96
5.0%	-1.46	-1.22	-1.09	-1.01	-1.23	-1.64
10.0%	-1.15	-1.00	-0.88	-0.80	-0.95	-1.28
90.0%	0.98	0.83	0.77	0.77	1.01	1.28
95.0%	1.29	1.13	1.04	1.01	1.33	1.64
97.5%	1.63	1.42	1.32	1.23	1.75	1.96
99.0%	2.01	1.78	1.61	1.51	2.23	2.33

Based on 2000 replications.

Table F.4
Distribution and Quantiles of BDS Statistic
Garch(1,1) Standardized Residuals
2500 Observations

	2	3	4	5		N(0,1)
			m			
$\epsilon = \sigma$						
Median	-0.05	-0.05	-0.04	-0.03		0.00
Mean	-0.03	-0.04	-0.03	-0.02		0.00
Std dev	0.79	0.68	0.60	0.56		1.00
Skewness	0.10	0.15	0.08	0.13		0.00
Kurtosis	3.02	3.14	3.16	3.13		3.00
Quantile						
1.0%	-1.79	-1.60	-1.38	-1.30		-2.33
2.5%	-1.56	-1.31	-1.19	-1.07		-1.96
5.0%	-1.36	-1.14	-1.01	-0.93		-1.64
10.0%	-1.05	-0.92	-0.82	-0.72		-1.28
90.0%	0.95	0.84	0.73	0.68		1.28
95.0%	1.25	1.09	0.98	0.88		1.64
97.5%	1.59	1.31	1.17	1.10		1.96
99.0%	1.88	1.59	1.44	1.37		2.33

	6	7	8	9	10	N(0,1)
			m			
$\epsilon = \sigma$						
Median	-0.02	-0.01	-0.01	-0.02	-0.03	0.00
Mean	-0.02	-0.01	0.00	0.01	0.02	0.00
Std dev	0.54	0.55	0.57	0.60	0.65	1.00
Skewness	0.14	0.18	0.23	0.28	0.30	0.00
Kurtosis	3.06	3.08	3.13	3.16	3.23	3.00
Quantile						
1.0%	-1.28	-1.24	-1.28	-1.32	-1.34	-2.33
2.5%	-1.03	-1.03	-1.06	-1.12	-1.16	-1.96
5.0%	-0.87	-0.87	-0.88	-0.93	-0.97	-1.64
10.0%	-0.70	-0.69	-0.70	-0.72	-0.78	-1.28
90.0%	0.68	0.69	0.73	0.76	0.85	1.28
95.0%	0.90	0.92	0.97	1.05	1.14	1.64
97.5%	1.06	1.08	1.22	1.34	1.44	1.96
99.0%	1.27	1.34	1.40	1.55	1.66	2.33

Based on 2000 replications.

References

Abel, A. 1988. Stock Prices Under Time-Varying Dividend Risk: An Exact Solution in an Infinite-Horizon General Equilibrium Model, *Journal of Monetary Economics* 22: 375–394.

Aiyagari, S., Eckstein, Z., and Eichenbaum, M. 1985. Inventories and Price Fluctuations under Perfect Competition and Monopoly, Carnegie-Mellon University.

Akgiray, V. 1989. Conditional Heteroscedasticity in Time Series of Stock Returns: Evidence and Forecasts, *Journal of Business* 62: 55–80.

Alogoskoufis, G., and Stengos, T. 1989. Testing for Nonlinear Dynamics in Historical Unemployment Rates, Department of Economics, Birbick College, London, U.K., and Department of Economics, University of Guelph.

Anderson, P., Arrow, K., and Pines, D., eds. 1988. *The Economy As An Evolving Complex System*, Sante Fe Institute Studies in the Sciences of Complexity, Vol. V, Redwood City, CA: Addison-Wesley.

Ariel, R.A. 1987. A Monthly Effect in Stock Returns, *Journal of Financial Economics* 18: 161–174.

Arrow, K., and Hahn, F. 1971. *General Competitive Analysis*, San Francisco: Holden Day.

Arthur, W. 1988. Self-Reinforcing Mechanisms in Economics, in Anderson, P., Arrow, K., and Pines, D., eds., *The Economy As An Evolving Complex System*, Sante Fe Institute Studies in the Sciences of Complexity, Vol. V, Redwood City, CA: Addison-Wesley.

Ashley, R., and Patterson, D. 1989. Linear Versus Nonlinear Macroeconomies: A Statistical Test, *International Economic Review* 30: 685–704.

Ashley, R., Patterson, D., and Hinich, M. 1986. A Diagnostic Test for Nonlinearity and Serial Dependence in Time Series Fitting Errors, *Journal of Time Series Analysis* 7 (3): 165-178.

Baek, E. 1987. Contemporaneous Independence Test of Two IID Series, University of Wisconsin, Madison.

Baek, E., and Brock, W. 1988a. A Nonparametric Test for Temporal Dependence in a Vector of Time Series, University of Wisconsin, Madison.

Baek, E., and Brock, W. 1988b. An Alternate Approach to Specification Error Test, Iowa State University and University of Wisconsin, Madison.

Barnett, W., Berndt, E., and White, H., eds. 1988. *Dynamic Econometric Modelling, Proceedings of the Third Austin Symposium*, Cambridge: Cambridge University Press.

Barnett, W., and Chen., P. 1988. The Aggregation-Theoretic Monetary Aggregates Are Chaotic and Have Strange Attractors, in Barnett, W., Berndt, E., and White, H., eds., *Dynamic Econometric Modelling, Proceedings of the Third Austin Symposium*, Cambridge: Cambridge University Press.

Barnett, W., Geweke, J., and Shell, K. 1989. *Economic Complexity, Chaos, Sunspots, Bubbles, and Nonlinearity: Proceedings of the Fourth International Symposium in Economic Theory and Econometrics*, Cambridge: Cambridge University Press.

Barnett, W., and Hinich, M. 1990. Has Chaos Been Discovered With Economic Data? Department of Economics, Washington University, St. Louis, and Department of Government, University of Texas, Austin.

Barnett, W., Powell, J., and Tauchen, G., eds. 1991. *Nonparametric and Semiparametric Methods in Econometrics and Statistics: Proceedings of the Fifth International Symposium in Economic Theory and Econometrics*, Cambridge: Cambridge University Press.

Barnett, W., and Singleton, K. 1987. *New Approaches To Monetary Economics: Proceedings of the Second International Symposium in Economic Theory and Econometrics*, Cambridge: Cambridge University Press.

Bates, D. 1987. The Crash Premium: Option Pricing Under Asymmetric Processes, With Applications to Options on Deutschemark Futures, Princeton University.

Baumol, W., and Benhabib, J. 1989. Chaos: Significance, Mechanism, and Economic Applications, *Journal of Economic Perspectives* 3 (1): 77–105.

Ben-Mizrachi, A., Procaccia, I., and Grassberger, P. 1984. Characterization of Experimental (Noisy) Strange Attractors, *Physical Review* 29: 975–977.

Benhabib, J., and Rustichini, A. 1989. A Vintage Model of Investment Growth: Theory and Evidence, Department of Economics, New York University, W.P. #89-26.

Bewley, T. 1983. Dynamic Implications of the Form of the Budget Constraint, in Sonnenschein, H., ed., *Models of Economic Analysis*, New York: Springer-Verlag.

Bickel, P., and Friedman, D. 1981. Some Asymptotic Theory for the Bootstrap, *Annals of Statistics* 9 (6): 1196-1217.

Black, F. 1976. Studies of Stock Price Volatility Changes, in
*Proceedings of the 1976 Meetings of the Business and Economics
Statistics Section of the American Statistical Association*, 177—181.

Black, F. 1986. Noise, *Journal of Finance* 41: 529—543.

Black, F. 1987. *Business Cycles and Equilibrium*, Oxford: Basil
Blackwell.

Blum, J., Kiefer, J., and Rosenblatt, M. 1961. Distribution Free
Tests of Independence Based on the Sample Distribution Function,
Annals of Mathematical Statistics, 32: 485-498.

Boldrin, M. 1988. Persistent Oscillations and Chaos in Dynamic
Economic Models: Notes for a Survey, in Anderson, P., Arrow, K.,
and Pines, D., eds., *The Economy As An Evolving Complex System*,
Sante Fe Institute Studies in the Sciences of Complexity, Vol. V,
Redwood City, CA: Addison-Wesley.

Boldrin, M., and Montrucchio, L. 1986. The Emergence of Dynamic
Complexities in Models of Optimal Growth: The Role of
Impatience, *Journal of Economic Theory* 40: 26—39.

Boldrin, M., and Woodford, M. 1990. Equilibrium Models
Displaying Endogenous Fluctuations and Chaos, *Journal of
Monetary Economics* 25 (2): 189—222.

Bollerslev, T. 1986. Generalized Autoregressive Conditional Heteroskedasticity, *Journal of Econometrics* 31: 307-327.

Bollerslev, T. 1987. A Conditionally Heteroskedastic Time Series Model for Security Prices and Rates of Return Data, *Review of Economics and Statistics* 69: 542–547.

Bollerslev, T., Engle, R., and Wooldridge, J. 1988. A Capital Asset Pricing Model with Time Varying Covariances, *Journal of Political Economy* 96: 116–131.

Box, G., and Jenkins, G. 1976. *Time Series Analysis: Forecasting and Control*, San Francisco: Holden Day.

Brock, W. 1982. Asset Prices in a Production Economy, in McCall, J.J., ed., *The Economics of Information and Uncertainty*, Chicago: University of Chicago and NBER.

Brock, W. 1986. Distinguishing Random and Deterministic Systems, *Journal of Economic Theory* 40: 168–195.

Brock, W. 1987. Notes on Nuisance Parameter Problems in BDS Type Tests for IID, University of Wisconsin, Madison (revised November 1989).

Brock, W. 1988. Nonlinearity and Complex Dynamics in Finance and Economics, in Anderson, P., Arrow, K., and Pines, D., eds., *The Economy As An Evolving Complex System*, Sante Fe Institute

Studies in the Sciences of Complexity, Vol. V, Redwood City, CA: Addison-Wesley.

Brock, W. 1990. Chaos and Complexity in Economics and Financial Science, in von Furstenberg, G.M., ed., *Acting Under Uncertainty: Multidisciplinary Conceptions*, Boston: Kluwer Academic Publishers, Chap. 17, 423–450.

Brock, W. 1991. Causality, Chaos, Explanation and Prediction in Economics and Finance, in Casti, J., and Karlqvist, A., eds., *Beyond Belief: Randomness, Prediction, and Explanation in Science*, Boca Raton, FL: CRC Press.

Brock, W., and Baek, E. 1991. Some Theory of Statistical Inference for Nonlinear Science: Gauge Functions, Complexity Measures, and Instability Measures, *Review of Economic Studies*, forthcoming.

Brock, W., and Dechert, W. 1988a. Theorems on Distinguishing Deterministic and Random Systems, in Barnett, W., Berndt, E., and White, H., eds., *Dynamic Econometric Modelling, Proceedings of the Third Austin Symposium*, Camgridge: Cambridge University Press.

Brock, W., and Dechert, W. 1988b. A General Class of Specification Tests: The Scalar Case, *Proceedings of the Business and Economic Statistics of the American Statistical Association*, 70–79.

Brock, W., Dechert, W., and Scheinkman, J. 1987. A Test for Independence Based On the Correlation Dimension, University of

Wisconsin, Madison, University of Houston, and University of Chicago.

Brock, W., Dechert, W., Scheinkman, J., and LeBaron, B. 1990. A Test for Independence Based On the Correlation Dimension, University of Wisconsin, Madison, University of Houston, University of Chicago, and University of Wisconsin, Madison.

Brock, W., Lakonishok, J., and LeBaron, B. 1990. Simple Technical Trading Rules and the Stochastic Properties of Stock Returns, SSRI W.P. #9022, Department of Economics, University of Wisconsin, Madison.

Brock, W., and LeBaron, B. 1990. Liquidity Constraints in Production-Based Asset Pricing Models, in Hubbard, R., ed., *Asymmetric Information, Corporate Finance, and Investment*, Chicago: University of Chicago Press, p. 231-255.

Brock, W., and Sayers, C. 1988. Is The Business Cycle Characterized by Deterministic Chaos? *Journal of Monetary Economics* 22: 71—90.

Burt, J., Kaen, F., and Booth, G. 1977. Foreign Market Efficiency under Flexible Exchange Rates, *Journal of Finance* 32: 1325—1330.

Casdagli, M., and Eubank, S. 1991. Nonlinear Modeling and Forecasting, *SFI Studies in the Sciences of Complexity*, Redwood city, CA: Addison-Wesley, forthcoming.

Casti, J. 1991. *Searching for Certainty: What Scientists Can Know About the Future*, New York: William Morrow & Co.

Chen, P. 1990a. Searching for Economic Chaos: A Challenge to Mainstream Econometric Practice and Nonlinear Numerical Experiments, IC^2 Institute, University of Texas, Austin, W.P. #90-08-02.

Chen, P. 1990b. The Bridge Between The Two Cultures: Some Fundamental Issues in Advancing Empirical Economic Science, IC^2 Institute, University of Texas, Austin, W.P. #90-09-02.

Christiano, L. 1986. On The Accuracy Of Linear Quadratic Approximations: An Example, Federal Reserve Bank of Minneapolis.

Christiano, L. 1987. Dynamic Properties of Two Approximate Solutions to a Particular Growth Model, Federal Reserve Bank of Minneapolis.

Cornell, B. 1977. Spot Rates, Forward Rates, and Market Efficiency, *Journal of Financial Economics* 8: 55–69.

Das, S. 1990. Economic Inequality and Business Cycles: The Asymmetric Rent Externality Effect, Department of Economics, University of Indiana, Bloomington.

Dechert, W. 1987. A Program to Calculate BDS Statistics for the IBM PC, University of Houston and University of Wisconsin, Madison.

Dechert, W. 1988. A Characterization of Independence for a Gaussian Process in Terms of the Correlation Dimension, SSRI W. P. #8812, Department of Economics, University of Wisconsin, Madison.

De Grauwe, P., and Vansanten, K. 1990. Deterministic Chaos in the Foreign Exchange Market, Centre for Economic Policy Research, Discussion Paper, No. 370, 6 Duke of York Street, London SW1Y 6LA.

Denker, M., and Keller, G. 1983. On U-Statistics and Von Mises Statistics for Weakly Dependent Processes, *Z. Wahrscheinlichkeitstheorie verw. Gebiete* 64: 505-522.

Denker, M., and Keller, G. 1986. Rigorous Statistical Procedures for Data From Dynamical Systems, *Journal of Statistical Physics* 44: 67–93.

Diebold, F. 1988. *Empirical Modeling of Exchange Rate Dynamics*, New York: Springer-Verlag.

Diebold, F., and Nason, J. 1990. Nonparametric Exchange Rate Prediction, *Journal of International Economics* 28: 315-332.

Diebold, F., and Nerlove, M. 1989. The Dynamics of Exchange Rate Volatility: A Multivariate Latent Factor ARCH Model, *Journal of Applied Econometrics* 4: 1—21.

Diebold, F., and Pauly, P. 1988. Endogenous Risk in a Rational-Expectations Portfolio Balance Model of the Deutschemark/Dollar Rate, *European Economic Review* 32: 27—54.

Domowitz, I., and Hakkio, C. 1985. Conditional Variance and the Risk Premium in the Foreign Exchange Market, *Journal of International Economics* 19: 987—1007.

Durlauf, S. 1990a. Locally Interacting Systems, Coordination Failure, and the Behavior of Aggregate Activity, Department of Economics, Stanford University.

Durlauf, S. 1990b. Spectral Based Testing of the Martingale Hypothesis, Department of Economics, Stanford University.

Eckmann, J., Kamphorst, S., Oliffson, S., Ruelle, D., and Scheinkman, J. 1988. Lyapunov Exponents for Stock Returns, in Anderson, P., Arrow, K., and Pines, D., eds., *The Economy As An Evolving Complex System*, Vol. V, Sante Fe Institute Studies in the Sciences of Complexity, Redwood City, CA: Addison Wesley.

Eckmann, J., Kamphorst, S., and Ruelle, D. 1986. Recurrence Plots of Dynamical Systems, Departement de Physique Theorique,

Universite de Geneve, and IHES, F-91440 Bures-sur-Yvette, France.

Eckmann, J., and Ruelle, D. 1985. Ergodic Theory of Chaos and Strange Attractors, *Reviews of Modern Physics* 57: 617-656.

Efron, B. 1982. *The Jackknife, The Bootstrap and Other Resampling Plans*, Regional Conference Series in Applied Mathematics, Vol. 38, Philadelphia: Society for Industrial and Applied Mathematics.

Efron, B., and Tibshirani, R. 1986. Bootstrap Methods for Standard Errors, Confidence Intervals, and Other Measures of Statistical Accuracy, *Statistical Science* 1: 54—77.

Engle, R. 1982. Autoregressive Conditional Heteroscedasticity With Estimates of The Variance of U.K. Inflations, *Econometrica* 50: 987-1007.

Engle, R. 1987. Multivariate ARCH with Factor Structures-Cointegration in Variance, University of California, San Diego.

Engle, R., and Bollerslev, T. 1986. Modelling the Persistence of Conditional Variances, *Econometric Reviews* 5: 1—50.

Engle, R., and Granger, C. 1987. Co-Integration and Error Correction: Representation, Estimation and Testing, *Econometrica* 55: 251—276.

Engle, R., Hendry, D., and Trumble, D. 1985. Small–Sample Properties of ARCH Estimators and Tests, *Canadian Journal of Economics* 18: 66—93.

Engle, R., Hong, C., and Kane, A. 1990. Valuation of Variance Forecasts with Simulated Option Markets, unpublished manuscript, Department of Economics, University of California, San Diego.

Engle, R., and Mustafa, C. 1989. Implied ARCH Models from Options Prices, University of California, San Diego, W.P. #89—29.

Engle, R., Ng, V., and Rothschild, M. 1990. Asset Pricing with a Factor-ARCH Covariance Structure: Empirical Estimates for Treasury Bills, *Journal of Econometrics*, 45: 213-237.

Epstein, L. 1987. The Global Asymptotic Stability of Efficient Intertemporal Allocations, *Econometrica*, 55: 329—356.

Eubank, S., and Farmer, D. 1989. An Introduction to Chaos and Randomness, 1989 Lectures in Complex Systems, *SFI Studies in the Sciences of Complexity*, Redwood City, CA: Addison Wesley.

Fama, E. 1970. Efficient Capital Markets: A Review of Theory and Empirical Work, *Journal of Finance* 25: 383—417.

Fama, E. 1976. *Foundations of Finance*, New York: Basic Books.

Fama, D., and French, K. 1988. Permanent and Temporary Components of Stock Prices, *Journal of Political Economy* 96: 246–273.

Farmer, J. D., and Sidorowich, J. J. 1987. Predicting Chaotic Time Series, *Physical Review Letters* 59: 845–848.

Feigenbaum, M. 1983. Universal Behavior in Nonlinear Systems, in Barenblatt, G., Iooss, G., and Joseph, D., eds., *Nonlinear Dynamics and Turbulence*, Boston: Pitman.

Ferson, W., and Merrick, J. 1987. Non-Stationarity and Stage-of-The-Business-Cycle Effects in Consumption-Based Asset Pricing Relations, *Journal of Finance* 18: 127-146.

Flood, R., Hodrick, R., and Kaplan, P. 1986. An Evaluation of Recent Evidence on Stock Market Bubbles, NBER W. P. No. 1971.

Frank, M., and Stengos. 1989. Measuring the Strangeness of Gold and Silver Rates of Return, *Review of Economic Studies* 56: 553–568.

French, K., Schwert, G., and Stambaugh, R. 1987. Expected Stock Returns and Volatility, *Journal of Financial Economics* 19: 3–29.

Gallant, A., Hsieh, D., and Tauchen, G. 1991. On Fitting a Recalcitrant Series: The Pound/Dollar Exchange Rate, 1974-83, in Barnett, W., Powell, J., and Tauchen, G., eds., *Nonparametric and*

Semiparametric Methods in Econometrics and Statistics: Proceedings of the Fifth International Symposium in Economic Theory and Econometrics, Cambridge: Cambridge University Press, p. 199–240.

Gallant, A., Rossi, P., and Tauchen, G. 1990. Stock Prices and Volume, North Carolina State University, University of Chicago, and Duke University.

Gallant, A., and Tauchen, G. 1989. Seminonparametric Estimation of Conditionally Constrained Heterogeneous Processes: Asset Pricing Applications, *Econometrica* 57: 1091–1120.

Gallant, A., and Tauchen, G. 1991. A Nonparametric Approach to Nonlinear Time Series Analysis: Estimation and Simulation, University of Minnesota, Institute for Mathematics and its Applications Volume, New York: Springer-Verlag, forthcoming.

Gallant, A., and White, H. 1988. *A Unified Theory of Estimation and Inference For Nonlinear Dynamic Models*, Oxford: Basil Blackwell.

Gennotte, G., and Marsh, T. 1986. Variations in Ex Ante Risk Premiums on Capital Assets, University of California at Berkeley.

Geweke, J. 1987. Modelling Nonlinearity With Normal Polynomial Expansions, Duke University.

Giddy, I., and Dufey, G. 1975. The Random Behavior of Flexible Exchange Rates: Implications for Forecasting, *Journal of International Business Studies* 6: 1—32.

Giovannini, A. 1989. Uncertainty and Liquidity, *Journal of Monetary Economics* 23: 239—258.

Gleick, J. 1987. *Chaos*, New York: Viking.

Grandmont, J. 1985. On Endogenous Competitive Business Cycles, *Econometrica* 53: 995—1045.

Grandmont, J., ed. 1986. *Symposium on Nonlinear Economic Dynamics, Journal of Economic Theory* 40.

Granger, C. 1987. Stochastic or Deterministic Non-linear Models? A Discussion of the Recent Literature in Economics, University of California, San Diego.

Granger, C. 1990. Developments in the Nonlinear Analysis of Economic Series, Department of Economics, University of California, San Diego.

Granger, C., and Andersen, A. 1978. *An Introduction to Bilinear Time Series Models*, Göttingen: Vandenhoeck & Ruprecht.

Grassberger, P., and Procaccia, I. 1983a. Measuring the Strangeness of Strange Attractors, *Physica* 9D: 189-208.

Grassberger, P., and Procaccia, I. 1983b. Estimation of the Kolmogorov Entropy From a Chaotic Signal, *Physical Review A* 28: 2591-2593.

Hall, R. 1989. Temporal Agglomeration, NBER W. P. No. 3143.

Hansen, L. 1982. Large Sample Properties of Generalized Method of Moments Estimators, *Econometrica* 50: 1029—1054.

Hardle, W. 1990. *Applied Nonparametric Regression Analysis*, Cambridge: Cambridge University Press.

Haubrich, J., and Lo, A. 1988. The Sources and Nature of Long-Term Memory in the Business Cycle, Department of Finance, The Wharton School, University of Pennsylvania.

Haugen, R. 1987. *Introductory Investment Theory*, Princeton, N.J.: Prentice Hall.

Hausman, J. 1978. Specification Tests in Econometrics, *Econometrica* 46: 1251—1272.

Heimstra, C. 1990. Applications to Macroeconomics, Finance, and Forecasting of Recently Developed Statistical Tests and Estimates Arising from Nonlinear Dynamical Systems Theory, Ph.D. dissertation, University of Maryland.

Hinich, M. 1982. Testing for Gaussianity and Linearity of a Stationary Time Series, *Journal of Time Series Analysis* 3: 169-176.

Hinich, M., and Patterson, D. 1985. Evidence of Nonlinearity in Stock Returns, *Journal of Business and Economic Statistics* 3: 69-77.

Hinich, M., and Patterson, D. 1986. A Bispectrum Based Test of The Stationary Martingale Model, University of Texas, Austin and Virginia Polytechnic Institute.

Hoeffding, W. 1948. A Non-Parametric Test of Independence, *Annals of Mathematical Statistics* 19: 546-557.

Hornik, K., Stinchcombe, M., and White, H., 1989. Universal Approximation of An Unknown Mapping and its Derivatives Using Multilayer Feedforward Networks, Department of Economics, University of California, San Diego.

Hsieh, D. 1983. A Heteroscedasticity-Consistent Covariance Matrix Estimator for Time Series Regressions, *Journal of Econometrics* 22: 281—290.

Hsieh, D. 1988a. The Statistical Property of Daily Foreign Exchange Rates: 1974—1983, *Journal of International Economics* 24: 129—145.

Hsieh, D. 1988b. A Nonlinear Stochastic Rational Expectations Model of Exchange Rates, University of Chicago.

Hsieh, D. 1989a. Testing for Nonlinear Dependence in Foreign Exchange Rates, *Journal of Business* 62: 339–368.

Hsieh, D. 1989b. Modeling Heteroscedasticity in Daily Foreign-Exchange Rates, *Journal of Business and Economic Statistics* 7: 307–317.

Hsieh, D. 1991. Chaos and Nonlinear Dynamics: Application to Financial Markets, *Journal of Finance*, forthcoming.

Hsieh, D., and LeBaron, B. 1988. Finite Sample Properties of the BDS Statistic, University of Chicago and University of Wisconsin, Madison.

Ibbotson R., and Sinquefield, R. 1977. Stocks, Bonds, Bills, and Inflation: The Past (1926-1976) and The Future (1977-2000), University of Virginia.

Jeong, K. 1990. A New Misspecification Test for Funcational Form of Regression Functions, University of Wisconsin, Madison.

Keim, D. 1983. Size-Anomaly and Stock Return Seasonality, *Journal of Financial Economics* 12: 13-32.

Kendall, M., and Stuart, A. 1970. *The Advanced Theory of Statistics*, Vol. 2, London: Griffin & Co., Ltd.

Kent, J. 1979. Time-Reversible Diffusions, *Advances In Applied Probability* 10: 819-836.

King, R., Plosser, C., and Rebelo, S. 1988. Production Growth and Business Cycles: I. The Basic Neoclassical Model, *Journal of Monetary Economics* 21: 309—342.

King, R., Plosser, C., Stock, J., and Watson, M. 1987. Stochastic Trends and Economic Fluctuations, University of Rochester, Harvard University, and Northwestern University.

Knuth, D. 1969. *The Art of Computer Programming: Seminumerical Algorithms*, Vol. 2, Reading, MA: Addison-Wesley.

Kohn, R. 1979. Asymptotic Estimation and Hypothesis Testing Results for Vector Linear Time Series Models, *Econometrica* 47: 1005-1030.

Laaksonen, M., and Luhta, I. 1990. Can The Business Cycle be Analyzed by Correlation Dimension, University of Vaasa, Raastuvankatu 31, SF-65100, Vaasa, Finland.

Lai, K., and Pauly, P. 1988. Time Series Properties of Foreign Exchange Rates Re-examined, University of Pennsylvania.

Lapedes, A., and Farber, R. 1987. Nonlinear Signal Processing Using Neural Networks: Prediction and System Modelling, Los Alamos W. P. No. LA-UR-87-2662.

Leamer, E. 1987. Specification Problems in Econometrics, *The New Palgrave*, Vol. 4, New York: Macmillan Press, 432—435.

Learmonth, G., and Lewis, P. 1973. Statistical Tests of Some Widely Used and Recently Proposed Uniform Random Number Generators, Naval Postgraduate School, Monterey, CA.

LeBaron, B. 1988a. Nonlinear Puzzles in Stock Returns, University of Chicago.

LeBaron, B. 1988b. The Changing Structure of Stock Returns, University of Chicago.

LeBaron, B. 1990a. Some Relations Between Volatility and Serial Correlations in Stock Market Returns, Department of Economics, University of Wisconsin, Madison.

LeBaron, B. 1990b. Forecast Improvements Using a Volatility Index, Department of Economics, University of Wisconsin, Madison.

Lee, T., White, H., and Granger, C. 1989. Testing for Neglected Nonlinearity in Time Series Models: A Comparison of Neural Network Methods and Alternative Tests, University of California, San Diego.

Liu, T. 1990. How to Decide if a Series is Chaotic: Estimation of the Correlation Exponent, Department of Economics, University of California, San Diego.

Lo, A., and MacKinley, A. 1988. Stock Market Prices Do Not Follow Random Walks: Evidence From a Simple Specification Test, *Review of Financial Studies* 1: 41–66.

Lo, A., and MacKinlay, C. 1990. Data-Snooping Biases in Tests of Financial Asset Pricing Models, *Review of Financial Studies* 3: 431-467.

Loeve, M. 1963. *Probability Theory*, Princeton: Van Nostrand.

Logue, E., and Sweeney, R. 1977. 'White-Noise' in Imperfect Markets: The Case of the Franc/Dollar Exchange Rate, *Journal of Finance* 32: 761–768.

Logue, E., Sweeney, R., and Willett, T. 1978. Speculative Behavior of Foreign Exchange Rates During the Current Float, *Journal of Business Research* 6: 159–174.

Lorenz, H.W. 1989. *Nonlinear Dynamical Economics and Chaotic Motion*, Lecture Notes in Economics and Mathematical Systems, #334, New York: Springer-Verlag.

Lucas, R.E. 1978. Asset Prices in an Exchange Economy, *Econometrica* 46: 1429–1445.

McCaffrey, D., Ellner, S., Gallant, R., and Nychka, D. 1990. Estimating Lyapunov Exponents with Nonparametric Regression, Department of Statistics, North Carolina State University.

Mackey, M., and Glass, L. 1977. Oscillation and Chaos in Physiological Control Systems, *Science* 50: 287-289.

McLeod, A., and Li, W. 1983. Diagnostic Checking ARMA Time Series Models Using Squared-Residual Autocorrelation, *Journal of Time Series Analysis* 4: 269–273.

Manas-Anton, L. 1986. *Empirical Behavior of Flexible Exchange Rates: Statistical Analysis and Consistent Models*, Ph.D. dissertation, University of Chicago.

Mandelbrot, B. 1963. The Variation of Certain Speculative Prices, *Journal of Business* 36: 392–417.

Mandelbrot, B. 1982. The Many Faces of Scaling: Fractals, Geometry of Nature, and Economics, in Schreve, W., and Allen, P., eds., *Self-Organization and Dissipative Structures*, Austin: University of Texas Press.

Manoukian, E. 1986. *Modern Concepts and Theorems of Mathematical Statistics*, New York: Springer-Verlag.

Manski, C. 1991. Regression, *Journal of Economic Literature*, 29: 34-50.

Marimon, R. 1989. Stochastic Turnpike Property and Stationary Equilibrium, *Journal of Economic Theory*, 47: 282—306.

Marsaglia, G., and Bray, T. 1968. One-Line Random Number Generators and Their Use in Combinations, *CACM* 11: 757—759.

Marsh, T., and Rock, K. 1986. The Transaction Process and Rational Stock Price Dynamics, University of California, Berkeley.

Mayer-Kress, G. 1986. *Dimensions and Entropies in Chaotic Systems*, New York: Springer-Verlag.

Mayfield, E., and Mizrach, B. 1989. On Determining the Dimension of Real-Time Stock Price Data, Department of Economics, Boston College, and Department of Finance, The Wharton School, University of Pennsylvania.

Meese, R., and Rogoff, K. 1983. Empirical Exchange Rate Models of the Seventies: Are Any Fit to Survive, *Journal of International Economics* 14: 3—24.

Milhøj, A. 1987. A Conditional Variance Model for Daily Deviations of an Exchange Rate, *Journal of Business and Economic Statistics* 5: 99—103.

Mizrach, B. 1989. Multivariate Nearest Neighbor Forecasts of EMS Exchange Rates, Department of Economics, Boston College.

Monastersky, R. 1990. Forecasting Into Chaos: Meteorologists Seek to Foresee Unpredictability, *Science News* 1: 280–282.

Montroll, E., and Badger, W. 1974. *Introduction to Quantitative Aspects of Social Phenomena*, New York: Gordon and Breach.

Mosekilde, E., Larson, E., and Sterman, J. 1989. Entrainment Between The Economic Long Wave and Other Macroeconomic Cycles, Physics Laboratory III, The Technical University of Denmark, Lyngby, Denmark, and Sloan School of Management, MIT.

Mussa, M. 1979. Empirical Regularities in the Behavior of Exchange Rates and Theories of the Foreign Exchange Market, in Brunner, K., and Meltzer, A., eds., *Carnegie-Rochester Series on Public Policy*, Vol. 11, Amsterdam: North-Holland.

Nelson, D. 1988. Conditional Heteroskedasticity in Asset Returns: A New Approach, Massachusetts Institute of Technology.

Nelson, D. 1990. Filtering and Forecasting With Misspecified ARCH Models I: Getting the Right Variance With the Wrong Model, University of Chicago.

Nelson, C., and Plosser, C. 1982. Trends and Random Walks in Macroeconomic Time Series, *Journal of Monetary Economics* 10: 139-162.

Newey, W. 1985. Maximum Likelihood Specification Testing and Conditional Moment Tests, *Econometrics* 53: 1047—1070.

Newey, W., and West, K. 1987. A Simple, Positive-Definite, Heteroskedasticity and Autocorrelation Consistent Covariance Matrix, *Econometrica* 55: 703—708.

Pagan, A., and Hall, A. 1983. Diagnostic Tests As Residual Analysis, *Econometric Reviews* 2: 159—218.

Patterson, D. 1987. BISPEC: A Program for the IBM PC to Test for Gaussianity and Linearity of Time Series Using the Bispectrum, Virginia Polytechnic Institute.

Pemberton, J., and Tong, H. 1981. A Note on the Distributions of Non-Linear Autoregressive Stochastic Models, *Journal of Times Series Analysis* 1: 47—71.

Pierrehumbert, R. 1989. Dimensions of Atmospheric Variability, Department of Geology, University of Chicago.

Potter, S. 1989. Nonlinear Time Series and Economic Fluctuations, Ph.D. dissertation, Department of Economics, University of Wisconsin, Madison.

Potter, S. 1990. A Nonlinear Approach to the Univariate Time Series Properties of Post 1945 U.S. GNP, Department of Economics, University of California, Los Angeles.

Prescott, D., and Stengos, T. 1988. Nonparameteric Kernel Estimation of the Nonlinear Structure of Rates of Returns: The Case of Gold, University of Guelph.

Priestley, M. 1980. State-dependent Models: A General Approach to Non-linear Time Series Analysis, *Journal of Time Series Analysis* 1: 47–71.

Priestley, M. 1981. *Spectral Analysis and Time Series*, Vols. I, II, New York: Academic Press.

Prigogine, I. 1980. *From Being to Becoming*, New York: W. Freeman.

Ramsey, J., Sayers, C., and Rothman, P. 1988. The Statistical Properties of Dimension Calculations Using Small Data Sets: Some Economic Applications, *International Economic Review* 31:991- 1020.

Ramsey, J., and Yuan, H. 1989. Bias and Error Bias in Dimension Calculation and Their Evaluation in Some Simple Models, *Physical Letters A*, 134: 287–297.

Randles, R. 1982. On the Asymptotic Normality of Statistics With Estimated Parameters, *Annals of Statistics*, 2: 462-474.

Randles, R., and Wolfe, D. 1979. *Introduction to the Theory of Nonparametric Statistics*, New York: Wiley.

Robinson, P. 1977. The Estimation of a Non-linear Moving Average Model, *Stochastic Processes and Their Applications* 5: 81—90.

Robinson, P. 1990. Consistent Nonparametric Entropy-Based Testing, Department of Economics, London School of Economics.

Rogalski, R., and Vinso, J. 1978. Empirical Properties of Foreign Exchange Rates, *Journal of International Business Studies* 9: 69—79.

Sakai, H., and Tokumaru, H. 1980. Autocorrelations of a Certain Chaos, *IEEE Transactions on Acoustics, Speech and Signal Processing* 1: 588—590.

Sargent, T. 1987a. *Macroeconomic Theory*, 2nd Ed., New York: Academic Press.

Sargent, T. 1987b. *Dynamic Macroeconomic Theory*, Cambridge, MA: Harvard University Press.

Savit, R., and Green, M. 1989. Time Series and Dependent Variables, *Physica D*, forthcoming.

Sayers, C. 1990. Chaos and the Business Cycle, in Krasner, S., ed., *The Ubiquity of Chaos*, Publication No. 89-15S, Washington, D.C.: American Association for the Advancement of Science.

Scheinkman, J., and LeBaron, B. 1989a. Nonlinear Dynamics and GNP Data, in Barnett, W., Geweke, J., and Shell, K., eds.,

Economic Complexity: Chaos, Sunspots, Bubbles, and Nonlinearity: Proceedings of the Fourth International Symposium in Economic Theory and Econometrics, Cambridge: Cambridge University Press, 213–227.

Scheinkman, J., and LeBaron, B. 1989b. Nonlinear Dynamics and Stock Returns, *Journal of Business* 62: 311–337.

Schwarz, G. 1978. Estimating the Dimension of a Model, *Annals of Statistics* 6: 461–464.

Schwert, G.W. 1989. Business Cycles, Financial Crises, and Stock Volatility, *Carnegie Rochester Conference Series on Public Policy* 31: 83–126.

Sen, P. 1963. On the Properties of U-Statistics When the Observations are not Independent: Part One, *Calcutta Statistical Association Bulletin* 12: 69–92.

Serfling, R. 1980. *Approximation Theorems of Mathematical Statistics*, New York: Wiley.

Silverman, B. 1986. *Density Estimation for Statistics and Data Analysis*, London and New York: Chapman and Hall.

Simon, J. 1990. Duopoly and Chaos Theory: New Directions for Research and Public Policy? Department of Economics, University of Maryland.

Sims, C. 1983. Comments on the Grandmont paper, 'Endogenous Competitive Business Cycles,' in Sonnenschein, H., ed., *Models of Economic Analysis*, New York: Springer-Verlag, 37—40.

Sims, C. 1984. Martingale-Like Behavior of Prices and Interest Rates, University of Minnesota.

Shlesinger, M., and Weiss, G. 1985. *The Wonderful World of Stochastics: A Tribute to Elliot W. Montroll*, Amsterdam: North-Holland.

Smith, V. 1986. Experimental Methods in the Political Economy of Exchange, *Science* 234: 167-173.

Smith, V., Suchanek, G., and Williams, A., 1988. Bubbles, Crashes and Endogenous Expectations in Experimental Spot Asset Markets, *Econometrica* 56: 1119—1151.

Sterman, J. 1989. Deterministic Chaos in An Experimental Economic System, *Journal of Economic Behavior and Organization* 12: 1—28.

Stock, J. 1986. Measuring Business Cycle Time, *Journal of Political Economy* 95: 1240—1261.

Stock, J. 1988. Estimating Continuous Time Processes Subject to Time Deformation: An Application to Postwar U.S. GNP, *Journal of American Statistical Association* 83: 77—85.

Stock, J. H., and Watson, M. 1989. Interpreting the Evidence on Money-Income Causality, *Journal of Econometrics* 40: 161–181.

Subba Rao, T., and Gabr, M. 1980. A Test for Linearity of Stationary Time Series, *Journal of Time Series Analysis* 1: 145-158.

Sugihara, G., Grenfell, B., and May, R. 1990. Distinguishing Error from Chaos in Ecological Time Series, Scripps Institution of Oceanography, University of California, San Diego, Department of Zoology, Cambridge University, Department of Zoology, Oxford University.

Sugihara, G., and May, R. 1990. Nonlinear Forecasting as a Way of Distinguishing Chaos From Measurement Error in Time Series, *Nature* 344: 734-741.

Summers, L. 1986. Does the Stock Market Rationally Reflect Fundamental Values? *The Journal of Finance* 41: 591-635.

Swinney, H. 1985. Observations of Complex Dynamics and Chaos, in Cohen, E., ed., *Fundamental Problems in Statistical Mechanics: VI*, Amsterdam: North Holland.

Takens, F. 1984. On The Numerical Determination of the Dimension of an Attractor, in *Dynamical Systems and Bifurcations*, Lecture Notes in Mathematics 1125, Berlin: Springer-Verlag.

Tauchen, G. 1985. Diagnostic Testing and Evaluation of Maximum Likelihood Models, *Journal of Econometrics* 30: 415—443.

Terasvirta, T. 1990. Power Properties of Linearity Tests for Time Series, Department of Economics, University of California, San Diego, Discussion Paper, 90-15.

Theiler, J. 1990a. Statistical Precision of Dimension Estimators, *Physical Review A* 42: 3038—3051.

Theiler, J. 1990b. Estimating Fractal Dimension, *Journal of Optical Society of America A* 7: 1055-73.

Tong, H. 1983. *Threshold Models in Non-linear Time Series Analysis*, Lecture Notes in Statistics, #21, New York: Springer-Verlag.

Tong, H., and Lim, K. 1980. Threshold Autoregression, Limit Cycles, and Cyclical Data, *Journal of the Royal Statistical Society*, 42 (Series B): 245—292.

Tsay, R. 1986. Nonlinearity Tests for Time Series, *Biometrica* 73: 461-466.

Wahba, G. 1990. *Spline Models for Observational Data*, Vol. 59, CBMS-NSF Regional Conference Series in Applied Mathematics, SIAM, Philadelphia, PA, March.

Weigend, A., Huberman, B., and Rumelhart, D. 1990. Predicting the Future: A Connectionist Approach, Department of Physics and Psychology, Stanford University.

Weiss, A. 1986. ARCH and Bilinear Time Series Models: Comparison and Combination, *Journal of Business and Economic Statistics* 4: 59-70.

White, H. 1982. Maximum Likelihood Estimation of Misspecified Models, *Econometrica* 50: 1-25.

White, H. 1987. Specification Testing in Dynamic Models, in Bewley, T., ed., *Advances in Econometrics*, New York: Cambridge University Press.

White, H. 1988. Economic Prediction Using Neural Networks: The Case of IBM Daily Stock Returns, University of California, San Diego.

White, H. 1989. Some Asymptotic Results for Learning in Single Hidden Layer Feedforward Network Models, *Journal of the American Statistical Association* 84: 1003-1013.

White, H., and Domowitz, I. 1984. Nonlinear Regression with Dependent Observations, *Econometrica* 52: 143-162.

Wolf, A., Swift, J., Swinney, J., and Vastano, J. 1985. Determining Lyapunov Exponents from a Time Series, *Physica* 16D: 285–317.

Wood, R., McInish, T., and Ord, J. 1985. An Investigation of Transactions Data for NYSE Stocks, *Journal of Finance* 40: 723-741.

Woodford, M. 1987. Three Questions About Sunspot Equilibria as an Explanation of Economic Fluctuations, *American Economic Review* 77: 93-98.

Woodford, M. 1989a. Imperfect Financial Intermediation and Complex Dynamics, in Barnett, W., Geweke, J., and Shell, K., eds., *Economic Complexity: Chaos, Sunspots, Bubbles, and Nonlinearity*, Cambridge: Cambridge University Press.

Woodford, M. 1989b. Equilibrium Models of Endogenous Fluctuations: An Introduction, Department of Economics, University of Chicago.

Yakowitz, S. 1987. Nearest-Neighbor Models for Time Series Analysis, *Journal of Time Series Analysis* 9: 235–247.

Index

Aggregation theory, 190

Akaike Information Criterion (AIC), 193

ARCH-M model, 138

ARCH model, 20—21, 80, 105, 142

    BDS statistic and, 57—58

    development of, 83

    Engle test for, 60—62, 93

    LWG test for linearity and, 173

    popularity of, 21—22

    third moment test and, 138

ARCH(1) model, 73

ARMA process, 22

AR(1) model, 55, 71—72, 78, 138

AR process, 133

Asset returns, 201

Autocorrelation, 82, 93—94, 201

Autocovariance function, 13

Autoregressive conditional heteroskedasticity. *See* ARCH model

Backward expectations, 35

Backward perfect foresight dynamics, 37

BDS statistic, 18

vs. alternative specification tests, 172

ARCH model and, 57—58

asymptotic distribution of, 42—47, 143—144, 196

distributions of, 225—231

finite sample distribution of, under IID, 48—53

finite sample distribution of, with nuisance parameters, 71—74

first order asymptotic null distribution of, 177

first order autoregression and, 54

first order moving average and, 55

fitted GARCH(1,1) residuals and, 95—96

fitted model residuals and, 101

in foreign exchange applications, 130—131

GARCH model and, 58—59

on GARCH residuals, distribution and quantities of, 276—279

linear dependence and, 133

for Mackey and Glass data, 94

nonlinearity in foreign exchange rates and, 132—133, 148—150

nonlinearity in tent map and, 93

nonlinear moving average and, 57

nuisance parameter property of, 235—267

power comparison and, 54—62, 77, 172, 173, 218—224

quantiles of, 232—234

rejection by, 75—76

simulated GARCH data and, 90—91, 109

size and distribution of, 206—217

size of, on residuals, 268—275

as specification test, scalar case, 62—71

standardized residuals of GARCH and, 141

and stock return data, 97, 99, 112

tent map and, 55—56

theoretical asymptotic power of, 53—54

threshold autoregressive model and, 56—57

BDS test, 3—8

advantages of, 173—174

computer software for, 4

disadvantages of, 174

vs. Durbin-Watson test for autocorrelation, 175

first order asymptotic distribution of, 173—174

foreign exchange rates and, 134, 150, 151

as goodness-of-fit test, 179, 202, 203

lack of asymptotic consistence of, 177—178

locally linear methods and, 198—199

nonforecastable nonstationarity and, 186—187

nonstationarity and, 175

null class models of, 169—172

parametric conditional mean function models and, 176—177

P-linearity and, 195—196

power comparisons and, 175

rejection by, 21, 174, 186—187

vs. RESET specification test, 175

usefulness of, 4

Bilinear model, 20

Bispectrum test for linearity, 61

Boldrin and Montrucchio theorem, 39—40

Bootstrapped data, 28, 85, 133

Bootstrap p-values, 97

Cauchy distribution, 47
Center for Research in Security Prices (CRSP), 27—28
Chaos, 1
    definitions and concepts of, 8—19
    forecastability of, 184—185
    largest Lyapunov exponent and, 9
    low-dimensional, 2—3
    in overlapping generations models, 34—39
    period doubling route to, 14
    sensitive dependence upon initial conditions and, 9
    testing for, 15
Chaotic equilibrium dynamics
    Boldrin and Montrucchio theorem and, 39—40
    in overlapping generations models, 34—39
    pathways to, 30—40
Chaotic rational expectations equilibrium, 31
Chaotic systems, stochastic and deterministic, 15—16
Competitive equilibria, 31—32
Complete markets, 33
Complex dynamics theory
    confrontation of, 22—30
    recent work in, 187—190
    testing of, 169—179
Complex equilibrium dynamics, channels for, 32—34

Complexity

   dimension and, 16

   measurement of, 2

Computer generator of random numbers, invariant measures and, 10—11

Computer pseudo random number generator, 2

Conditional density

   estimations, 202—204

   semi-nonparametric methods and, 203—204

Conditional moment generating function prediction, 30

Conditional skewness prediction, 30

Conditional variance prediction, 30

Correlation dimension, 16

Correlation integral, 15, 18, 42

Cramer and von Mises-type statistics, 196

CRSP value weighted index, 95—98

Data limitations, for financial economists, 23

Deterministic chaos, 8—10, 13, 174

Deterministic data generators, 2—3

Deterministic equilibrium trajectories, 1

Deterministic models, 92—94

Dimension estimates, 186

Dimension plots, 5

   description of, 84—85

   of original data vs. random data, 5—6

Dow Jones Industrial Average, 10

Dow Jones stock returns, 201

Durbin-Watson test for autocorrelation, 175

Durlauf-type localized externalities, 189

Economic fluctuations, 26

Economic models, and generation of deterministic equilibrium
 trajectories, 1

Economists, natural nulls for, 182—187

Engle statistic, 91, 96—99

 for Mackey and Glass data, 94

 nonlinearity in tent map and, 93

 for stock return data, 99, 112

Engle test for ARCH, 60—62

Ergodic condition, 11

Ergodicity, 9

Estimated residuals, 19

Euler equations, 22

Exchange rates. *See* Foreign exchange rates

Exogenous shock, 26, 27

External sources of fluctuation, 26—27

Farmer and Sidorowich technique, 103

Feigenbaum period doubling route, 37

Firm size, 189

First order autoregression model. *See* AR(1) model

First order moving average. *See* MA(1) model

Fiscal policy, changes in, 26

Forecast errors, 4, 186

Forecasting

    long-run, 13

    and stock returns, 102—104

Foreign exchange rates, 2

    differentiation of nonlinearities in, 134—139

    and forecast errors, root mean squared, 135, 152

    GARCH model for, 139—143

    graphical depictions of nonlinearity in, 131—132, 161—163

    low-dimensional regular chaotic dynamics in, 135

    mean-nonlinearity in, 135—136, 138

    nonlinearity testing in, 131—134, 146—147, 158—160

    nonlinear stochastic dynamics in, 135

    recurrence plots of nonlinearity for, 132, 164—168

    third moment test of filtered data and, 139, 154

    variance-nonlinearity in, 135—137

Forward perfect foresight dynamics, 37

GARCH(1,1) generalized error distribution, 143

GARCH-M models, 100—101

GARCH model, 6, 7, 80

    BDS statistic and, 58—59

    detection of incorrect model and, 93

    development of, 83

    foreign exchange rates and, 139—143

    LWG test for linearity and, 173

    power of, 60—61

    residuals of, 95

    simulations of, 142—143

standardized residuals of, 91

stock return nonlinearity and, 104—105

third order cumulants of, 91

volatility changes and, 92

GARCH(1,1) model, 90, 94, 95, 142

standardized residuals of, 73—74, 140, 155—157

tests of nonlinearity and, 142, 155—157

Generalized Autoregressive Conditional Heteroskedastic model. *See* GARCH model

Goodness-of-fit test, 140, 142, 179, 202, 203

Government activity, in financial markets, 29

GP plots, 185

of bootstrapped data, 85

for CRSP value weighted series, 97—98

description of, 4—5, 89

for linearly filtered Mackey and Glass data, 94

of nonlinearity in exchange rates, 131—132, 161—163

for S&P series, 99—100

of tent map, 93

Granger's typical spectral shape, 188

Grassberger and Procaccia plots. *See* GP plots

Hausman test, 76

Hicksian temporary equilibria, 37

Independent and identically distributed (IID), 13, 18, 41, 48, 62, 195—196, 199

Infinite horizon growth model, 31

Instability, natural notion of, 5

Instability measures, 179—181

Instantaneously unpredictable process, 24—25

Interest rates, 28—29

Internal sources of fluctuation, 26—27

Intertemporal budget constraint, 35

Invariant measures, 9—11

Inventories, 187

Jeong's test, 176—177

Kalman filter, 10, 22

Kernel estimators, 178, 179

Kullback-Liebler measure, 178

Lagrange multiplier, 60

Lags, 34, 175

Lebesque measure, 9, 12

Linearity, 195

Linear predictor, 5

Liquidity constraints, 190

Locally linear methods, 197—199

Logistic map, long-run behavior of, 13—14

London Metals Exchange, 28

Low-dimensional chaos deterministic generators, 3, 26

Low-dimensional deterministic chaos, 17, 29

    in macroeconomic aggregates, 191—193

    testing for, in time series, 14—15

LWG test for linearity, 172—173

Lyapunov exponent, 11, 13
   estimates, 181
   estimation algorithms, 180
   largest, 5, 9, 28, 179, 180

Mackey and Glass equation, 92—94, 103

McLeod and Li test, 173

Macroeconomics, nonlinear time series work in, 190—194

Macroeconomic time series, disaggregative, 200

Macroeconomic variables, 2

MA(1) model, 55, 72, 78, 138

Market clearing conditions, 35

Mean-nonlinearity, third moment test and, 138, 153

Mean squared error (MSE), 195

Measurement error propagation, natural notion of, 5

Monte Carlo simulations, 169—170
   and finite sample distribution of BDS test, 132—133
   and power comparisons of BDS statistic, 59—62

MSE (mean squared error), 195

Natural nulls, for natural scientists vs. economists, 182—187

Network architecture, 199—200

Neural network (NN), 199—202

NMA model, 20, 57, 60, 74

Noises, 188—190

Nonlinearity, 2. *See also* Chaos
   definition of, 194—195

in foreign exchange, 130—168

general test for, 194—196

in macroeconomics, 190—194

in stock returns, 29

testing strategy for, 5

Tsay test for, 59—60

Nonlinearity tests

descriptions of, 83—88

future research and, 7

for macroeconomic series, 191

Nonlinear moving average. *See* NMA model

Nonlinear predictors, 196—197, 201

Nonlinear stochastic models, 20—22

Nonlinear time series analysis, 196—204

locally linear methods of, 197—199

in macroeconomics, 190—194

neural network methods of, 199—202

Nonparametric methods, 176, 204—205

Nonparametric regression, 178, 181

Nonstationarity or regime changes, 29

Null class models, covered by BDS test, 169—172

Null hypothesis, 41, 137, 176

Observer function, 10

One-step-ahead conditional density, 202

Orthogonality condition, 173, 177

Out-of-sample predictability, 201

Overlapping generations models, 34—39

Paley-Wiener condition, 195

Parametric methods, 202

Pareto Optimal, 31, 33

Parsimony, level of, 17

Period doubling route to chaos, 14

Persistence, degree of, 189—190

P-linearity, 195

Predictability, 192—193

Price volatility, 22—23

Pseudo random number generators, 2, 11

p-step-ahead predictability, 192

Put and call options, 30

$Q_{xx}(50)$ test, 142

Randomness multiplication phenomena, 5, 26

Random walk method, 135, 190

Rational expectations asset pricing models, 106—107

Rational expectations dynamics, 35, 36

Real Business Cycle school, 31, 189

Recurrence plots, 4—5

    dating of major economic events and, 6

    dating of monetary policy shifts and, 6

    description of, 87—88

    of nonlinearity in exchange rates, 132, 164—168

    for S&P 500 weekly returns series, 99

Recursive dynamic general equilibrium modeling, 188—189

RESET specification test, vs. BDS test, 175

Residuals, 19

    ARCH(1) model, 73

    AR(1) model, 71—72

    dimension of, 28

    GARCH(1,1) model, 73—74

    MA(1) model, 72

    NMA model, 74

Robinson's test statistic for independence, 178

Sample splitting technique, 176, 178

Sample weighting scheme, 178

Schwarz-preferred model, 203

Scientists, natural nulls for, 182—187

Semi-nonparametric methods (SNP), 203—204

Sensitive dependence upon initial conditions (SDIC), 9

Sign scrambling plots, description of, 86—87

SNP (semi-nonparametric methods), 203—204

Specification tests, 62—71, 76

S&P 500 index, 95, 99—100

Stationary parametric dynamics, 23—24

Stationary process, linearity of, 195—196

Stationary scalar valued stochastic process, linear in mean, 172

Stationary stochastic process, linearity of, 5

Stochasticity, test for, 15

Stochastic models, of stock returns, 89—92

Stochastic processes, fractionally differenced, 29

Stock market, 28

Stock returns, 2—3, 104—107

and CRSP value weighted index, 95—98

and deviation from random walk model, 83

forecasting, 102—104

instability measures and, 179—180

January effect for, 95

nonlinearity test descriptions for, 83—88

nonlinear structure in, 82—83

random walk hypothesis and, 190—191

simulations of, 88—94

tests of nonlinearity applied to, 95—101

unpredictability of, 24

week-of-the-month effect for, 95

TAR model, 20—21, 56—57, 60, 79

T-bill rates, 29

Tent map, 11—12, 79, 92—93

BDS statistic distribution and, 225—231

BDS statistic power and, 218—224

BDS test and, 178

correlation dimension for, 16

nonlinearity in, 93

power comparison and, 55—56, 60

Third moment test, 137—139, 153—154

Threshold autoregressive model. *See* TAR Model

Time series of data, temporal dependence of, 10

Trading volume, 22

Trajectories, generated by chaotic maps, 25

Treasury Bills, 28

Tsay statistic, 91, 96, 97
    GARCH-ARCH models and, 105
    for Mackey and Glass data, 94
    nonlinearity in tent map and large, 93
Tsay test, 91, 134, 140
    bispectrum test for linearity and, 61
    power comparisons and, 60
    problem with, 142
    steps in, 59—60
Tuning parameter, 14
Turbulence. *See* Chaos

Uncertainty amplification, 5
U-statistics, 43, 44

Variance, 4
Volatility, forecastable, 4

Weather forecasting, 26
White test, 76
Wold representation, 195
W-statistic, 18